"In this honest, insightful, informative, and provocative book, Enns offers readers an innovative way of reconciling their faith with evolutionary theory. In the course of fleshing out his argument, he provides readers with accessible introductions to the historical-critical approach to Scripture as well as to the cultural and literary backgrounds of the Bible's creation stories and of Paul's reflections on Adam. Whether one ends up agreeing with Enns or not, all readers will benefit enormously from reading this book. I heartily recommend *The Evolution of Adam!*"

—**Greg Boyd**, author of *The Myth of a Christian Nation*, *The Jesus Legend* (with Paul Eddy), and *Letters from a Skeptic*

"For far too long, evangelical Christians have dodged the implications of modern biology for our understanding of the Bible and theology. Foremost, we have failed to face the unassailable fact that death, rather than being the historical consequence of Adam's sin, was a part of the natural cycle that created our human forebears. What shall we do with Genesis and Paul in light of these facts? Enns blazes a trail that engaged Christians can follow."

—**Kenton L. Sparks**, Eastern University

"The evolution of humans from other organisms has always presented serious problems for conservative Christians, and the most serious problems have centered on the historicity of Adam. In this splendid book, Peter Enns confronts these problems with remarkable clarity and courage, offering a solution that is both biblically and scientifically informed."

—**Edward B. Davis**, Messiah College

"In this book, Peter Enns deals with one of the most challenging issues facing Christians today—the historicity of Adam. Was there really a man named 'Adam' from whom all men and women descend? How are we to understand the story of Adam? More importantly, how are we to understand Paul's theological use of Adam? Enns is well-equipped to deal with these volatile issues, holding a PhD from Harvard University in Old Testament studies and having taught for twenty years at various evangelical seminaries and colleges. With grace and incisive scholarship he offers a provocative thesis that will certainly interest and challenge the evangelical church. From my perspective, Enns fulfills Jesus's commandment that we 'love the Lord our God with all our mind' (Matt. 22:37), and he does so fearlessly and faithfully."

—**Denis O. Lamoureux**, St. Joseph's College, University of Alberta

THE EVOLUTION
of ADAM

WHAT THE BIBLE DOES AND DOESN'T
SAY ABOUT HUMAN ORIGINS

PETER ENNS

Brazos Press
a division of Baker Publishing Group
Grand Rapids, Michigan

For my teachers who influenced me most
BKW
TLIII
RBG
JDL
and JLK

And to many others, for your encouragement

John 8:32

© 2012 by Peter Enns

Published by Brazos Press
a division of Baker Publishing Group
P.O. Box 6287, Grand Rapids, MI 49516–6287
www.brazospress.com

Printed in the United States of America

Library of Congress Cataloging-in-Publication Data
Enns, Peter, 1961–
     The evolution of Adam : what the Bible does and doesn't say about human origins / Peter Enns.
        p.   cm.
     Includes bibliographical references (p.   ) and indexes.
     ISBN 978-1-58743-315-3 (pbk.)
     1. Theological anthropology—Biblical teaching. 2. Bible. O.T. Genesis—Criticism, interpretation, etc. 3. Bible. O.T.—Criticism, interpretation, etc. 4. Bible. N.T. Epistles of Paul—Theology. I. Title.
BS661.E56 2012
233′.11—dc23   2011030887

Unless otherwise indicated, Scripture quotations are from the New Revised Standard Version of the Bible, copyright © 1989, by the Division of Christian Education of the National Council of the Churches of Christ in the United States of America. Used by permission. All rights reserved.

Scripture quotations labeled NIV are from the Holy Bible, New International Version®. NIV®. Copyright © 1973, 1978, 1984, 2011 by Biblica, Inc.™ Used by permission of Zondervan. All rights reserved worldwide. www.zondervan.com

In keeping with biblical principles of creation stewardship, Baker Publishing Group advocates the responsible use of our natural resources. As a member of the Green Press Initiative, our company uses recycled paper when possible. The text paper of this book is composed in part of post-consumer waste.

12   13   14   15   16   17   18   7   6   5   4   3   2   1

0321

Contents

Part Two: Understanding Paul's Adam

Acknowledgments

I am thankful for the many who have given freely of their time to read through the manuscript at its early stages and make numerous and insightful comments: Steve Bohannon, Justin Dombrowski, Brad Gregory, Rob Kashow, Daniel Kirk, Nathan Mastenjak, David Vinson, and Brandon Withrow. Others read the manuscript but asked that their names not be included here, and I understand and support that decision. I have benefited greatly from all of their comments; yet, as is always the case, the final product remains entirely my own and does not necessarily reflect their own views. I would like to thank Rob Kashow and Steve Bohannon in particular for tracking down various sources for me. Rob Kashow also proofread the final version and compiled the Scripture index. Steve Bohannon compiled the always-tricky subject index. I am deeply grateful to both for their extra work.

Many others were involved in this project, albeit indirectly. I have had many conversations over the years with scientists of uncompromising Christian faith who have either struggled mightily with how their faith and scientific work can coexist or have given up the synthetic work and grown content to trade their time between parallel universes of faith and science. I also have before my mind's eye those Christians who are looking for constructive ways forward in the ever-present challenge of being thinking Christians in a modern world. Promptings from these communities have led me to write this book.

Further, I continue to be thankful to God for the intellectual and spiritual influences that have crossed my humble path. My seminary and doctoral work helped clarify for me the types of questions the Bible is prepared to answer. My spiritual guides—pastors, friends, coworkers—have helped me remember why we ask those questions at all. I trust that this book will honor them all, some of blessed memory.

Finally, my wife, Sue, and now-grown children, Erich, Elizabeth, and Sophie, have shown great strength over some difficult years, and I am proud of them. Each is also gifted with a highly calibrated nonsense meter, which seems to be turned on any time I become enamored of the sound of my own words. They've kept it real.

Introduction

Why This Book?

Evolutionary theory has been around for generations, but in recent years two factors are bringing the issue back into the public eye. The first is the relentless, articulate, and popular attacks on Christianity by the New Atheists. Jerry Coyne, Richard Dawkins, Daniel Dennett, and others have aggressively promoted evolution and argued that evolution has destroyed the possibility of religious faith, especially a faith like Christianity, whose sacred writings contain the story of Adam, the first man created out of dust several thousand years ago. The second factor has been well-publicized advances in our understanding of evolution, particularly genetics. The Human Genome Project, completed in 2003, has shown beyond any reasonable scientific doubt that humans and primates share common ancestry.

Evolution has crept back into the popular consciousness and has become a pressing issue for many Christians because evolution is typically understood to challenge, if not simply undermine, the story of origins presented in the Bible. Here my goal is not to arrive at final solutions, and it is certainly not to cover the many vital, complex, interwoven issues that evolution has brought to the theological table.[1]

My goal is to focus solely on how the Bible fits into all of this. The biblical authors tell a very different story of human origins than does science. For many Christians, the question that quickly surfaces is how to accept evolution and also value Scripture as God's Word.

In other words, "If evolution is true, what do I do with my Bible?" Even limiting the focus this way is far more than any one book can adequately handle. My intention here is somewhat modest. I hope to clear away some misunderstandings and suggest different ways of thinking through some perennial problems in order to put interested readers on a constructive path and thus hopefully encourage further substantive discussion.

Let me begin by explaining whom I see as my primary audience. I make two assumptions about my readers. The first is that they consider themselves Christian, of whatever tradition or stripe, and so respect Scripture and recognize that what it says must be accounted for somehow. A significant subset of this group is an evangelical readership, particularly in an American context. Evangelical readers generally tend to live more in the tensions between their deep, instinctual commitment to Scripture and the challenges to that commitment that arise in life in the modern world. Often those challenges come from the natural sciences. This type of burden does not seem to be as pressing in either mainline forms of Christianity or in fundamentalism, and in saying so I mean no slight to either. I am simply addressing here the audience that will likely connect more immediately to the types of arguments laid out in this book and the *need* for engagement that I presume about my readers. I also want so suggest that the matter of evolution, particularly as it touches notions of biblical authority and a historical Adam (the heart of the evolution challenge), seems to me—at least in my experience—more particularly an American evangelical problem than a British evangelical problem. I therefore expect that not all self-identified evangelicals will recognize their own frame of mind in this book (although I still hope something might be gained from reading it).

Second, these same people are convinced, for whatever reason, that evolution must be taken seriously. They may not all agree on how specifically life has evolved, but they accept that evolution is the proper word to describe the process. My aim, therefore, is not to convince people that the Bible is important, nor is it to make people see that evolution is true. My aim is to speak to those who feel that a synthesis between a biblically conversant Christian faith and evolution is a pressing concern. And my purpose here is certainly not to undermine the faith of those who see things differently.

I also wish to state—however briefly—my own precommitments as I engage this topic. My Christian faith is summed up in the Apostles' and Nicene Creeds, which are expressions of broad Christian orthodoxy. More specifically to the points that will occupy us below, I believe in the universal and humanly unalterable grip of both death and sin, and the work of the Savior, by the deep love and mercy of the Father, in delivering humanity from them. I also try to follow the teachings of Scripture as a whole and Jesus in particular in my life as a follower of Christ—as a husband, father, churchgoer, scholar, and human being.

With respect to Scripture, which is a topic that the ancient creeds do not address, I have sketched some of my views in a previous book.[2] I do not assume that readers of this book will have read that one, so allow me to state briefly my main thesis since it sits not too far in the background of virtually every topic I cover here.

The most faithful, Christian reading of sacred Scripture is one that recognizes Scripture as a product of the times in which it was written and/or the events took place—not merely so, but unalterably so. In my aforementioned book I tried to advocate for this commonly held position by drawing upon the analogy of the incarnation. As Jesus, the Word, is of divine origin as well as a thoroughly human figure of first-century Palestine, so is the Bible of ultimately divine origin yet also thoroughly a product of its time.

Stating the matter this way does not provide a solution for how the Bible should be interpreted in its particulars. Rather, it provides a general attitude for how readers today should approach the Bible: we should gladly accept and expect that the Bible will through and through bear the marks of its historical settings. In *Inspiration and Incarnation*, I touch on three specific areas, all of which play some role in this book, but in particular the first and third do: (1) Our knowledge of the cultures that surrounded ancient Israel greatly affects how we now understand the Old Testament—not only here and there but also what the Old Testament as a whole is designed to do. (2) Because Scripture is a collection of discrete writings from widely diverse times and places and written for diverse purposes, the significant theological diversity of Scripture we find there should hardly be a surprise. (3) How the New Testament authors interpret the Old Testament reflects the Jewish thought world of the time and thus accounts for their creative engagement of the Old Testament. It also helps Christians today understand how the New Testament authors brought together Israel's story and the gospel.

Further, this "human dimension" of Scripture is not an unfortunate state of affairs that must be tolerated, an unhappy condescension on God's part. Instead, the "incarnational" reality of Scripture is—as is the actual incarnation of Christ—a mark of God's great love for his people, evidence of how low he is willing to stoop in order to commune with his creation. I make no sort of ontological statement here; in other words, I do not suggest that Scripture is a union of divine and human "substances" in the same way that Jesus of Nazareth is. The incarnation is an analogy, a means of explaining one thing in terms of another. I only mean to make the point that we should expect of Scripture the same sort of embrace of the human that Jesus himself willingly took on, even to the point of emptying himself of his divine prerogative and becoming our brother (Phil. 2:6–8). I also emphasize that the incarnation is the grand mystery of the Christian faith—essentially incomprehensible. This by no means diminishes its value as an analogy for Scripture, although I readily admit that it means using such an analogy is hardly the final word—and I have never intended it to be.

Following upon that, I firmly believe that understanding Scripture from the vantage point of those historical circumstances in which it was written or its events took place is a vital responsibility of Christian readers (and where trained biblical scholars can be of help). I do not mean to suggest that historically oriented readings are the only viable approaches. The church has a grand history of contemplative readings of Scripture (*lectio divina*) or other similar methods that are aimed directly at communing with God in a deeply spiritual sense. The historical approach I take in this book is in no way a slight to such readings. Nor do I wish to say that academic readings of Scripture have greater worth than how Christians in general read the Bible for spiritual nourishment.

Yet the topic before us in this book requires nothing less than an enthusiastic engagement of Scripture in context, for the question of evolution cannot be addressed any other way. Hence, I wish to be crystal clear at this point—respecting at the outset differences of opinion on this matter—that the issues I raise in this book and the conclusions (exploratory and tentative at some points) that I reach are an *outworking of my Christian convictions* of what it means to be a responsible reader of Scripture in my time and place. Scripture records a story with deep historical impulses, and thus we must engage Scripture on that level when the situation calls for it, as it does here.

Although there is certainly a core set of convictions that define historic Christian doctrine, I believe that our theological articulations are always works in progress. The truth-value of any theological iteration cannot be judged simply by how well it conforms to past views. Certainly we must be careful to walk the thin line between hardened traditionalism for its own sake and airy speculation for the sake of novelty. Both are wrong, but I take it as axiomatic that a healthy theology is one that shows a willingness—even an expectation—to revisit ways of thinking and changing them when need be. Although veterans of the science-faith discussion will quickly see there is little truly novel in what follows, I realize that at least some readers will be venturing into new territory.

Finally, the title of the book, *The Evolution of Adam*, reflects my contention that our thinking about Adam must change—or perhaps better, continue to change. As will be clear from the chapters that follow, I am not arguing in this book that Adam evolved. Rather, I am arguing that *our understanding of Adam has evolved* over the years and that it must now be adjusted in light of the preponderance of (1) scientific evidence supporting evolution and (2) literary evidence from the world of the Bible that helps clarify the kind of literature the Bible is—that is, what it means to read it as it was meant to be read. Furthermore, all of this can be done in a way that respects and honors the authority of the Bible. Indeed, reflecting on the nature of Scripture like this is the very expression of honor and respect.

"Science and Faith" or "Evolution and Christianity"?

There are many thoughtful books out there that speak to the compatibility of natural science and faith.[3] But phrasing it this way is too general and therefore will be of little help in addressing the tensions between evolution and Christianity.

The biblical writers assumed that the earth is flat, was made by God in relatively recent history (about 4,000 years before Jesus) just as it looks now, and that it is the fixed point in the cosmos over which the sun actually rises and sets. Most Christians don't have a problem in reconciling this biblical view with science. I say "most" because there are groups that do not seem to be convinced. There is in fact a Flat Earth Society,[4] and one well-known group continues to advocate for a six-thousand-year-old earth where humans and dinosaurs coexisted.[5]

Others contend that the universe only looks old, that God created the cosmos with "apparent age."[6] In my opinion, these specific positions are problematic—scientifically and theologically—but I will leave it to others to explain how. As I said, the readers I have in mind here are already committed to keeping Scripture and natural science in conversation. These other views, rooted in a precommitment to read the Bible literally at virtually every point despite evidence to the contrary, avoid engaging science by reinterpreting it to conform to that conviction. To the contrary, it is clear that, from a *scientific* point of view, the Bible does not always describe physical reality accurately; it simply speaks in an ancient idiom, as one might expect ancient people to do. It is God's Word, but it has an ancient view of the natural world, not a modern one.

Evolution, however, is a game changer. The general science-and-faith rapprochement is not adequate because evolution uniquely strikes at central issues of the Christian faith.[7] Evolution tells us that human beings are not the product of a special creative act by God as the Bible says but are the end product of a process of trial-and-error adaptation and natural selection. This process began billions of years ago, with the simplest of one-cell life forms, and developed into the vast array of life on this planet—plants, reptiles, fish, mammals, and so forth—and humanity. These humans also happen to share a close common ancestry with primates. Some Christians reconcile their faith with evolution by saying that God initiated and guides this process, which is fine (and which I believe), but that is not the point here. The tensions that evolution creates with the Bible remain, and they are far more significant than whether the earth is at the center of the cosmos, how old it is, and whether it is round or flat.

If evolution is correct, one can no longer accept, in any true sense of the word "historical," the instantaneous and special creation of humanity described in Genesis, specifically 1:26–31 and 2:7, 22. To reconcile evolution and Christianity, some assert that there was a point in the evolutionary chain where God elevated two hominids (or a group of hominids) to the status of image-bearer of God (Gen. 1:26–27). According to this scheme, "image" is understood as the soul, God-consciousness, or other qualities that make us human. That way of thinking allows evolution and Genesis to coexist somewhat but eventually proves inadequate for me. One reason is that it does little to ease the tensions with the Bible, for this hybrid of modern and ancient accounts of human origins is hardly what the Bible depicts: two humans created specially by God. This hybrid view does not adhere to the Bible but rewrites it.

Also, although what "image of God" means in its fullest biblical witness may be open for discussion, in Genesis it does not refer to a soul or a psychological or spiritual quality that separates humans from animals. It refers to humanity's role of ruling God's creation as God's representative. We see this played out in the ancient Near Eastern[8] world, where kings were divine image-bearers, appointed representatives of God on earth. This concept is further reflected in kings' placing statues of themselves (images) in distant parts of their kingdom so they could remind their subjects of their "presence." Further, idols were images of gods placed in ancient temples as a way of having a distant god present with the worshipers.

Genesis 1:26 clearly operates within the same thought world: "Let us make humankind in our image, according to our likeness; and *let them have dominion* over the fish, . . . birds, . . .cattle, . . . all the wild animals, . . . every creeping thing" (emphasis added).[9] Humankind, created on day 6, is given authority to rule over what God had made on days 4 and 5. The image of God is not that spark in us that makes us human rather than animal—like reason, self-consciousness, or consciousness of God. In Genesis it means that humans represent God in the world, nothing less but certainly nothing more. This is not to dismiss the question of what makes us human and how humanity uniquely reflects God, especially given the challenge of evolution; but "image of God" is not the biblical way of addressing those ideas.

Attempts to reconcile Genesis and evolution are understandable, but they invariably lead to making some adjustments in the biblical story, and these adjustments always move us away from a strictly literal/historical reading of Genesis toward something else—call it "symbolic" or "metaphorical" or some other term. Unless one simply rejects scientific evidence (as some continue to do), adjustments to the biblical story are always necessary. The only question is what sorts of adjustments best account for the data. Part of this book is aimed at thinking through the parameters for answering that question.

Yet Christians have a bigger problem than dealing with Genesis if they want to reconcile Christianity and evolution: Paul. Here we come to the heart of the matter, what I believe is the ultimate source of concern for Christians who are seeking a synthesis between the Bible and evolution.

After a virtual silence in the Old Testament, Adam makes a sudden and unprecedented appearance in two of Paul's Letters (Rom. 5; 1 Cor. 15).[10] There Paul draws an important analogy between Adam and Jesus. Just as the first Adam introduced *sin and death* to all humanity through his *disobedience* in the garden of Eden (eating the forbidden fruit), now Jesus, the second Adam (see 1 Cor. 15:47), introduces *life* through his *obedience* (death on the cross and resurrection). The first Adam is a "pattern" for the second (Rom. 5:14), and Paul's point looks straightforward enough.

$$\text{Adam} \rightarrow \text{disobedience} \rightarrow \text{death}$$
$$\text{Jesus} \rightarrow \text{obedience} \rightarrow \text{life}$$

For Paul's analogy to have any force, it seems that both Adam and Jesus must be actual historical figures. Not all Christian traditions will necessarily see it that way, but this is clearly a commonly held assumption today and the root reason why Christianity and evolution are in such tension for many, in my opinion. A historical Adam has been the dominant Christian view for two thousand years. We must add, however, that the general consensus was formed before the advent of evolutionary theory. To appeal to this older consensus as a way of keeping the challenge of evolution at bay is not a viable option for readers today. The same argument from consensus was used against Galileo's observation that the earth revolves around the sun, and that old consensus eventually (slowly) failed to persuade. We should be cautious not to repeat that same mistake.

The problem is self-evident. Evolution demands that the special creation of the first Adam as described in the Bible is not literally historical; Paul, however, seems to require it. After all, what purpose does the actual obedience of the second Adam (Christ) have if there was no first Adam who disobeyed? So, as the argument often goes, if there was no first Adam, then there was no fall. If there was no fall, there is no truly inescapably sinful condition and so no need for a Savior. If evolution is true, then Christianity is false. When the issue is framed this way, the discussion tends to move toward one of two extremes: Christians either choose Paul over Darwin or abandon their faith in favor of natural science.

As we can see, the issue is not whether science and religion in general can be reconciled. The issue before us is more pressing: can evolution and a biblically rooted Christian faith coexist? When the biblical authors presented their view that the earth does not move (Pss. 96:10; 104:5), they were only expressing their assumptions about the nature of the cosmos and were hardly touching on matters central to the faith. But with Genesis and Paul on the origin of humanity, we seem to be dealing with biblical teachings that are of far greater importance: they address questions of who we are and why we do what we do. It is easy to see how, for some, a clear choice has to be made: either evolution is right about human origins, or Paul and Genesis are right. That is the dilemma many face. Deep Christian commitments lead one to read Paul and Genesis with utmost seriousness, but scientific sensibilities do not allow one to dismiss evolution.

As I see it, there are four options before us:

1. *Accept evolution and reject Christianity.* Plenty of people find themselves here, but their assumptions about how Genesis and Paul ought to be read may be part of the problem. If one is convinced of evolution and also assumes that the Bible—since it is the Word of God—is required to give a scientifically and historically accurate account of human origins, option 1 may be the only option. One of the purposes of this book is to offer a very different path for learning what to expect from the Bible where it touches on creation.

2. *Accept Paul's view of Adam as binding and reject evolution.* This option means that the overwhelming evidence for evolution must be rejected. Like the first option, it also assumes that the Bible is prepared to give us accurate information about human origins, and so one must choose between the two.

3. *Reconcile evolution and Christianity by positing a first human pair (or group) at some point in the evolutionary process.* This option is seriously considered by respected thinkers who are trying to bring evolution and Christianity into some meaningful conversation. I respect their efforts but, as I hinted above and hope to make clear in what follows, I do not think this is the best way to proceed. It seems to me that this approach is driven by a perceived theological need to preserve some sort of a first pair in order to preserve Paul's theology. The irony, however, is that in expending such effort to preserve biblical teaching, we are left with a first pair that is utterly foreign to the biblical portrait. As I see it, this is enough of a problem to warrant alternate solutions.

This third option also shares one shortcoming with the previous two: a failure to properly address Genesis as ancient literature and Paul as an ancient man. Once those ancient settings are adequately understood, there will be less of an urgency to align scientific models and biblical literature (an urgency that is far less pronounced in the third option, to be sure). This brings us to the fourth option.

4. *Rethink Genesis and Paul.* An alternate way forward is to reevaluate what we have *the right to expect* from Genesis and Paul. This will help us think synthetically about how Christianity and evolution can be in dialogue. I am writing this book to present one way of pressing forward that synthesis for those interested in such an exercise.[11]

Overview of the Book

This book is divided into two parts, the first dealing with Genesis and the second with Paul. In part 1 we will look at when Genesis was written and why, which are two related questions. Widely convincing answers to those questions have been offered over the last several generations of biblical scholarship, and becoming familiar with them may help us look more productively at the evolution-Christianity discussion.

Specifically, two important developments in biblical scholarship in the nineteenth century have had significant and deserved influence on how we read Genesis today. One was the new field of biblical archaeology. The other was an innovative answer to long-standing problems concerning when the Pentateuch was written and by whom. These developments are not above criticism, to be sure, but they started conversations that have shed considerable light on *when and why Genesis was written.* Answers to those questions in broad outline have been accepted in some form by most biblical scholars, including many evangelicals. Listening in on that conversation helps disarm the alleged "conflict" between Genesis and evolution, for it shows us that Genesis is an ancient Israelite narrative written to answer pressing ancient Israelite questions.

To anticipate the point, modern scholarship understands the Old Testament as a whole, and Genesis and the Pentateuch in particular, to be Israel's statement of national self-definition in the wake of Babylonian captivity (586–539 BC). The Old Testament is not aimed at simply providing objective historical information, and certainly not scientific information that conforms to modern expectations. Genesis in particular shows us how Israel thought about itself amid its own troubled history and among the surrounding nations. Having a good handle on what a portion of Scripture was written to do, especially the opening chapters of Genesis, reorients the kinds of questions we might ask of Genesis when the topic turns to evolution. To be direct, the more we understand the kind of information Genesis is prepared to offer, the less likely we will feel the need to reject Genesis in view of evolution, reject evolution in view of Genesis, or bring the two into uneasy "harmony." Science and Scripture speak two different languages and accomplish quite different things. My goal in part 1 is to reflect on the "language" of Genesis.

But again, the central concern for many Christians is not so much Genesis but Paul's appeal to Adam in Romans 5 and 1 Corinthians 15. As mentioned above, for many Christians the analogy requires that both Adam and Jesus be historical figures. But understanding Paul's Adam is actually quite challenging, much more than a matter of accessing the "plain meaning" of a few verses in his Letters. Paul's understanding of Adam has a much broader context. Clarifying that context has been the ongoing work of scholars of the New Testament and Second Temple Judaism.[12] The sheer volume of material those scholars have produced—even over the last fifty years—is absolutely overwhelming. Yet some dimensions of those scholarly conversations can filter down to where they are needed, and I hope I will do justice to those discussions. Among other things, to shed light on how Paul handles Adam specifically, we will look at how Paul uses the Old Testament in general.

I will show that Paul's use of the Adam story serves a vital theological purpose in explaining to his ancient readers the significance for all humanity of *Christ's death and resurrection*. His use of the Adam story, however, cannot and should not be the determining factor in whether biblically faithful Christians can accept evolution as the scientific account of human origins—and the gospel does not hang in the balance.

In the concluding chapter I offer nine theses for how Adam can be understood today. Some of these theses summarize main points in the book, while others add further points for consideration.

At this moment in history, the state of scientific knowledge is driving Christians to rethink some important issues. The challenge of evolution is here to stay, and its effect on how Christians read Genesis and Paul must be deliberately addressed. It is always a difficult subject to suggest that something outside the Bible can significantly affect how the Bible is to be read. We will come back to this now and then throughout the course of the book. Let me say here that I understand the theological sensitivities surrounding such reluctance; what we "have always believed" seems to be at the mercy of the dictates of science. The matter cannot be expressed quite so simply, however, as we shall see.

Moreover, as much attention as we might give to preserving the past, it is equally important to give adequate thought to preparing the church for the future. I feel that if we do not engage Scripture with future believers in mind, we will unwittingly erect unnecessary and tragic obstacles to belief. Part of what drives this book is my concern to help prevent that scenario.

PART ONE

GENESIS

AN ANCIENT STORY
OF ISRAELITE SELF-DEFINITION

1

Genesis and the Challenges of the Nineteenth Century

SCIENCE, BIBLICAL CRITICISM, AND BIBLICAL ARCHAEOLOGY

For Christians, the nineteenth century was rough. In the span of about twenty years, three independent, technical, and powerful forces converged to challenge the historical reliability of Genesis (not to mention other parts of the Old Testament). Separately each of these forces was a handful. Together they formed a relentless tidal wave that has had a lasting and powerful impact on how Genesis is read. The conflicts that ensued are the very stuff of the liberal-versus-conservative divide, particularly in the United States, that a century and a half later still generates considerable heat and precious little light.

Despite this relatively negative appraisal, familiarity with the legacy of the nineteenth century and its lasting impact on Genesis can ease evolution and Christianity toward meaningful dialogue. Understanding that legacy will also let us see more clearly the nature of the conflict that still exists for some today and so perhaps help us move beyond those tensions. In other words, moving forward requires first looking back.

One of those three forces that reared its head in the nineteenth century is natural science's advance and its effect on how we understand the history of our planet. Since the eighteenth century, geology had made its presence known, showing by means of the fossil record that the earth is millions upon millions of years old—far older than most people had taken for granted, far older than a literal interpretation of the Bible allows. Darwin's work in the nineteenth century followed on the heels of these discoveries. His theory of human origins further challenged the biblical view of the origin of life, to put it mildly. Understandably, evolution and the account in Genesis were deemed incompatible on the scientific level.

Almost everyone knows something about the basic impact of evolution—a theory claiming that humans and primates are cousins was bound to get its fair share of press. But the second and third forces, generally lesser-known, are as important for understanding the major shift in reading Genesis.

The second force is developments in biblical studies, often called biblical criticism. Biblical criticism is often understood as being condescending toward the Bible, or even atheistic. It is not uncommon to hear the objection that biblical criticism tends to undermine the Bible and even poison the faith of unsuspecting believers. Unfortunately, this has too often been the case, but such motivations hardly describe the heart of the matter.

Understood in a more neutral fashion, biblical criticism refers to the academic study of the Bible that is marked mainly by a historical investigation into the date and authorship of biblical books. In this sense, evangelical biblical scholars today are engaged in biblical criticism and in many cases find themselves in some level of agreement with secular counterparts (although this observation hardly does justice to the long history of dis-ease). At any rate, in the early years the focus of this investigation was the date and authorship of Genesis; it is even fair to say that the modern academic study of the Old Testament began as a series of questions about who wrote Genesis, which expanded to the Pentateuch as a whole.[1]

Biblical criticism is a far less exciting topic than evolution: no media coverage or mass controversy—just a lot of Hebrew and some other ancient languages. But the impact has been significant. The traditional view was that one man, Moses, living in the middle of the second millennium BC, was solely (more or less) responsible for writing the first five books of the Bible. A few premodern readers had already begun to question the traditional view, however gently, and we will look at two examples below. But it is not until the seventeenth and eighteenth centuries that we begin to see some earlier questions bubble over into detailed arguments for why the Pentateuch could not have been written by one man at one time.

The issue came to a boiling point in the work of the nineteenth-century German Old Testament scholar Julius Wellhausen (1844–1918), whom we will meet more properly in the next chapter. He proposed a theory about the authorship of the Pentateuch that, although both strongly contested and widely accepted, has had an unparalleled effect on how the Pentateuch is viewed—and Old Testament scholarship has not been the same since. The bottom line is that for Wellhausen and many other biblical scholars before and since, the Pentateuch *as we know it* (an important qualification) was not completed until the postexilic period (after the Israelites were allowed to return to their homeland from Babylon beginning in 539 BC). There were certainly long-standing written documents and oral traditions that the postexilic Israelites drew upon, which biblical scholars continue to discuss vigorously, but the Pentateuch as we know it was formed as a response to the Babylonian exile. The specifics of Wellhausen's work no longer dominate the academic landscape, but the postexilic setting for the Pentateuch is the dominant view among biblical scholars today.

This is extremely significant. Knowing something of when the Pentateuch came to be, even generally, affects our understanding of why it was produced in the first place—which is the entire reason why we are dipping our toes into this otherwise esoteric pool of Old Testament studies. The final form of the creation story in Genesis (along with the rest of the Pentateuch) reflects the concerns of the community that produced it: postexilic Israelites who had experienced God's rejection in Babylon. The Genesis creation narrative we have in our Bibles today, although surely rooted in much older material, was shaped as a theological response to Israel's national crisis of exile. These stories were not written to speak of "origins" as we might think of them today (in a natural-science sense). They were written to say something of God and Israel's place in the world as God's chosen people.

Complementing the work of biblical criticism was a third factor, the growing field of archaeology of ancient Israel and the surrounding area, or as it is commonly referred to, biblical archaeology. This field posed serious challenges of its own, in some respects more serious than the work of Wellhausen and other biblical critics. Wellhausen worked wholly with "internal data," the Bible itself. But archaeology introduced "external data": texts and artifacts from the ancient Near Eastern world, Israel's neighbors and predecessors. These findings have helped us understand more deeply the intellectual world in which the Bible was written. Israel now had a context, which meant that scholars could compare and contrast Israel's religious beliefs with those of the surrounding nations.

The most famous of these findings are Babylonian texts that look very similar to Genesis 1 and the flood story (Gen. 6–9), both of which we will explore in chapter 3. These texts do not directly affect the question of Adam, which is the central issue for the evolution-Christianity dialogue. Other texts that later came to light are more immediately relevant for Adam, but we will only glimpse at them, leaving our discussion of Adam mainly for part 2. Here in part 1 we will focus on the profound and lasting impact these other nineteenth-century discoveries had—and continue to have—on our understanding of the opening chapters of Genesis in general (chaps. 1–11). Focusing there is not beside the point, however. A proper understanding of the Adam story is directly affected by how we understand Israel's primordial stories as a whole in light of the nineteenth-century developments in biblical scholarship.

These Babylonian texts helped scholars to see how Genesis functioned for Israel, and in this sense they complemented the internal analysis of Wellhausen and other biblical critics. Placing Genesis in its ancient Near Eastern setting strongly suggests that it was written as a self-defining document, as a means of declaring the distinctiveness of Israel's own beliefs from those of the surrounding nations. In other words, Genesis is an argument, a polemic, declaring how Israel's God is different from all the other gods, and therefore how Israel is different from all the other nations.

This is all well and good, but here is the problem: the ancient Israelites, in making this polemical case, freely adapted the themes of the much-older stories of the nations around them. It quickly became self-evident that the rather bizarre Babylonian stories were disturbingly (if only partly) similar to the creation and flood stories of Genesis, which raised the obvious question of the historical value of Genesis 1–11 as a whole: if these chapters look so much like Mesopotamian myth, how can they still be God's revealed Word? The stories of the early chapters of Genesis may have seemed fanciful to modern readers beforehand—with a talking serpent and trees with magical fruit. But there was now external, corroborating evidence that Genesis and pagan mythologies were connected somehow, at least indirectly.

It is not hard to understand why traditionalists reacted vigorously and unyieldingly to these two developments in biblical scholarship. For some the truth of the gospel itself was under attack—casting doubt on the historical value of Genesis was only a few steps removed from casting doubt on anything the Bible says, including Jesus and the resurrection. After all, if God is the author of all of Scripture, undermining one part undermines the whole.

Given the assumption that inspiration and historical accuracy are inseparable, conservatives sensed that the trapdoor to the slippery slide to unbelief was cracking open, and it needed to be slammed shut quickly. That is why there was such resistance to biblical criticism of the Pentateuch and to accepting the implications of the ancient Near Eastern evidence. And with all that going on, as if conservatives did not have enough to worry about from biblical scholars, throw Darwin into the mix. Now we have a scientific theory of origins that, along with biblical criticism and biblical archaeology, converged to produce powerfully coherent and persuasive explanations for what Genesis is and how it should be understood. The tensions that resulted were considerable and, from a historical point of view, wholly understandable.

I do not mean to imply that Genesis got a free pass before the nineteenth century. As I mentioned above, European scholars (such as the philosopher Spinoza, 1632–77) began challenging traditional views of Genesis (and other portions of the Bible) as early as the seventeenth century, and geology had already been a force to be reckoned with since the eighteenth century. But the nineteenth century was a profoundly influential time. It did away with any hope for pasting new ideas piecemeal onto old views. Now the one-two-three punch of biblical criticism, biblical archaeology, and science demanded a fresh *synthesis* of new and old.

That synthesis proved to be a difficult step for many to take, for it required rethinking some long-held beliefs about the Bible, particularly regarding its historical value, and whether the books were written by eyewitnesses or long after the events they describe. Instead of synthesis, there was deep conflict, and clear battle lines were quickly drawn. Generations of traditionally minded biblical scholars dedicated their entire careers to defending the Bible from these threats, and separatist Bible colleges and seminaries began dotting the landscape with greater density. Contemporary evangelicalism and fundamentalism arose out of this conflict; although some of the emotion has subsided, the debris from early bombshells still clutters much of the evangelical and fundamentalist landscape, and neutrality is rare. Those who are part of an American mainline denomination or were reared in evangelical or fundamentalist denominations likely owe their ecclesiastical identity to this unfolding of events; they are living among these old tensions.

The question of Genesis was not settled forever during the nineteenth century—far from it, as anyone familiar with Old Testament studies can attest. Important trajectories were set, but in the same way that evolutionary theory has not stood still since Darwin, neither has Old Testament scholarship. Not every theory posed during that generative era has remained convincing, and some things have been rejected. Biblical scholarship has moved beyond some initially unguarded conclusions, and rightly so. So to be clear, I am not advocating a return to the glory days of the nineteenth century any more than contemporary evolutionists are advocating a return to Darwin.

Still, the nineteenth century was unquestionably a pivotal moment in recent intellectual history, with huge implications for a good many things, including how we read Genesis, and thus also for the evolution discussion. These developments are foundational to the academic study of Scripture, but they are not always understood where they most need to be: in on-the-ground discussions concerning evolution and Christianity. In the remaining chapters of part 1, we will look at these academic developments a bit more closely for what they have to say about when Genesis was written and why, and what difference that makes for how we think about Genesis and evolution.

2

When Was Genesis Written?

I mentioned above that some see biblical criticism as simply undermining or unnecessarily complicating what the Bible says. But a blanket negative appraisal can obscure a seldom-appreciated fact: modern scholarship on the Pentateuch did not come out of nowhere. The question of when the Pentateuch was written and why is not an outside imposition of modern biblical critics. Rather, many of the questions that modern scholars address are generated by the Pentateuch itself and had already captured the attention of some readers long before the modern period (as we will see below). Modern biblical scholarship, whatever its promises and pitfalls—and there are both— grew out of earlier attempts to address obvious questions.

It is hard to appreciate where modern scholarship has landed on the issue of Genesis and the Pentateuch without first understanding how it got there. Toward that end, we begin this chapter by looking at how the Pentateuch itself raises its own questions about who wrote it and when. Then we will move to how the problem of the Pentateuch was generally settled in modern scholarship, and especially in the nineteenth century. This will lead us briefly beyond the Pentateuch to the Old Testament as a whole to see the impact that the Babylonian exile had on the formation of Israel's Scripture as a self-defining statement. Seeing the Old Testament as a whole in this light, and Genesis in particular, can also be a model for how contemporary Christians can appropriate the theology of Genesis.

This chapter intentionally takes a step back from the evolution discussion to sketch a bigger picture of what the Old Testament is and what we have the right to expect from it. Adjusting our expectations about the Old Testament and Genesis is perhaps the first and most important step to take when discussing the relationship between evolution and Christianity. Any meaningful talk of Adam's place in that discussion, which will come up more specifically in the chapters to follow, must take place against that larger backdrop.

The Problem of the Pentateuch

For a very long time, careful readers have noticed that the Pentateuch needs some explaining, since it raises its own questions. This is especially true of Genesis, particularly the creation stories in its opening chapters.[1] These chapters, so pivotal for setting the stage for much of the following drama of the Old Testament, are nevertheless a veritable minefield of interpretive challenges. Seeing these challenges does not require vast learning but arises naturally from the text itself during the normal course of reading. For example:

- In Genesis 1, how can there be days 1, 2, and 3 (1:3–13) before a sun and moon are created on day 4 (1:14–19)?
- Why doesn't Genesis 1 mention the creation of angels, since they are part of God's creation and play such prominent roles later in the Old Testament?
- Why does God say, "Let *us* make humankind" (1:26; 3:22)?
- What does it mean to be made in the image and likeness of God (1:26)?
- How does the formation of one man (Adam, in 2:7) and one woman (Eve, in 2:21–25) relate to the creation of humanity as a whole, male and female (1:26–27)?
- Are Adam and Eve created perfect and immortal?
- Why does God not want Adam to have the knowledge of good and evil (2:15–17)? What does it mean to be like God (3:22) if Adam does acquire that knowledge?
- What drives Adam and Eve to disobey God and Cain to kill Abel?
- Is Adam's sinfulness hereditary in some way?
- Who is really to blame, Adam or Eve?

- Why are Adam and Eve only banished for eating the forbidden fruit (3:22–24) when God said they would die on the very day they eat of it (2:17)?
- If Adam and Eve are the first humans, and Cain their only surviving offspring, how can Cain be afraid of retaliation for murdering his brother (4:13–16)? Where did he get his wife (4:17)?
- Who/what is the serpent in the garden, and what is it doing there in the first place (3:1–7)?
- Why does God need to ask where Adam and Eve are in the garden (3:9)?

These questions are among those asked by the earliest known biblical interpreters—beginning with Jewish interpreters living two hundred years or so before Christ. And these and other questions continued to be addressed by Jewish and Christian interpreters for hundreds of years. No doubt many reading this will recognize a good number of these questions, and one or two may even have been a source of embarrassment in teaching children's Sunday school. (What teacher has not been asked by a precocious eight-year-old where Cain found his wife?) The above questions come from the first four chapters of Genesis, and this list is not exhaustive. If we continue reading Genesis—the flood story, tower of Babel, Abraham and his descendants—similar questions will come up, and they all require some sort of answer for people who look to the Bible for divine guidance.

For this reason the long history of Jewish biblical interpretation has been anything but bashful about engaging the many interpretive challenges of Genesis.[2] These writings are so voluminous that theological libraries have shelf after shelf of commentaries and other books dealing with how Genesis and the rest of the Bible were handled by these early interpreters—apparently showing that there has always been a need to apply a lot of energy and creativity in addressing a myriad of interpretive problems. Such creative engagement can be seen in the Dead Sea Scrolls (first or second century BC), other generally pre-Christian Jewish works (Pseudepigrapha and Apocrypha), and early interpreters like Philo and Josephus (first century AD). Later Judaism continued such careful interaction with the biblical texts in its official documents (Mishnah and Talmud, second to fifth centuries AD), Aramaic paraphrases of Scripture (targumim, from before Christ to well into the medieval period), and medieval commentaries (midrashim).

Likewise, Christians from the earliest years produced writings that record their own attempts to address the interpretive challenges of Genesis. Second-century church fathers such as Justin Martyr, Melito of Sardis, Theophilus of Antioch, and Irenaeus of Lyons all wrote on Genesis and dealt not only with some of the questions listed above but also with the added concern of showing how the creation narratives and the gospel of Jesus Christ are related. Later writers of the third century (Tertullian, Origen) and fourth century (Cyril of Jerusalem, Athanasius of Alexandria, Basil of Caesarea, Gregory of Nazianzus, Gregory of Nyssa) continued spirited discussions and debates about how to understand the biblical creation narratives. Rounding out our list of early Christian writers is Augustine (354–430), especially his work *The Literal Meaning of Genesis*, where he shows, among other things, how much intellectual effort is required to handle Genesis well, and how ill-advised it is to read the creation stories literally.

> It is a disgraceful and dangerous thing for an infidel to hear a Christian, presumably giving the meaning of Holy Scripture, talking nonsense on these [cosmological] topics, and we should take all means to prevent such an embarrassing situation, in which people show up vast ignorance in a Christian and laugh it to scorn.[3]

This is not the place to look into the vast history of premodern Jewish and Christian interpretation on Genesis; we are only scratching the surface here. My point is that Genesis is not now and never has been an easy book to understand. It raises its own questions and requires skill and learning to handle well; thoughtful people have been doing that since long before the modern era. To be sure, some may be convinced that answers to at least some of these questions are clear, but it would not take much digging to appreciate the diversity of compelling opinions offered on some of these questions. (In chap. 6 we will look at some of that diversity concerning Jewish interpretations of Adam.)

What distinguishes modern biblical scholarship from some of this early history we have just glimpsed is not the pointing out of ambiguities and inconsistencies in Genesis. That is old hat. Rather, modern scholars have tended to focus on the historical questions raised by those ambiguities and inconsistencies; namely, how did such an ambiguous and inconsistent text come to exist in the first place? In other words, the questions are about authorship and date. In addition to ambiguities and inconsistencies, an added impetus for asking these questions of Genesis pertains to perceived anachronisms. The following reflect these various modern concerns at various points in Genesis:

- Why are there two such clearly different creation stories at the very beginning of the Bible? (1:1–2:3 and 2:4–25)[4]
- Why is proper sacrifice mentioned so suddenly at the dawn of time? Why does it play such a big role with Cain and Abel? (Gen. 4)
- Why is the flood story so choppy, repetitive, and internally inconsistent? (Gen. 6–9)
- Why are there two stories of the nations being dispersed? (Gen. 10 and 11:1–9)
- Who is Melchizedek? How can he be a priest of "God Most High" way back in Abraham's day? (14:18)
- Why are there two covenant-making stories with Abraham? (Gen. 15 and 17)
- How can Abraham be described as a law keeper long before the law was given? (26:5)
- How can the concept of Israelite kingship be mentioned long before Israel existed as a nation? (36:31)

These and other questions (summarized later in the chapter) led modern biblical scholars to question seriously—and eventually reject—the traditional view that Genesis and the Pentateuch were written in the second millennium BC by one man, Moses. Again, modern scholarship is hardly beyond fault, and all arguments need to be judged on their own merits. But modern biblical scholars, beginning especially in the eighteenth century, did not create a problem where there had been none. They were heirs to a long-standing history of probing the meaning of Genesis, because Genesis itself demands close inspection. Genesis generates its own questions.

Two Early Examples

The question of authorship that defines much of modern scholarship is not an entirely modern issue. Let me illustrate with two examples. The first concerns Deuteronomy, the fifth book of the Pentateuch. Deuteronomy is largely a series of speeches by Moses, given on the brink of the promised land. (He was not allowed to enter Canaan; see Num.

20:12.) The traditional view is that Moses wrote this book along with the other four, but Deuteronomy nowhere claims that. More important, the content of the book argues against it. Specifically, the beginning and end of Deuteronomy raise serious questions about Moses's role in writing Deuteronomy, and at least one early interpreter from about AD 400, whom we will meet in a moment, picked up on this.

The first five verses of Deuteronomy present the entire book as a third-person account *about* Moses. Thus in 1:5 we read, "Moses undertook to expound this law as follows," followed by a third-person account of what Moses said. It seems that someone other than Moses wrote this (see also 4:41, 44; 5:1). In 1:1 we see a more compelling piece of evidence. We are told that the following words are what "Moses spoke to all Israel *beyond the Jordan*" (emphasis added). This comment *about* Moses, in the *past* tense, is spoken by someone who apparently made it into *Canaan*—on the other (west) side of the Jordan River from where Moses gave his speeches on the plains of Moab. According to Numbers 20:12 and Deuteronomy 32:48–52, Moses never made it into Canaan, and so it is safe to conclude that Moses did not write at least the opening portion of the book.

Some have tried to maintain Mosaic authorship by saying that the Hebrew phrase translated "beyond the Jordan" is a fixed geographic term—like "The East River" or "South Central Los Angeles" today; these locations are "east" or "south central" regardless of where the speaker is. So, as the argument goes, perhaps "beyond the Jordan" simply means "East Jordan," which some believe opens the door to the possibility that Moses could have written Deuteronomy 1:1–5. But this approach cannot gain traction. First, we still have the rather odd scenario of Moses's writing about himself in the third person and in the past tense. Second, the same Hebrew phrase "beyond the Jordan" is spoken by Moses in Deuteronomy 3:25 and 11:30 and refers to the promised land: west of the Jordan. In other words, "beyond the Jordan" means just what it says: the side you are not on. It is a relative geographic term, not a fixed one.

There is good reason, therefore, to conclude that the first five verses of Deuteronomy—which sets up the entire book—are indisputably written by someone who made it to the promised land after Moses died. But there is no indication of how long afterward. I suppose Moses's contemporary Joshua is a possible candidate, although there is no real reason to name him specifically. It is true that Joshua is a *possible* author, but only one possibility among many. It is equally possible that

David wrote it, or Hezekiah, or Ezra, or anyone. Raising a possible solution should not be mistaken for argument. The real issue is what is convincing and persuasive. Joshua is a tempting candidate for some because, if Moses is not the author, at least Joshua would be an eyewitness to the events. The concern for some seems to be the accuracy of what is recorded, which would allegedly be assured if a contemporary of Moses wrote Deuteronomy. But enlisting Joshua as a candidate is arbitrary and will only be convincing if it finds support elsewhere. A reluctance to see Deuteronomy as written long after Moses's lifetime is not a good-enough reason to insert Joshua's name.

The report of Moses's death in chapter 34 is an even bigger problem, for it suggests a time much later than that of Moses. Specifically, verses 6 and 10 sound as though they were written a good time after Moses died. After we read of Moses's death and burial, verse 6 says, "No one knows his burial place *to this day*" (emphasis added). Verse 10 adds, "*Never since* has there arisen a prophet in Israel like Moses" (emphasis added). The fact that his gravesite is unknown suggests that a lengthy time has transpired.[5] To maintain Mosaic authorship, one would need to argue that Moses wrote about his future death in the third person and past tense and that he also anticipated that his gravesite would become unknown. In my opinion, this is an extremely unlikely scenario. Verses 6 and 10 also make very unlikely the notion that Joshua is responsible since that would mean that within a few short years the eyewitnesses had trouble locating Moses's burial site. The same holds for verse 10. This statement makes little sense if only a generation or two (or three or four) has transpired. The whole gravity of verse 10 is lost unless we presume that a considerable length of time has transpired: "Moses was great, and even after *all this time* no one like him has come along" (emphasis added).

It is hard to avoid the conclusion that the book of Deuteronomy comes to us from someone who lived a long time after Moses.[6] So who is responsible for all this if not Moses? The church father Jerome (AD 347–420), without any fanfare or elaboration, suggested a sober explanation for the account of Moses's death, and this explanation can be seen in one form or another in various modern interpreters. Jerome proposed that "to this day" in Deuteronomy 34:6 refers to the time of Ezra, the mid-fifth-century-BC returnee from Babylonian exile.[7]

One can only speculate whether Jerome thought Ezra was responsible for more than just this one verse; yet we should be careful not to expect more from Jerome than he is prepared to deliver. Nevertheless,

at least in this one instance, Jerome saw a problem that clearly needed
an explanation and offered one that anticipates a commonly held
view among biblical scholars. Jerome was not adamant about the
point, but neither did he seem all that concerned to defend it. And he
certainly wasn't undermining the Bible by suggesting that Moses did
not write this. He was addressing an interpretive issue and exercised
common sense in doing so.

A second early interpreter is the twelfth-century rabbi Abraham Ibn
Ezra. Ibn Ezra was brilliant and respected. He also was reluctant to break
with tradition too quickly—including the tradition that Moses wrote
the Pentateuch. Still, Ibn Ezra found some biblical evidence difficult to
reconcile to that tradition and was forthright in noting it:

1. Moses did not cross the Jordan (the problem of Deut. 1:1–5).
2. With respect to Moses's writing the Pentateuch, Ibn Ezra refers
   cryptically to a "mystery of the twelve." The seventeenth-cen-
   tury philosopher Spinoza (see below) understood this to refer
   to Deuteronomy 27 and Joshua 8:32, where the entire book of
   Moses was inscribed on an altar that consisted of twelve stones.
   Apparently the "book of Moses" was small enough to fit on
   such a small space and so could not have included the entire
   Pentateuch during Moses's day.
3. Ibn Ezra felt that the third-person account of Moses's life was
   a problem for Mosaic authorship, citing Deuteronomy 31:9
   ("Moses wrote down this law").
4. According to Genesis 22:2, 14, the mountain of God is called
   Mount Moriah. Moriah is mentioned elsewhere only in
   2 Chronicles 3:1, as the site of the temple. By citing this example, Ibn Ezra may have thought that a reference to Moriah
   in Genesis is anachronistic. Hence the writer of Genesis lived
   much later and placed a reference to Mount Moriah in Abraham's day to legitimate the temple site. This would require
   a date at least in the fifth century for Genesis 22:2, 14, since
   Chronicles was written no earlier than the middle of the fifth
   century BC (see the discussion later in this chapter).
5. According to Deuteronomy 3:11, the nine-cubit-long bed of
   iron of Og king of Bashan "can still be seen in Rabbah."
   This sounded to Ibn Ezra like an explanation for an ancient
   relic. He attributed this comment to the time of David, who
   conquered the city (2 Sam. 12:30).

6. At Genesis 12:6, during Abraham's sojourn through the promised land, the narrator comments, "*At that time* the Canaanites were [still] in the land." Ibn Ezra concluded that this was written when the Canaanites were no longer in the land—pointing to a time after the final conquest of Canaan under David, a thousand years later. Ibn Ezra, understanding the implications of this passage, writes: "There is a secret meaning to the text. Let the one who understands it remain silent."[8]

Ibn Ezra seems to have thought that a date of authorship from around the time of David would explain at least some of what the Pentateuch says. Biblical scholars would later adopt a similar position, for the time of David and Solomon was one of relative peace for this fledgling nation, a good time to compose their national story. Later scholars, however, would also argue that the time of the early monarchy was only the beginning of a writing process that did not come to an end until after the exile, a point that Ibn Ezra was in no position to adopt in his historical moment. Also, unlike Jerome, Ibn Ezra's difficulties with the Pentateuch are numerous, not just with a verse in Deuteronomy. Although Ibn Ezra's list of difficulties is modest, it has raised an important question for later scholars: is the Pentateuch an essentially Mosaic document that was merely updated here and there, or do these examples indicate when Genesis and the Pentateuch as a whole were written (no earlier than the time of David)?

A concerted exploration of that question would have to wait for a different moment in European history, when open questioning of received traditions came into vogue. Such a critical climate arose in Europe beginning in the seventeenth century, and an early formidable and influential figure was the Jewish philosopher Benedict Spinoza (1632–77). In his 1670 work *Theologico-Political Treatise*, Spinoza lays out his views of the Bible as a whole[9] and spends his share of time on the Pentateuch. He draws explicitly on Ibn Ezra's work but makes a far grander claim: "From all this [Ibn Ezra's list plus his own observations] it is clearer than the noonday sun that the Pentateuch was not written by Moses but by someone else who lived many generations after Moses."[10] That someone, Spinoza argues, was Ezra the scribe, echoing Jerome's suggestion thirteen hundred years earlier but applying it to the entire Pentateuch, not simply to Moses's death in Deuteronomy 34.

Spinoza's work was influential, and his words were a revealing early indication of where things were headed: the widespread belief that the Pentateuch is essentially a document written long after Moses lived.[11] As bold as this claim was, it still fell short of a comprehensive theory for how the Pentateuch came to be. Such a theory would have to wait until the next century, when a physician, not a philosopher, would chart a course leading to a true paradigm shift in the dating of the Pentateuch and, in subsequent generations, the entire Bible.

God Has Two Names

Modern Old Testament scholarship began in earnest in the eighteenth century, and questions about Genesis led the way. One issue in particular came to the forefront: why does God have two names in Genesis, Elohim (God) and Yahweh (typically translated LORD)? It is no exaggeration to say that the answers given to that question gave rise not only to the modern study of the Pentateuch but also to Old Testament biblical scholarship as a whole.

The man typically credited for unwittingly spearheading this revolution in biblical scholarship was Jean Astruc (1684–1766), a French professor of medicine and physician to Louis XV. He apparently was quite industrious. In addition to teaching and tending to the French monarch, Astruc also read a lot of Hebrew and came up with a theory about Genesis that formed the basis for the work of every scholar after him, including Wellhausen and beyond.

Astruc was not out to make a name for himself as a biblical scholar. He was just curious as to how Moses could have written Genesis when he was not an eyewitness to the events.[12] In pondering this question, he noticed that Genesis 1 refers to Israel's God as Elohim but that Genesis 2–4 uses the name Yahweh (startling since that name seems to be introduced to Moses only later, in Exod. 3:13–15). Astruc thought the name change in Genesis was interesting because the difference in name coincided with the different perspectives on creation in those chapters. (We will look more at the differences between the two creation stories in chap. 3.)

Astruc wondered if he could detect a similar pattern elsewhere in Genesis, and so he undertook a systematic analysis of the Hebrew text. He concluded that the presence of two names for God is best accounted for by positing two hypothetical, originally independent documents that he named, rather unimaginatively, A (Elohim) and B (Yahweh). (Astruc's sources ran through the letter M, but the others are not important for us here.) He thought these documents were ancient memoirs that eventually came to Moses, who then arranged them to form the book of Genesis. Wherever those memoirs overlapped in subject matter, Moses laid them side by side (as in Gen. 1 and 2) or wove them together (as in the flood story). In other words, Moses was the editor of Genesis.

Since he was not a trained biblical scholar, Astruc was not confident about his conclusions. He was also concerned that his views would be misused to undermine the Bible, the very opposite of his intention. He was encouraged by a friend, however, and decided to publish his views anonymously in order to subject his theory to professional criticism and to abandon it if need be. Instead of criticism, however, his argument received wide acclaim, thanks in part to the work of Johann Gottfried Eichhorn (1753–1827), a biblical scholar whose own work corroborated that of Astruc.[13]

Here is why Astruc's work became important. As later biblical scholars thought more about Genesis and Astruc's idea of memoirs— or "sources," as they would come to be called—they noticed something: the patterns Astruc saw in Genesis can also be seen elsewhere in the Pentateuch, which suggested that *Astruc's theory of sources for Genesis could also be applied to the entire Pentateuch*. This was a significant shift, for it suggested (1) that not only Genesis but also the entire Pentateuch was *edited* and (2) that the editing process must have happened *long after Moses*, since the Pentateuch has such long-recognized post-Mosaic elements.

With this we have moved beyond Ibn Ezra and Spinoza's procedure of simply pointing out problems in the Pentateuch and offering piecemeal solutions. Now we have arrived at the threshold of a theory that claims to explain how those problems came to exist in the Pentateuch to begin with. Astruc's theory was the key: *different documents written by different authors at different times, compiled together by a later editor.*

For the next generation or two, Old Testament scholars would be working with this basic template to see how best to explain the properties of the Pentateuch. Theories were posed—some accepted, some rejected, some modified—all of which paved the way for crucial and lasting, if also controversial, developments in the nineteenth century.

Wellhausen and a Postexilic Pentateuch

No Old Testament scholar has had more of a lasting impact on his field than Julius Wellhausen.[14] Not unlike Darwin in his field, Wellhausen synthesized a lot of data and developed a theory that caught on quickly with most specialists at the time yet was also hotly contested by others and even maligned and reviled by some. Like Darwin, Wellhausen's ideas have had to be refined, adjusted, and in some cases abandoned as further discoveries came to light. Today many of the details of Wellhausen's arguments no longer dominate the academic conversation, but two general insights remain as a virtually unquestioned foundation for subsequent work: (1) that parts of the Pentateuch were composed over several centuries, and (2) that the Pentateuch as a whole was not completed until after the Israelites returned from exile. Because of Wellhausen's towering importance, it is worth our while to take a few moments and look at the basic outline of his theory.

Wellhausen argued that a careful reading of the Pentateuch reveals various patterns, such as distinct theological viewpoints and use of vocabulary (esp. the names of God). Working from what Astruc, Eichhorn, and several others proposed, Wellhausen grouped together sections of the Pentateuch that exhibited similar characteristics. Wellhausen concluded, as others had before him, that these groupings of texts dispersed throughout the Pentateuch were originally four distinct documents that were put together in the present form by an editor living after the return from exile.

Specifically, Wellhausen identified these four sources (or documents) as J, E, D, and P, and in that order.[15] J stands for "Jahwist" (Astruc's B), whom Wellhausen identifies as an anonymous tenth-century-BC author who hailed from the southern kingdom of Judah and preferred to use Yahweh to refer to God ("Yahweh" is spelled "Jahweh" in German, hence the J). The E (Elohist) source is a ninth-century work from the northern kingdom of Ephraim, reflecting that author's preference to refer to God by the Hebrew word "Elohim." A lot of Genesis is made up of J and E.

Next comes D (Deuteronomist), which stands for Deuteronomy and other parts of the Pentateuch that express similar theological themes. The D source dates to the late seventh to sixth century BC, near the time when the southern kingdom, Judah, was taken into exile in Babylon. The final source, considered postexilic by Wellhausen, is P (priestly, Astruc's A). Like E, this author preferred Elohim. He was also responsible for the kinds of things that Wellhausen thinks priests would produce: the tabernacle section in Exodus, the regulations in Leviticus, and laws in general—almost anything that sounds like ritual and legalism. According to Wellhausen, all of this was brought together by an editor in the middle of the fifth century BC.

As radical as all this might seem, dividing the Pentateuch into sources was not earth shattering in that academic climate. Even conservative scholars acknowledged (and continue to acknowledge) that there were some sources behind the Pentateuch, although they typically assigned the editing job to Moses, as did Astruc.

Wellhausen was controversial for another reason. He claimed that the editor responsible for cutting and pasting the sources to create the Pentateuch was driven by a striking—for some, disturbing—agenda. Wellhausen argued that the legal and ritualistic material (P), which the Bible says was given to Moses on Mount Sinai, was written last, about one millennium after Moses. The postexilic editor, however, wishing to lend support to priestly authority, *put the law at the very beginning of Israel's history*. His editing job was only partially successful, however, for all sorts of clues were left that people like Wellhausen claimed to have found—such as anachronisms and theological contradictions.

Wellhausen's theory, if correct, completely overturned—frankly, obliterated—any sense of the Pentateuch's value as a historical document, and so one can easily understand the controversy that Wellhausen generated. The historical picture the Pentateuch gives is actually a deception. Only after we untangle the mess created by the propagandist editor and put the sources into their proper order is the true history of Israel revealed. That picture shows a movement of Israel's religion from simple to complex, or better, from free to legalistic, and this is why Wellhausen placed the sources in their particular order.[16]

The sources J and E are the earliest, where we see a simple, free, unencumbered relationship with God, devoid of ritual, as when Abraham builds altars wherever he travels (e.g., Gen. 12:8; 13:18). Ritual is a later imposition, which begins with D and starts to squelch spontaneous religious expression. According to Wellhausen, here we see the beginning of Jewish dogma, carefully guarded by the developing ruling and priestly class. Worship is now to be controlled by a clergy and performed under their careful gaze in only one place, the place Yahweh will "choose" (Deut. 12, esp. v. 21): Jerusalem. For Wellhausen, D does not give us a second-millennium-BC, divinely inaugurated, Mosaic legislation that sets the template for Israel's legal history.

Rather, Deuteronomy is revisionist history, mid-first-millennium propaganda, where words are put into Moses's mouth.[17]

What D began was carried through with greater force in P. Here Wellhausen saw priests running amok, making all sorts of regulations for what should be sacrificed when, how many, and for what reason. Thus P is legalism pure and simple and, according to Wellhausen, would eventually give rise to Judaism, a religion completely contrary to the spirit of free religious expression depicted in J and E. So D and P and the Judaism that arose from them were a different religion altogether from what the Old Testament itself really describes—provided one knows how to decipher the clues left in the text, which Wellhausen claimed to have done. For Wellhausen, the law was not the starting point for the history of ancient Israel, but for the history of Judaism.

Wellhausen is important to us because of how pivotal his work has been in establishing the importance of the postexilic period for the compilation of the Pentateuch, despite the shortcomings of his theory that were brought to light from the beginning and ever since. For one thing, his specific theory is laced with a distinct tinge of anti-Semitism, which has not helped his legacy, especially among Jewish scholars.[18] Many Christians were not too happy with him either. If the law was postexilic propaganda rather than Israel's premonarchic national foundation, the biblical presentation of Israel's history would be turned completely upside down and thus call into question the general reliability of the Old Testament as a historical source. In his mind, ironically, Wellhausen's theory was an attempt to rescue the Old Testament for Christianity. He understood true Israelite religion to be reflected in J and E. The legalism of D and P were later impositions. The antilegalistic teachings of Jesus reflected Israel's true faith as seen in J and E (and one can perhaps see here Wellhausen's German Lutheranism coming through, with its tendency to dichotomize Old Testament law and New Testament grace).

Regardless of what might have motivated Wellhausen, the theory itself was far from problem-free. For example, it is hard to maintain the notion that Israel's legal and ritual dimensions are entirely postexilic when we consider that other ancient Near Eastern religions displayed similar patterns of legal and ritualistic behaviors centuries—even millennia—before the exile. This has come to light more clearly from archaeological discoveries after Wellhausen's time, so perhaps he can be forgiven for jumping the gun. Hence Wellhausen's theory that the "legalism" of the Pentateuch arose only after the exile has been abandoned. Some scholars today argue that P is preexilic, even if the

Pentateuch as we know it came to be only after the exile. Further, even to speak of discrete sources appearing in strict chronological sequence seems a bit quaint in today's scholarly atmosphere.

Also, soon after Wellhausen presented his Documentary Hypothesis, other scholars posed theories that were in some measure complementary but also headed in different directions. For example, as early as the turn of the twentieth century, Hermann Gunkel (1862–1932) felt the need to go beyond simply identifying written sources to pondering the existence of smaller oral or written units that lay behind the sources. (This approach is known in English by the nondescript term *form criticism*, which reflects the German term.) Gunkel did not dismiss Wellhausen, but he was influenced by studies in folklore at the time that focused on oral, prewritten tradition. Since Gunkel's time a significant amount of work has been done on oral "sources," which for some scholars has called into question the very notion of written sources as Wellhausen thought of them. Truth be told, source criticism has had an interesting journey throughout the twentieth century and first decade of the next. It remains a pillar of Old Testament study in most research universities and seminaries, although by no means the sole or even preferred method everywhere. Source critics certainly disagree on many details, and other schools of thought advocate approaches that have little to do with analyzing sources.

This is not the place to trace that in-house debate, however. For our purposes, the important point is that Wellhausen's theory brought together many generations, even centuries, of observations about the content of the Pentateuch. He posed his theory in a compelling manner, and the heart of the matter continues to be a stable element in current scholarship: *The Pentateuch was not authored out of whole cloth by a second-millennium Moses but is the end product of a complex literary process—written, oral, or both—that did not come to a close until the postexilic period.* This summary statement, with only the rarest exception, is a virtual scholarly consensus after one and a half centuries of debate. To admit this point does not in any way commit someone to one particular theory of how the Pentateuch came to its present form (and it does not in and of itself disallow some writing by Moses, hypothetically). It is only to admit that what we have cannot be explained as an early (second-millennium-BC) document written essentially by one person (Moses). Rather, the Pentateuch has a diverse compositional history spanning many centuries and was brought to completion after the return from exile.

To round out our discussion on this last point, the following is a summary of the evidence that supports the contemporary scholarly consensus

1. *The entire Pentateuch is written in the third person and in the past tense.* The Pentateuch is self-evidently a story about characters in Israel's past: Adam, Noah, Abraham, Isaac, Jacob—and Moses. The clear impression is that all of these figures, including Moses, are presented as figures from the distant past. When seen from this perspective, comments such as Numbers 12:3, where Moses is called the most humble man on earth, make sense. (Otherwise Moses would be pridefully claiming world-renowned humility for himself.) It also helps explain much of what follows below.

2. *There is no claim in the Pentateuch that Moses is its author,* and only certain passages refer to Moses as doing any writing (Exod. 17:14; 24:4; 34:27–28; Deut. 31:9, 24). Taken at face value, this actually implies that Moses's authorial role was quite limited at best and that his writings were combined by a later editor. Some argue that the biblical witness to Moses's limited writing activity is evidence that he was the essential or primary author of the *entire* Pentateuch, but most do not find this compelling.[19]

3. *The Pentateuch contains numerous explanatory comments that reflect a time well beyond that of Moses.* In addition to the beginning and end of Deuteronomy and Ibn Ezra's list, other examples include the reference to Edomite kings as ruling "before any Israelite king reigned" (Gen. 36:31 NIV). This comment assumes that the nation of Israel with a monarchy already existed even though that state of affairs did not come to pass until around 1000 BC (with Saul and then David).

4. *The Pentateuch assumes that conditions present at the time of writing were in existence in ancient times.* For example, Genesis 14:14 refers to the city of Dan; yet according to Joshua 19:47, Laish/Leshem was not renamed Dan until the conquest of Canaan. Also, there are various references to Philistines as existing in patriarchal and prepatriarchal times (Gen. 10:14; 21:32, 34; 26:1, 8, 14–15, 18), although the archaeological record indicates that they did not settle in Canaan until the twelfth century BC.

5. There are a number of "doublets" in the Pentateuch (two versions of the same story). *The presence of these doublets suggests a complex literary (perhaps oral) history* rather than just one author repeating himself in various ways on the same topic (e.g., two creation accounts in Gen. 1 and 2; two stories of the Abrahamic covenant in

Gen. 15 and 17; two incidents of Abraham's passing Sarah off as his sister in Gen. 12 and 20 [and Isaac also tried it in Gen. 26]; two calls of Moses in Exod. 3 and 6; two incidents of Moses and water from the rock in Exod. 17 and Num. 20).

6. Related to the previous point, *these doublets are not easily harmonized but present significantly different points of view.* As Astruc concluded long ago, these doublets are best understood as originally independent traditions (although not necessarily written documents) that were brought together by an editor respectful of maintaining both traditions, rather than one author working in one place and time (e.g., Gen. 1 and 2 are not just two creation accounts, but very different and independent accounts; likewise for the genealogies in Gen. 10 and 11).

7. Although beyond our scope, the Hebrew in which the characters of the Pentateuch speak did not exist during the second millennium BC. Rather, by comparing Hebrew with other languages of the ancient Near Eastern world, linguists have demonstrated that *the language of the Pentateuch reflects the state of Hebrew in the first millennium BC.* Whatever language the characters of Genesis might have spoken in history, it was at best a distant precursor to what we know as "Biblical Hebrew," and so the Pentateuch as we know it is a first-millennium product.

Other issues could be mentioned, but the factors outlined above are clear enough for our purposes. Nuances may be disputed, but the overall point remains. As Spinoza says, "It is clearer than the noonday sun" that the Pentateuch was not written by Moses.[20] This does not mean that the Pentateuch was written out of whole cloth during this time, however. Daniel Fleming suggests an analogy with Renaissance paintings where Madonna and Child are redressed like Italian nobles: "The stories [of Genesis] are imbued with the details of their tellers' own time."[21] Older traditions are shaped later.

It is only fair to mention that some more traditionally minded scholars (Christian and Jewish) have contested at least some of these points, and they are more than free to do so. Leaving aside relatively uninformed lay reactions to biblical scholarship, classic treatments can be found for those interested in looking into the issue for themselves.[22] There should be no objection raised to the presence of countervoices or looking at old problems in fresh ways. The questions of pentateuchal scholarship are fair game for everyone, and no one can predict from whom the next great insights will come. (Remember that Astruc was a physician.)

It is unlikely, however, that debunking the postexilic setting of the Pentateuch as we know it is likely to succeed. We may not know exactly the mechanisms by which the Pentateuch came about historically—and we may never know. But the evidence from the Pentateuch itself, in the opinion of an overwhelming majority of biblical scholars over the last several generations, is best explained by the hypothesis that the Pentateuch as we know it was shaped in the postexilic period.

In a book on evolution, why is it so important for us to see the Pentateuch as a postexilic work? Because it helps us understand the broad *purpose* for which it was compiled. That purpose can be put into sharper relief by taking a step back from the Pentateuch and looking at the Old Testament as a whole. The date of the Pentateuch is one part of a larger cluster of issues: *What is the Old Testament? When was it written? Why was it written?* As with the Pentateuch, the strong scholarly consensus is that the Old Testament as a whole owes its existence to the postexilic period. Although our focus is on Genesis, looking at the Old Testament as a whole, even briefly, will flesh out what we have seen about the date of Genesis and Israel's self-definition. The next chapter will make the same point from a different angle.

The Old Testament, the Exile, and Israel's Self-Definition

It is common for Christians to think of the "biblical period" of the Old Testament as extending from Genesis to the fall of Jerusalem and Israel's deportation to Babylon in 2 Kings 25 (about 586 BC). This is the bulk of the story, and Ezra, Nehemiah, and a couple of the Minor Prophets form a postexilic postscript to bring the whole sad story to a stuttering, anticlimactic ending. The exilic and postexilic periods become something of a postbiblical dark age. All that is worth knowing has happened: Israel has failed, and it is time to move on.

But such a scenario hardly tells the whole story. This alleged "post-biblical" period is actually the *biblical* period, meaning the time in which the Hebrew Old Testament as we know it took shape as a final and *sacred* collection of texts. There is little serious question that Israel documented, recorded, told, and retold its own story—orally and in writing—long before the exile. Few would dispute this. It is unlikely, however, that these early records of ancient deeds, court politics, and temple liturgies were thought of as sacred Scripture at the time. That is a later development, and the motivation for it was Israel's national crisis.

The exile was the most traumatic event in Israel's ancient national history and was therefore extremely influential on how the Israelites thought of themselves as the people of God. The Israelites understood themselves to be God's chosen people: they were promised the perpetual possession of the land, the glorious temple as a house of worship, and a son of David perpetually sitting on the throne. With the exile, all of this came to a sudden and devastating end. Exile in Babylon was not simply a matter of relocating. It meant to the Israelites that their God had turned his back on them. It also meant that God could no longer be worshiped in the Jerusalem temple as required. Israel's connection with God was severed: no land, no temple, and no sacrifices. Rather than prompting the other nations to acknowledge the true God, which was Israel's national calling, Israel was humiliated by these nations. Rather than the nations streaming to them (Isa. 2:2–4), they were slaves in a foreign land. Israel was estranged from God.

The impact of this series of events cannot be overstated. Since these long-standing ties to Yahweh were no longer available to them, the Israelites turned to the next best thing: bringing the glorious past into their miserable present by means of an official collection of writings. Some of these writings were collected and edited at that time, with additions and thorough updating—like the Pentateuch. Others only came into existence then. Either way, the trauma of the exile was a significant factor—if not the driving factor—in the creation of what has come to be known to us as "the Bible." Old Testament theologian Walter Brueggemann puts it well:

> It is now increasingly agreed that *the Old Testament in its final form is a product of and response to the Babylonian Exile*. This premise needs to be stated more precisely. The Torah (Pentateuch) was likely completed in response to the exile, and the subsequent formation of the prophetic corpus and the "writings" [poetic and wisdom texts] as bodies of religious literature (canon) is to be understood as a product of Second Temple Judaism [postexilic period]. This suggests that by their intention, these materials are . . . an intentional and coherent response to a particular circumstance of crisis. . . . Whatever older materials may have been utilized (and the use of old materials can hardly be doubted), the exilic and/or postexilic location of the final form of the text suggests that the Old Testament materials, under-stood normatively, are to be taken [understood] precisely in an acute crisis of displacement, when old certitudes—sociopolitical as well as theological—had failed.[23]

The central question the exilic and postexilic Jews asked themselves concerned their identity: "Are we still the people of God? After all that has happened, are we still connected to the Israelites of old, with whom God spoke and showed his faithfulness?" Their answer to these questions was to tell their story from the beginning (creation) and from their postexilic point of view—which meant editing older works and creating some new ones. The creation of the Hebrew Bible, in other words, is *an exercise in national self-definition in response to the Babylonian exile.*

An example may help illustrate this, and it comes from Israel's parallel histories: Chronicles and Samuel–Kings, which sit side by side in our English Bibles. This canonical placement is a shame, since for many readers there hardly seems to be any sense in reading Samuel–Kings and then continuing right along and reading "the same thing" in Chronicles. But Chronicles is not merely a repetition of Samuel–Kings: it tells Israel's story quite differently.

The fact that Chronicles comes right after the previous history no doubt contributes to its misunderstanding. In the Jewish canon, however, Chronicles is last.[24] It was not until the Greek translation (Septuagint)[25] of the Hebrew Old Testament that Chronicles was tucked neatly away after 2 Kings. The Greek translators gave Chronicles a name that betrays their attitude: *Paraleipomenōn*, which means "[book] of things omitted" (from Samuel–Kings). This is hardly a way to encourage readers to dive in. Being placed last in the Hebrew canon is a signal, though, that this is not just a repetition of Samuel–Kings but a book with its own story to tell. Chronicles is a retelling of Israel's story in light of the return from exile. It is Israel's declaration that, despite the exile, the same God back then is still with his people today. Whatever else may have changed, Yahweh is still their God.

For example, compare these two accounts of Nathan's prophecy to David, one from 2 Samuel and the other from 1 Chronicles. Nathan the prophet is speaking for God and makes a promise to David about the longevity of his dynasty.

2 Samuel 7:16: *Your* house and *your* kingdom shall be made sure forever before me; *your* throne shall be established forever. (emphasis added)

Nathan refers to David's "house"—David will have descendants on his throne perpetually. Compare this to how Chronicles relays the same episode:

1 Chronicles 17:14: I will confirm him in *my* house and in *my* kingdom forever, and his throne shall be established forever. (emphasis added)

There is clearly a lot of overlap between these two accounts, especially the idea that God is going to do something concerning David that will endure "forever."[26] Still, the two accounts report the same event differently. In 1 Chronicles, the house and kingdom are God's, but in 2 Samuel they are David's. Likewise, the throne is David's in 2 Samuel, but in 1 Chronicles it is "his," referring to Solomon, who built the temple, and who for the author of Chronicles is Israel's ideal king (not David), the model for Israel's restored glory in the postexilic period. The message of 2 Samuel is "Don't worry, David, *your* line is safe," but the message of 1 Chronicles is "Remember, it is *my* throne and *my* kingdom, and I will put the right person there in time."

What accounts for this difference? Some might suggest that there really is no significant difference at all—just a minor variation in expression that can easily be harmonized. But that solution is difficult to accept. Not only is the wording of Chronicles different, but also Chronicles as a whole thoroughly and consistently tells its own version of Israel's history.[27] Harmonizing these verses obligates one to harmonize everywhere, and that would quickly become an exercise in futility.

The differences between these accounts are theological and must be explained on the basis of their differing historical settings. The focus of 2 Samuel is still on the hope of continuing David's line. But the author of Chronicles wrote long after the Israelites had already returned from Babylon—no earlier than the mid-fifth century BC, judging from the names listed toward the end of the genealogy in 1 Chronicles 1–9. He had a different perspective. David's perpetual line had been broken in exile. For the author of Chronicles, the lesson of the exile is that Israel's royal dynasty is not dependent on the establishment of David's house and throne, as 2 Samuel has it. It is not really David's throne at all but God's, and God will put the right person there when and how he wishes.

It is a scholarly consensus that the author of Chronicles was working from the text of Samuel–Kings (although not necessarily the exact version we have, and perhaps also from sources older than Samuel–Kings). That means that he changed the wording of this older text in order to communicate the theological convictions of his postexilic community. The author of Chronicles changed a dashed promise into a messianic hope.[28] He is declaring that Israel's ultimate hope is not in whether David's literal line has continued but in what God is doing with *his* throne to return Israel to its bygone days of favor. Connecting postexilic Israel to its preexilic glory days is why 1 Chronicles begins with nine chapters of names. Most readers today gladly skip over them, but for postexilic Israelites, the genealogy made a vital point: it traced Israel's history from the postexilic period all the way back to Adam. (1 Chron. 1:1 is the only explicit reference to Adam in the Old Testament after Gen. 5.) Thus Chronicles is a postexilic rewriting of Israel's entire history to remind the Israelites that they are still the people of God—regardless of all that has happened, and regardless of how much they have deserved every bit of misery they received. They remain God's people, and their lineage extends to the very beginning, to Adam.[29] The exile prompted the Israelites to write a new national history that would be meaningful to them. Rather than simply repeating the stories of the past, they rewrote them to speak to their continued existence as God's people; they rewrote the past in order to come to terms with their present. Chronicles is not a "history" such as we might expect as modern readers. It is a "theological history" that can only be properly understood as a response to the exile.

This is just one example from one book that illustrates a larger principle about the Old Testament as a whole. As Brueggemann says above, the Pentateuch was brought into its final form during this time. The other portions of the Old Testament (Poetical, Historical, Prophetic books) also owe their existence to the experience of exile because they were either written or reshaped then. Below is a snapshot of how the Old Testament as a whole is a product of the exilic and postexilic periods. This information can be verified and elaborated upon by looking at almost any Old Testament introduction, introductions to commentaries, or in some cases a good study Bible.

• The *Deuteronomistic History*[30] (Joshua–2 Kings) was likely written around the time of the exile, although it clearly relies on earlier documents and traditions (e.g., the Book of the Annals of the Kings of Judah [1 Kings 15:23] and of Israel [1 Kings 15:31]). Some postulate a second edition at some later point. Either way, this collection of books recounts Israel's history from just after Moses's death to the Babylonian exile and the release of King Jehoiachin (2 Kings 25:17–30, about 561 BC), which means these books reached their final form no earlier than the exilic period.

• In addition to 1 and 2 Chronicles, *Ezra and Nehemiah* are obviously postexilic historical books, since they recount Israel's return to the land after the Babylonian captivity. Other details indicate that these books were written no earlier than the latter half of the fifth century BC. Likewise, *Esther* was written no earlier than the middle of that century, since it is set during the reign of the Persian king Xerxes. Given its well-known and numerous historical inaccuracies, the book is typically dated between the fourth and third centuries BC.

• Of the Poetic books, few would dispute a postexilic date for *Ecclesiastes*, and many suggest the Hellenistic period (after the conquest of Alexander the Great in 332 BC). Granting a Solomonic core, which is debated, *Proverbs* has multiple authors and an editorial history that at least extends beyond the time of Hezekiah (d. 687 BC; see Prov. 25:1). Many scholars see good reason to pose a postexilic date, although the setting of the book of Proverbs is a thorny issue. There is no clear consensus on the date of *Job*: dates range from 700 to about 200 BC, with perhaps an older oral tradition behind it. The final form of the *Psalter* is a big topic of discussion. The shape of the Psalter is clearly intentional: "five books," mimicking the Pentateuch, which alone suggests a time well after the return from exile. The Dead Sea Scrolls show that books 4 and 5 of the Psalter were still in considerable flux near the time of Jesus. Further, there are numerous postexilic psalms (e.g., Ps. 137). *Song of Songs* is notoriously difficult to date, in part due to the lack of any reference to historical events. Some argue that linguistic evidence points to a postexilic date, while others see the parallels between Song of Songs and earlier Egyptian love poetry as pointing to a date as early as the tenth century BC. At present it is best to remain open to different possibilities.

• Among the Prophetic books, *Jeremiah*, *Ezekiel*, and *Daniel* clearly deal with the exile and subsequent events. Still controversial to some is the book of *Isaiah*. Chapters 40–66 seem to assume that the exile is a past event (e.g., 42:22–25; 47:6). This is one of several factors that have led to the virtually unanimous scholarly consensus that Isaiah (like the Pentateuch) was written over several centuries extending well past the exile, which means that the final form of that book as a whole stems from that period. *Daniel* is routinely dated to the second century. Also, there has been much work in recent years on the twelve *Minor Prophets*. Scholars are seeing more clearly how those books are a collective literary product (hence referred to as "the Book of the Twelve"). At least Haggai, Zechariah, and Malachi are clearly written during the exilic and postexilic periods. The final collection of the Book of the Twelve is dated to the Persian period (539–322 BC), if not later.

There is good reason to believe that the Old Testament as a whole is fundamentally a postexilic document. Again, few scholars would care to deny a prehistory—in some cases a lengthy and extensive prehistory, whether oral or written—to at least some portions of the Old Testament. Also, there are some parts that cannot be dated with any certainty. Still, there is a strong consensus that the postexilic period played a vital role in (1) the production of numerous books or parts of books and (2) the final editing of older material and eventually shaping of the entire Old Testament as sacred Scripture.

It was after the exile that Israel's sacred collection of books came to be—not out of a dispassionate academic interest on the part of some scribes but as a statement of self-definition of a haggard people who still claimed and yearned for a special relationship with their God. The Bible, including the Pentateuch, tells the old story for contemporary reasons: Who are we? Who is our God?

The questions that led to the formation of the Old Testament are the same ones that have occupied the minds and hearts of people of faith ever since. The Bible already models that process of bringing the past to bear on the present, which leads to the following and final point of this chapter.

The Creation Story and the Church's Self-Definition

In this chapter we have looked at some interpretive questions raised within the Pentateuch itself—particularly how they affect the issue of authorship, how these questions are addressed, and how that discussion came to a head in the nineteenth century. How the Pentateuch came to be and the importance of the postexilic period for forming the Pentateuch and the Old Testament are not side issues. These factors help reorient our expectations of what questions the Bible as a whole and Genesis in particular are prepared to answer. The crisis of the exile prompted Israel to put down in writing once and for all an official declaration: "This is who we are, and this is the God we worship." The Old Testament is not a treatise on Israel's history for the sake of history, but a document of self-definition and spiritual encouragement: "Do not forget where we have been. Do not forget who we are—the people of God."

The creation stories are to be understood within this larger framework, as part of a larger theologically driven collection of writings that answers ancient questions of self-definition, not contemporary ones of scientific interest. Later in part 1 we will look more closely at what this self-definition looks like. For now, we will content ourselves with the following observation. Christians today misread Genesis when they try to engage it, even minimally, in the scientific arena. Rather, they must follow the trajectory of the postexilic Israelites and ask their own questions of self-definition as the people of God: *In view of who and where we are, what do these ancient texts say to us about being the people of God today?*

Israel's historical moment, that of national crisis, drove their theologians to engage their past creatively. The first Christians were in an analogous situation. Their view of that same history was shaped by a defining moment—not one of crisis but of good news, the appearance of the kingdom of heaven and the Son of God, crucified and raised. *That defining moment shaped how the New Testament writers engaged Israel's story*—better put, it forced a fresh engagement of that story. They believed Jesus to be the focal point of that drama. In my estimation, demonstrating how Jesus both confirms and reshapes that story is a central concern of the New Testament writers. Its authors echo the pressing question of the postexilic Israelites: in view of what has just happened, what does it mean to be the people of God? In answering that question, the New Testament constantly refers to the Old Testament—about 365 citations and over 1,000 allusions.[31] With each citation and allusion we see the New Testament authors at work, rethinking and transforming Israel's story in view of this new thing that God has done in Christ—bringing past story and present reality into conversation.

The defining moment for the New Testament writers remains the defining moment for Christians today. The Old Testament—including Genesis—is the church's *theological* self-defining document recast in light of the appearance of God's Son. Proper contemporary appropriation of Israel's self-defining documents, therefore, requires a theological engagement, not scientific harmonization. Reducing Genesis to a book of scientific interest is not just awkward and off topic; it also is sub-Christian since it fails to follow the path blazed for us by the New Testament writers. (I will say more in chap. 6 on how Paul specifically handles his Bible in the light of Jesus's resurrection.)

This theme of self-definition will become clearer as we focus next on the creation stories in Genesis and what they tell us about how the Israelites saw themselves and their God vis-à-vis the surrounding cultures. Israel's creation stories are potent claims about who they were. Understanding those claims against the backdrop of the world in which they were written, in my opinion, lays to rest any notion that these writings have any relevance to modern debates over human origins. Once that is understood, we can move to a discussion about Paul and how all of this bears on evolution and Christianity, which is the topic of part 2.

3

Stories of Origins
from Israel's Neighbors

Genre Calibration

Beginning around the middle of the nineteenth century, archaeologists began to unearth a body of evidence from the cultures and religions contemporary to and older than Israel. These discoveries for the first time—and irrevocably—placed Israelite religion in a larger context. It was inescapable that discerning readers would begin comparing and contrasting Israel to its newfound neighbors and forebears. This put Old Testament scholarship on a whole new footing and has deeply affected our understanding of the type of literature Genesis is and therefore what we should expect of it.

Placing Israel in its broader cultural and religious context has been referred to as the "comparative approach." Although accurate, this term is often maligned because it is unfortunately understood by some to imply that Israelites were simply copying or "borrowing" what was around them. This is not the case, and the reality is certainly much more complicated.

Perhaps a better way of thinking about the issue is to introduce the phrase "genre calibration." Placing Genesis side by side with the primordial tales of other ancient cultures helps us gain a clearer understanding of the nature of Genesis and thus what we as contemporary readers have a right to expect from Genesis. Such comparisons have made it quite clear that Israel's creation stories are not prepared to answer the kinds of questions that occupy modern scientific or even historical studies. Genesis is an ancient text designed to address ancient issues *within the scope of ancient ways of understanding origins*. However one might label the genre of the opening chapters of Genesis (myth, legend, suprahistorical narrative, story, metaphor, symbolism, archetypal, etc.) is not the point here. The point is that Genesis and the modern scientific investigation of human origins do not overlap. To think that they do is an error in genre discernment.

Reading Genesis by ancient standards will actually help us to articulate positively how Genesis contributes to Christian thought. The synthesis of Christianity and evolution is all too often simply perceived as taking something away from Genesis (its literal, historical, scientific value) and leaving nothing behind. Rather, a proper understanding of the genre of Genesis helps us understand its theology, which aligns us with the very purpose for which Genesis was written. If we want to have a meaningful conversation between evolution and Christianity, we must hear Genesis in its ancient voice, not impose upon it questions it will not answer or burdens it will not bear. The only way to bring Genesis into our world is first to understand the world of Genesis and what this book is trying to say in its world. Then we will be in a position to understand how Genesis can be appropriated by Christians today as a theological statement, not as a statement of modern scientific interest.

One might think that our increased knowledge of Israel's surrounding cultures would be universally welcome. After all, the importance of the historical setting of the Bible is central to both evangelicalism and fundamentalism, as seen in their strong support for the grammatical-historical method of interpretation (i.e., the Bible is to be interpreted in the original languages and in view of its historical contexts). But placing Israel's stories of origins in their grammatical and historical contexts has caused some stress as well. One need only glance at the primeval history, Genesis 1–11, to see that these stories are of a different flavor from what we read elsewhere in Genesis or throughout the historical books of the Old Testament. They take us back to primordial time: the formation of the cosmos, the beginnings of humanity, an ancient flood after which everything begins all over again. It is precisely these chapters that intersect with the nineteenth-century discoveries of texts from other ancient Near Eastern cultures, findings that have done so much to illuminate our understanding of Genesis. But they have also challenged certain traditional Christian notions of the historical and revelatory nature of these chapters.

The crisis of nineteenth-century archaeological discoveries is this: if the foundational stories of Genesis seem to fit so well among other—clearly ahistorical—stories of the ancient world, in what sense can we really say that Israel's stories refer to fundamentally unique, revealed, historical events? This serious doctrinal challenge continues to affect many Christians today, in part because it is very difficult to avoid or massage this evidence. Wellhausen and the entire discipline of pentateuchal studies focused on assessing "internal evidence," giving an account for why the Pentateuch looks the way it does by discerning clues within. Archaeology, however, has introduced "external evidence." In earlier centuries the Old Testament could safely be read in isolation; now archaeological discoveries of the nineteenth century introduced an external control by which to assess the nature of Genesis, to calibrate its genre. Counterarguments had to deal with concrete evidence, regardless of what ambiguities might accompany their interpretation, and explain the similarities between an inspired text and pagan myths. As the debate developed, this external factor has proved to be much more challenging to traditional views than Wellhausen's work.

The specific archaeological discoveries that rocked the boat in the nineteenth century were ancient Mesopotamian stories that looked strikingly similar to two episodes in Genesis 1–11, the first creation story (Gen. 1) and the flood (Gen. 6–9). At least the existence of these texts, if not their content, is probably familiar to anyone who has ever taken a high school or college introductory Old Testament class or watched educational programs on television. Israel's creation and flood stories are certainly unique to them in the sense that any culture is "unique" when compared to others. But Genesis also bears doctrinally uncomfortable similarities to the clearly mythical stories of the Mesopotamian world. Regardless of how some have addressed this issue, all agree that from the very outset these discoveries have posed a problem for traditional conceptions of Genesis, which needed to be addressed.

The Mesopotamian material discovered in the nineteenth century persuasively accounts for why the opening chapters of Genesis look the way they do. With that in mind, we begin by turning to the major archaeological discoveries of the nineteenth century that raised these issues, and then turn to the second creation story, the all-important story of Adam, in its ancient context.

Genesis 1 and *Enuma Elish*

Beginning in 1847 and continuing for several decades, major archaeological excavations were performed in the library of King Ashurbanipal (668–627 BC) in the ancient city of Nineveh (the capital city of ancient Assyria). Archaeologists discovered thousands of clay tablets written in Akkadian, which is the English translation of the term the speakers of this language used themselves: *Akkadum*. Akkadian was the main language of a number of Mesopotamian peoples, notably the Babylonians and Assyrians, and spanned the third, second, and first millennia BC. It is a somewhat distant uncle to Hebrew.

Many different kinds of texts were found among these writings (e.g., legal, economic, and historical texts), and from them we gain many valuable insights into what life was like in the ancient Near East three to four thousand years ago. But what was most striking at the time—and a bit unsettling—were the religious texts found there. One of these texts bore clear similarities to Genesis 1. How people viewed Genesis would never be the same again.

That text is a Babylonian story of origins referred to as *Enuma Elish*, its title taken from the opening words of the story ("When on high"). It is sometimes referred to as the "Babylonian Genesis" because of the similarities it bears to the biblical story. The version found in Ashurbanipal's library consists of seven tablets and dates to the seventh century BC (just before Israel's captivity in Babylon). In ancient Near Eastern terms, this is quite recent, but the original story is certainly many hundreds of years older. Determining the age of the story depends on a combination of linguistic and historical factors, not to mention the rich but unchartable oral tradition that preceded any writing. Bearing in mind these factors, the consensus is a second-millennium-BC date for *Enuma Elish*, in part because this version of the story extols the victory of the god Marduk, who rose in prominence within the Babylonian pantheon around 1800 BC.[1] It also seems that this Babylonian version has much older Sumerian antecedents, which pushes back the date of the basic story to the third millennium BC.

Settling on a firm date for *Enuma Elish* is not important other than to emphasize that the general story is far older than Israel's creation story—and far older than Israel. It is a creation story with Sumerian antecedents (third millennium BC), written by a dominant culture in the early second millennium, which continued to be handed down and changed for centuries thereafter. Furthermore, biblical scholars commonly accept that Genesis 1 was written in the postexilic period (perhaps with earlier versions) and expresses Israel's faith in Yahweh against the backdrop of the familiar creation-story idioms of the ancient Near East in general and of their recent Babylonian hosts in particular. In other words, the Israelites who first heard Genesis 1 likely had some knowledge of the Babylonian story as reflected in the copy of *Enuma Elish* known to us from Ashurbanipal's library. Genesis 1 is not the prototype but presumes and interacts with the far older Babylonian theology of the dominant culture.

More important than haggling about the date is understanding the content. Genesis and *Enuma Elish* exhibit several commonly agreed-upon similarities:[2]

- Matter exists independently of the divine spirit. In other words, Genesis 1 does not describe creation out of nothing, but the establishment of order out of "chaos."[3]
- Darkness precedes creation.
- In *Enuma Elish* the chaos symbol is the goddess Tiamat. In Genesis the chaos symbol is in Hebrew *tehom* ("the deep"), which is linguistically related to Tiamat.
- Light exists *before* the creation of the sun, moon, and stars.
- In *Enuma Elish*, Marduk fillets the body of the slain Tiamat; with half of it, Marduk forms a barrier to keep the waters from escaping. Genesis 1:6–8 depicts the sky not as a slain goddess but as a solid dome ("firmament") to keep the waters above where they belong.
- The sequence of the days of creation is similar, including the creation of the firmament, dry land, luminaries, and humanity, all followed by rest.[4]

These similarities are striking and when they first came to light prompted a heated debate about whether Genesis 1 was directly dependent on the older *Enuma Elish*. This debate is sometimes referred to as the "Bible and Babel" controversy ("Babel" coming from one of the Hebrew words for Babylon; see Gen. 11:9). A related view, called "Pan-Babylonianism," asserted that not only Genesis 1 but all world myths, including Christianity, owed their existence to Babylonian culture. As time went on, scholars came to see that earlier views exaggerated Babylonian influence and so began to assess the relationship between the two stories more carefully.

For one thing, some scholars have argued that the theological themes we see in *Enuma Elish* might have been mediated to the Israelites through their neighbors the Canaanites in the centuries before the exile. The story of Baal, a Canaanite god well known to readers of the Old Testament, reflects similar themes as *Enuma Elish*. Much of our knowledge of this Baal story comes from discoveries in the ancient city of Ugarit, which flourished from about 1450–1200 BC and was discovered in 1928. There are also noted similarities between Genesis 1 and the Egyptian Memphite Theology (eighth-century text, second-millennium origin), which may have been mediated to the Israelites through the Phoenicians, whose cultural influence pervaded Canaan well before the Israelites arrived on the scene. The details are not important here, only the larger point that literary dependence is very difficult to establish in general, let alone dependence on one specific story like *Enuma Elish*. It is also relatively unimportant. Conceptual similarity is more pertinent and more clearly demonstrated.

Even at each of the points listed above, the Babylonian and biblical stories have many significant differences, suggesting that something other than simple "borrowing" has taken place. To give one example, a chief difference is that there is no divine conflict in Genesis, whereas conflict is a major theme in *Enuma Elish*. The Babylonian story depicts a cosmic battle between numerous gods, particularly the god Marduk and his great-great-grandmother, the goddess Tiamat. After a protracted period of tensions, Marduk kills Tiamat, splits her slain body in half, and with one half forms the heavens and with the other half the earth, an act that wins him notoriety and thus eventually the head seat in the Babylonian pantheon. Slaying Tiamat is dimly reflected in God's taming the deep (*tehom*) in Genesis 1:1–2, 6, 9–10. Yet the deep is not a god but an impersonal entity. Genesis depersonalizes the symbol of chaos.

Scholars are no longer eager to draw a direct line of dependence from *Enuma Elish* to Genesis. Instead, the two texts participate in a similar conceptual world concerning the nature of beginnings. *Enuma Elish* is older than Genesis and so sets the stage for Genesis 1. But the similarities between Genesis and *Enuma Elish* are due to a matrix of cultural factors that are bigger than both. Unquestionably they share common ways of speaking about the beginning of the world, as seen in the list above.

What bearing does the relationship between Genesis 1 and *Enuma Elish* have on the evolution issue? It means that any thought of Genesis 1 providing a scientifically or historically accurate account of cosmic origins, and therefore being wholly distinct from the "fanciful" story in

Enuma Elish, cannot be seriously entertained. Apart from the obvious scientific problems with such an idea, it simply ignores the conceptual similarities between Genesis 1 and *Enuma Elish*. Whether or not the author of Genesis 1 was familiar with the text known to us as *Enuma Elish*, he was certainly working within a similar conceptual world, where solid barriers keep the earth safe from the heavenly waters, where chaotic material existed before order, and where light existed before the sun, moon, and stars.

Although we should not exaggerate the similarities, we should not move to the opposite extreme of keeping the two at arm's length from each other. It is sometimes argued that *since* dependence of Genesis 1 on *Enuma Elish* is not a scholarly accepted view (correct), therefore the similarities between them are superficial and inconsequential (incorrect). This logic misses the point that similarity derives from a shared culture—in this case, influence of the dominant culture—and direct literary dependence is not required to produce these similarities. The Genesis account cries out to be understood in its ancient context, and stories like *Enuma Elish* give us a brief but important glimpse at what that context is. *Enuma Elish* helps us calibrate the genre of Genesis 1.

Accepting the conceptual similarities between these stories high-lights an important dimension of Genesis 1: its polemical function. Israel's God is portrayed as truly mighty in that he is solely and fully responsible for forming the cosmos. From this story we learn some-thing about Israel's understanding of God and therefore of itself as God's people. Israel's God alone created the world (established order out of chaos) by an act of his sovereign will, not as the result of a power struggle within a dysfunctional divine family. Again, there is no "cosmic battle" in Genesis 1, although the imagery of the battle between Tiamat and Marduk is in the background. (We will come back to this in chap. 4.) Not only is Tiamat depersonalized, but so are the sun, moon, and stars. These are not gods to be reckoned with as they are in some other ancient stories, but objects placed at the true God's command, put in the heavens where he wishes. By depict-ing God's work of creation so differently while drawing on a set of familiar themes, Genesis argues that Israel's God is superior to the gods of the surrounding nations.[5]

I want to stress that the polemical character of Genesis 1 does not mean that the author of Genesis was insulated from the mythic themes of *Enuma Elish*. It is a common popular apologetic to argue that, since the author of Genesis was inspired by God, he knew better than to be taken in by these fanciful stories; he just willingly adopted the "errant" view of his contemporary culture to make a theological point. The assertion that Genesis must keep a safe distance from its historical moment is rooted in what I consider to be a faulty theological assumption about the Bible: "The Bible is inspired by God and therefore simply can't reflect the sort of nonsense we see in the ancient world. God is the God of truth and wouldn't perpetuate lies, but correct them."

We should be more reticent about claiming to know what God would or would not say. Every ancient culture, Mesopotamian or otherwise, had stories that reflected ancient, nonscientific, ahistorical ways of thinking of primordial time. To claim that Israel, of all world cultures, somehow escaped that influence is, frankly, a peculiar assertion, resting on a theological presumption that it is beneath God to adopt these forms of speech. But what would that say about God himself? The Christian and Jewish God is not one who refuses to enter into the particularities of history. Rather, this is a God who gets dirty, who constantly shows up and allows himself to be described according to a particular people's ways of thinking.[6]

Keeping God at arm's length from a biblical text's ancient context does not "protect" him. Instead, it gives us a God that neither the Jewish nor the Christian Bible can support—a God who will do neither sacred book much good. Isolating Israel from its environment like this violates a foundational principle of interpretation, one ironically championed by conservatives as much as any: a text's meaning is rooted in its historical and literary context. With Genesis and the nineteenth-century discoveries, that principle started becoming uncomfortable, but that does not mean it should be abandoned. Rather, it may be signaling to us that we have to adjust our expectations of what the Bible can or cannot do; that is, we need to calibrate our genre expectations of Genesis in view of newer historical information.

The polemical thrust does not isolate Genesis from its environment. Rather, the polemic is effective only because of the shared cultural/ religious categories. The Israelites were not on a "higher plain" with a more "accurate" (modern) cosmology. Rather, in a world full of stories about gods' creating through violence, the Israelites bucked the trend by ascribing to their one God a complete and utterly effortless act of ordering creation. We must try to appreciate how counterintuitive Israel's theology was in an ancient Mesopotamian context. That world was swimming in notions of various pantheons of gods bringing the world into existence. A world without a pantheon was unimaginable to ancient Israel's neighbors. The theological message in Genesis 1 was that their God is not like the other gods. He alone can claim the title "Creator," which makes him alone worthy of allegiance and worship.

Genesis 1 and Monolatry

This polemical dimension raises an extremely important point about the theology presented in Genesis 1 that we must address here, even if briefly. It is widely recognized that Israelite faith in Yahweh was not consistently monotheistic, which is the belief that only one god exists. Rather, the Israelites were monolatrous, at least throughout portions of their history, meaning they worshiped only one God, Yahweh, but without denying the existence of other gods. (The Greek word for worship is *latreuō*, hence monolatry.)

Acknowledging the existence of other gods is found on Yahweh's own lips in Exodus 12:12: "For I will pass through the land of Egypt that night, and I will strike down every firstborn in the land of Egypt, both human beings and animals; *on all the gods of Egypt I will execute judgments*. I am the LORD" (emphasis added). This is not rhetoric: it actually describes the central drama of the book of Exodus.

The exodus story is not about the humanitarian liberation of slaves. Rather, Yahweh is laying claim on his own people, that they might serve him rather than Pharaoh and the Egyptian gods. Egyptian religion is notoriously difficult to map, but Pharaohs were considered to be the earthly representations of the high god. So, god-Pharaoh wants to hold on to his slave population so that they might "serve" him. The Hebrew here is *'avad* (e.g., Exod. 1:13–14), and it refers to slave labor. But Moses tells god-Pharaoh to let the people go so that they might "serve" (*'avad*) Yahweh instead (Exod. 4:23; 7:16; see also 3:12). Here we see a play on the word *'avad*. It can mean both being bound as a slave and bound as a worshiper. So the question throughout Exodus is, "Whom will Israel *'avad*: god-Pharaoh as *slaves* or God-Yahweh as *worshipers*?"

Some scholars see the plague narrative, at least in part, as a battle between Yahweh and the Egyptian pantheon to see who will claim the right to Israel. This battle is not much of a contest, however, which is the whole point—the gods are no match for Yahweh. Yahweh even prolongs the battle so that his power might be on full display (see esp. Exod. 9:15–16). In his sights he has not simply the political powers of Egypt to liberate the slaves but also the underlying religious structure.

We see this in the very first plague, turning the Nile to blood. The Nile, Egypt's source of survival, was personified and worshiped as a god. By turning the Nile to blood, Yahweh is showing mastery over the god responsible for Egypt's very existence. Other plagues seem to carry forward this polemic. The goddess of childbirth, Heqet, was depicted with the head of a frog, and we see the swarming frogs (second plague) as a foreshadowing of the death of the Egyptian firstborn in the tenth plague. The mother- and sky-goddess Hathor was depicted as a cow (fifth plague, on livestock). The hailstorm (seventh plague) shows Yahweh's supremacy over the Egyptian gods associated with storms (e.g., Seth). Pharaoh was considered to be the earthly representative of the sun-god, Re (or Ra), and in the ninth plague Yahweh blots out the sun. Osiris is the Egyptian god of the dead, yet Yahweh will lay claim on the firstborn of Egypt by putting them to death (tenth plague).

The exodus story is about Israel's God—the God of first a wandering and then an enslaved people—who marches into the territory of the superpower of the day and effortlessly defeats their gods and their king. Exodus is a story of monolatry, not monotheism. To miss this is to miss the theological depth of Exodus.

The first and second commandments (Exod. 20:3–6) reflect the same theology. The first commandment famously states, "You shall have no other gods before me." If read in the context of the polytheistic world in which Israel lived, this is a statement of monolatry, not monotheism. The command does not say that there *are* no other gods but that Israel is to *have* no other gods rivaling Yahweh. The second commandment clarifies that Yahweh is not to be worshiped the way the nations worship their gods (idols), but as Yahweh commands. In other words, the first two commandments amount to "Worship me *alone* and in the *way* I tell you" because Yahweh is a "jealous God" (20:5). Yahweh does not want to share Israel's allegiance with any other god. This way of reading the first two commandments may seem counterintuitive, even theologically suspect to some. But if we read Exodus in the context of the ancient thought world in which the Israelites lived, it makes perfect sense.

Monolatry can also be seen in numerous psalms, where Yahweh is praised for being greater than the gods of the surrounding nations:

- *Among the gods* there is none like you, O Lord; no deeds can compare with yours. (86:8; emphasis added in each verse)
- For the LORD is the great God, the great King *above all gods*. (95:3)

- For great is the LORD and most worthy of praise; he is to be *feared above all gods*. (96:4)
- For you, O LORD, are most high over all the earth; you are exalted far *above all gods*. (97:9)
- I know that the LORD is great, that our Lord is *greater than all gods*. (135:5)
- Give thanks to the *God of gods*, for his love endures forever. (136:2)

Some might argue that the psalmists simply use poetic license: they did not intend for their words to be taken literally. But that argument is not convincing, particularly since monolatry is not restricted to poetic texts, as we have seen. Moreover, the purpose of the comparison is to exalt Yahweh by way of contrast. For the comparison to have any real punch, both entities must be presumed to be real.

The Old Testament is not uniformly monolatrous (e.g., see Deut. 4:39; Isa. 44:6–20; Jer. 10:1–16), but that does not affect the point I am making. Genesis 1 reflects the same argument we find in Exodus and the Psalms: Yahweh alone is worthy of worship, and none of the other gods can compare to him. This is a radical claim that would have spoken volumes to a small, beleaguered nation surrounded by polytheism. Yahweh spoke[7] and things fell into place quickly and effortlessly. Even the sun and moon—deities in the ancient world—are impersonal objects fixed in the heavens by God's command not until day 4. The placement of the stars, thought to be keys to revealing the will of the gods, is almost an afterthought.

The theology of Genesis 1 becomes clearer when we read it in its ancient literary-religious context. For those who wish to see support in Genesis for modern science, it may seem a bit of a letdown that God is "only" said to have tamed a preexisting chaos, for example. After all, if he were truly almighty, would he not create out of nothing? But in the ancient world of the Israelites, this was not an active question. In that world, the theology of a chaos-tamer working solo, commanding the elements to line up, was counterintuitive and set Israel apart theologically. Genesis 1 is not in any way a modern scientific statement, but an ancient religious one. It drew on the thought categories available at the time to create a powerful statement within its own context for the uniqueness of Israel's God and his worthiness to be worshiped.

The Flood, *Gilgamesh*, and *Atrahasis*

The main focus of part 1 is the creation stories in Genesis, but the flood story also deserves our attention, for two reasons. First, our understanding of the flood story has been even more deeply affected by nineteenth-century discoveries than Genesis 1, and so it has contributed significantly to the genre calibration of Genesis that we discussed earlier. Second, the flood story is conceptually tied to the creation narrative in Genesis: it is a story of the second creation of the cosmos. Therefore, looking at the flood story will give us a backdrop for understanding more clearly Israel's creation theology.

The Mesopotamian stories known to us as the *Atrahasis Epic* and the *Gilgamesh Epic* both include narratives of a cataclysmic flood. They are not the only ancient versions of the story (cf. other Akkadian versions as well as Sumerian), but *Atrahasis* and *Gilgamesh* are the most relevant to Genesis.

Atrahasis is the name of the story's Noah-like figure and means "exceedingly wise." The story was found in fragmentary form in the mid-nineteenth century among the ruins of Ashurbanipal's library (as was *Enuma Elish*). A more complete version was found in 1965 and was dated to the seventeenth century BC. This fuller depiction of the story has helped tremendously in showing the conceptual similarities with not only the biblical flood story but Adam as well (see below). Yet as with *Enuma Elish*, the date of the text that archaeologists happened to find does not indicate how old the story actually is. All of the examples we are looking at, including the biblical examples, retell much older stories for contemporary audiences.

The *Gilgamesh Epic* is named after the Sumerian king of Uruk who ruled sometime between 2800 and 2500 BC. The story itself has a complex literary history. The earliest copies of *Gilgamesh* are Sumerian, from the first half of the second millennium BC. Some have argued for a date in the middle of the third millennium since this was the time when Sumerian poets began recounting the tales of their hero, Gilgamesh. The earliest versions, however, do not include a flood story. That was added in the latter part of the second millennium and was deliberately adopted from *Atrahasis*.

It goes without saying that the two Mesopotamian flood stories have their own qualities and are subjects of study in their own right. For us, however, we can take the two together and compare them to Genesis, and the result is illuminating. It is hard to deny that some direct connection exists between them. The following summarizes the shared elements:[8]

- A flood and a huge boat, built to precise dimensions and sealed with pitch.
- Clean and unclean animals come on board.
- A Noah figure and his family are saved. (*Gilgamesh* includes some others.)
- The boat comes to rest on a mountain.
- A raven and doves are sent out. (*Gilgamesh* includes a swallow.)
- The Deity/deities proclaim that animals will fear humans.
- The Deity/deities smell the pleasing aroma of the sacrifices afterward.
- A sign of an oath is given (rainbow in Genesis, precious lapis lazuli necklace for *Gilgamesh*).

Again, the similarities in themes and details suggest that the three stories are related in some way. As mentioned above, *Gilgamesh* seems to have a direct literary tie to *Atrahasis*. Some scholars also feel that the episode of the birds in Genesis 8:6–12 is dependent on *Gilgamesh*. But for us, it is not important to demonstrate the direct literary dependence of Genesis on these ancient Mesopotamian stories. As with *Enuma Elish*, it may be that they share common motifs about how this story should be told.

What can be ruled out, however, is any notion of Genesis being the original. The Genesis story we have is written in a dialect of Hebrew that did not exist until the first millennium BC. Hebrew culture is also a later development than Babylonian culture, and it strains credulity to think that Mesopotamian superpowers would bind their national story to that of a tribe of wanderers. There is really little question among scholars of Scripture and the ancient Near East that the Hebrew version is later and owes its existence to its Akkadian predecessors, in terms of shared cultural and literary motifs if not actual retellings of those Akkadian precursors.

We must remember too that the flood story, like Genesis 1, has a polemical dimension vis-à-vis its Mesopotamian antecedents. That polemic requires an established and well-known flood ideology against which the Israelite version can make its theological point. Like all ancient flood stories, the Israelite version is aimed at saying something distinct about its beliefs, not simply relaying some meteorological information. And the distinct elements of Genesis carry forward its theology, all the while working within the familiar, older, established conventions of the time.

One important distinction of the Israelite version is the reason given for the flood. In *Atrahasis* we see the lesser gods (the Igigi) staging mass rebellion against the slave labor to which the higher gods have subjected them. To solve the problem, protohumans (*Lullû*) were created from the remains of one of the Igigi slain in the rebellion. They increased in population and became so noisy that the gods could not sleep, so the god Enlil sent a flood to wipe them out.

Genesis at best captures a hint of this scenario, but on the whole the biblical story presents a God who is hardly this cranky. In Genesis, two reasons are given for the flood. The first is the curious incident of interspecies cohabitation in Genesis 6:1–4 between the "sons of God" and the "daughters of humans." Throughout the history of biblical interpretation, readers have made numerous attempts to make sense of this. The most straightforward explanation is that the "sons of God" are divine beings (alluded to perhaps in the "let us" of Gen. 1:26) who had begun cohabiting with the "daughters of humans" (clearly meaning human women)—which certainly raises questions about the historical nature of this passage.[9] The second reason is given in Genesis 6:5: human wickedness and wholly corrupt thinking had become a worldwide problem and intolerable to God.

In the biblical flood story, God kills every human being on earth except for one family because one man, Noah, is deemed to be "blameless in his generation" (6:9). Throughout history, no less in today's world, God's destruction of all life has raised serious questions about the nature of Israel's God. He seems here to be quite satisfied to give in to his temper rather than to find some means of redeeming humankind. At least one early Jewish interpreter was quite sensitive to this charge and hence portrayed the flood story as one of God's patience: Cain's murder was cause enough for destruction, but God allows the human drama to play out to see if things will get better (Mishnah, tractate 'Abot 5.2). This is not the place to work through the moral issues surrounding the flood, but whatever moral questions the biblical story may raise, the behavior of Israel's God is driven by an entirely different issue from what we see in *Atrahasis*.

The biblical flood is not the impulsive act of a cranky, sleep-deprived God. The actions of both the "sons of God" and of the human population threaten the created order established by God in Genesis 1. God has put everything in its place and assigned all things their role. The earth is the abode of created life, not of divine beings. When the sons of God cohabit with human women, they cross that boundary, which in effect means that they are reintroducing chaos to the created order. Likewise, humans are created to be image-bearers of God (Gen. 1:26–28). We recall that "image" of God refers to humanity's role in being representatives of God in the world, much like earthly kings in the ancient Near East embodied the presence of a distant god or made a king "present" among his distant subjects. Curiously, the flood story does not lay out exactly what humanity is doing to make God so angry. Regardless, image-bearers—representatives of God in creation—are required to act accordingly. Whatever behavior is left unspoken in Genesis 6:5, there is much more to it than people being very naughty, and so God kills them. Humanity is not fulfilling the role in God's created order for which it was made. Humanity has becomes an agent of disruptive chaos.

The flood is not a divine fit of rage but, theologically speaking, the proper response. Heavenly and divine beings have become forces of chaos, not order. God responds by reintroducing chaos in earnest, wiping the slate clean, and starting over with a second creation. The flood, therefore, is not a really bad rainstorm but the unleashing of the waters of chaos that God has held at bay in Genesis 1:6–8. The "fountains of the great deep burst" up through the earth, and the "windows [NIV: "floodgates"] of the heavens were opened" to release the waters above that had been held back by the firmament (Gen. 7:11). The sea and the land were given their proper boundaries, and now those boundaries are obliterated, returning the earth to its precreation state of chaos.

As horrific as the biblical flood story is, it makes a distinct point about Israel's God and the status of humanity vis-à-vis *Atrahasis*. Israel's God does not need his sleep, nor are humans his slaves. Humans are God's image-bearers, representative rulers in creation, not a class of slaves created so the gods can be in repose. The distinct theology of the biblical flood story, however, does not imply that it is of a higher historical or scientific order than the other ancient flood stories. It does seem likely that there is a historical basis for the flood stories of the ancient Near East, perhaps the cataclysmic deluge in Mesopotamia around 3000 BC. (Some suggest earlier dates.) The ancient Near Eastern stories in this case would be attempts to explain this great deluge from a religious point of view: "What happened between us and the gods to cause this?"

The biblical account reflects this same mind-set. It is not a journalistic report of an event but Israel's answer to Mesopotamian theology. For the biblical writer, along with every other ancient writer, the entire world was as it appeared, small and flat, and so it was presumed that the local flood (from the point of view of modern geology) covered the entire earth. This is fully to be expected. It is true that there are flood stories from around the world, but this does not imply that one global flood was responsible for those stories. It simply reflects the ubiquity of floods and the devastation that massive ones would bring in pretechnological antiquity (and still do, as in the Indian Ocean tsunami of December 26, 2004, which swept away about 300,000 people; and the similar tsunami that hit northeastern Japan on March 11, 2011). The fact that the stories across the world are so different from each other reflects how each culture told the story of their local floods in their own way. The biblical and Mesopotamian versions are similar, but that is because they share a conceptual world. The differences between them, as I mentioned, are due to their different theologies.

Like the story of creation, Israel's flood story is a theological expression of self-definition. Like all of the other Mesopotamian versions, it answers the question, "Why did this massive flood occur?" But the answer it gives is different because it presumes a different idea of who God is as creator. Together Genesis 1 and the flood story in chapters 6–9 present not a picture of history but a picture of how Israel sees itself as God's people amid the surrounding world. This point is essentially self-evident and so shapes our expectations of what Genesis is prepared to deliver for those who read it today. These early chapters are the Word of God, but they are not history in any normally accepted sense of the word today. And they are most certainly not science. They speak another language altogether.

Israel's Second Creation Story

Thus far we have focused on the creation story in Genesis 1 and the flood story in Genesis 6–9. We have taken the time to look at these stories because understanding how they came to be and what they are meant to convey provides the backdrop for the all-important second creation story—the story of Adam—found in chapters 2–3.

The Adam story (due in part to Paul's influence on Christian readers) is too often treated in isolation from the larger primordial narrative that extends from Genesis 1 through 11, which itself reflects the broader ancient Near Eastern context we glimpsed. Even though the Adam story is where evolutionary theory and the Bible come into direct conflict, and so one may be tempted to home in on it directly, it is actually part of a larger package. As with Genesis 1 and the flood story, it is clear that the second creation story is not a historical account as we normally think of it, nor is it a scientific explanation. It too reflects religious beliefs that the Israelites were intent to communicate. Missing this means getting off on the wrong foot altogether.

To understand the second creation account, it is helpful to begin by comparing it to Genesis 1. As can be seen in the chart below, the differences between the two creation stories are significant, not superficial, and should therefore be respected rather than harmonized. Particularly telling is the sequence of creation in the third row.[10]

Table 3.1 Comparison of the Two Creation Accounts

	Genesis 1:2–2:3	Genesis 2:4–25
Duration of creation	Six days	One day implied (see "in the day" in 2:4b)
Primordial scenario	Dark, watery chaos	An oasis amid desert
Sequence of creation	Light Firmament Dry land Plants Lights in the sky Sea and sky creatures Land animals Humans (male and female)	Man (Adam) Garden with trees and river Land animals and birds as potential helpers to Adam Woman as the fitting helper to Adam
Method of creation	God speaks, separates, names, blesses	God forms, breathes, plants, puts to sleep, builds
Portrait of God	Transcendent Sovereign over creation Some anthropomorphism God is called Elohim	Immanent Actively involved in creation Lots of anthropomorphism God is called Yahweh Elohim
Portrait of humanity	Unspecified number of humans (ʾadam), males (zakar) and females (neqevah), created simultaneously Royals, created in divine image, given dominion over the earth	One male (ʾadam) from the ground (ʾadamah), then one woman (ʾishah) from the man (ʾish)—in two separate acts of creation Servants, made caretakers of the garden

These two stories are clearly significantly different, and they cannot be harmonized by saying that the first gives the overview and the second fills in some of the details. The presence of two different creation accounts is troublesome for readers who assume that Genesis 1 and 2 are historical in nature and that the Bible's first priority is to recount history accurately. Yet the divergence of these stories cannot be reasonably questioned. To stitch them into a seamless whole would dismiss the particular and distinct points of view that the authors were so deliberate in placing there. The differences between the two creation accounts are further complemented by differences seen in other Old Testament passages such as Psalms 77:16–20; 89:5–37; Job 9:4–15; 26:5–14; 38:4–38; and Isaiah 40:12–31; 44:24–28. It does not seem to be a concern of the biblical writers to provide God's people with a "unified" story of creation.

Relevant here too are other parallel stories in Genesis 1–11: two divergent genealogies of Adam's line are given in 4:17–26 and 5:3–32, and differing genealogies of the postflood repopulation of the earth appear in 10:1–32 and 11:10–32. Whoever is responsible for Genesis 1–11 certainly seems comfortable allowing distinct accounts to rest side by side. The reason for this may simply be that the final editor of Genesis wished to preserve Israel's own diverse traditions, or perhaps needed to, owing to the weight of tradition behind them. I certainly think this is true, but there is still more going on. The placement of these stories side by side has theological value: Genesis 1 tells the story of creation as a whole by the one sovereign God, and Genesis 2 focuses early and specifically on *Israel's* story. I come back to this in chapters 4 and 6 and summarize the point in theses 4 and 5 in the conclusion. For now, however, I do not want us to be distracted from the point that the two accounts differ from each other, and those differences should not be minimized.

Once the differences are accepted for what they are, one implication for the evolution discussion becomes immediately apparent: concern over the historical or scientific value of these accounts seems anachronistic. Faced with these clear differences in perspective between the accounts, some assign an essential historical value to the Adam story and assign less historical value to Genesis 1. It is claimed that Genesis 1 is less historical because of its poetic-like structure. Genesis 2–3, because it is written in a narrative style, is considered to be of greater historical value.

In the Old Testament there certainly is such a thing as poetic license; generally speaking, readers should not make historical conclusions on the basis of, say, Yahweh as one "who rides upon the clouds" (Ps. 68:4). But the matter of Genesis 1 is not so straightforward. First, it is not entirely clear the style of Genesis 1 is poetic. Second, surely narrative is not an automatic indication of historical veracity, either in the Bible or any other literature, ancient or modern: fiction as well as nonfiction can be written in narrative style. Genesis 1 is not the symbolic, less historical, "poetic" account of creation and Genesis 2–3 the narrative and *therefore* more historical one. Both reflect ancient ways of thinking; we need to understand them first on their own terms and appreciate the tensions between them for what they tell us about their theologies.

Adam and *Atrahasis*

Our understanding of the second creation story has been enhanced by ancient texts, particularly the *Atrahasis Epic*. We discussed *Atrahasis* earlier in relation to the biblical flood story, but there is more to *Atrahasis* than that.

The general story line of *Atrahasis* is similar to Genesis 2–8 as a whole: creation, population growth, flood. Some argue that Genesis 2–8 is actually an Israelite version of *Atrahasis*. Perhaps we cannot be dogmatic about this, but given their striking similarities, it is a reasonable suggestion. Table 3.2 shows the places where, either by comparison or contrast, the two stories follow a very similar structure.[11]

One would be hard-pressed to find an ancient text that has such clear implications for understanding the biblical stories of Adam, of population growth, and of the flood as *Atrahasis*. These similarities are widely recognized by biblical scholars and are tremendously significant for addressing the type of literature that Genesis is. Whether or not Genesis is actually modeled after *Atrahasis* deliberately, there is no question that they share a common way of describing the primordial world. Seeing the similarities between these two stories should discourage us from expecting the Adam story to contribute to contemporary scientific debates about human origins (let alone guide those debates). Likewise, the similarities between Genesis and *Atrahasis* suggest that the biblical account cannot be labeled "historical," at least not in any conventional sense of the word. What can be said of the first creation story and cosmological origins can—and indeed must—be said of the second creation story and human origins: they are ancient texts addressing ancient concerns. Precisely how the Adam story functioned for Israel we will leave for later chapters.

Table 3.2 Comparison of *Atrahasis* and Genesis 2–8

Atrahasis	Genesis 2–8
Agriculture by irrigation	Eden watered by irrigation
Lesser gods (Igigi) as original laborers	Yahweh as original laborer (plants garden)
High gods (Anunnaki) enjoying privileges of divine rank	Yahweh's private garden with magic trees of life and wisdom
Protohumans (*Lullû*) created as laborers to replace Igigi modeled from clay + rebel god's blood implicitly immortal (no natural death)	Primeval human (*ha-ʾadam*) created to care for Yahweh's garden modeled from clay + divine breath potentially immortal (tree of life)
Institution of marriage	Institution of marriage
Lullû anger the gods (making too much noise)	*Ha-ʾadam* rebels against God (eating forbidden fruit)
Lullû punished: life diminished by plague, drought, and famine	*Ha-ʾadam* punished: life diminished by exile from garden, denial of access to tree of life, and hard labor
As a last resort, the god Enki sends a flood to drown out humanity's noise and control overpopulation	Yahweh sends a flood to punish humanity's wickedness and cleanse the creation
The god Enki tells Atrahasis to build an ark and escape the flood	Yahweh tells Noah to build an ark and escape the flood
Atrahasis survives the flood and offers a sacrifice	Noah survives the flood and offers a sacrifice
The gods smell the sacrifice and bless the survivors; Enlil is reconciled to noisome humanity	Yahweh smells the sacrifice and blesses creation; Yahweh is reconciled to sinful humanity
Limitations imposed on humans: *Lullû* become normal humans	Limitation of 120-year lifespan imposed on humans: *ha-ʾadam* become normal humans
Sign of divine goodwill: mother-goddess Nintu's fly necklace	Sign of divine goodwill: duration of seasons (and Yahweh's bow [9:12–17])

In addition to the *Atrahasis Epic*, other texts—Sumerian, Babylonian, and Egyptian—have come to light since the nineteenth century and further illuminate the second creation story. To round out our discussion, here is a list of the biblical scenes with the relevant extrabiblical texts in parentheses. I have tried to be fairly complete in this list, but I make no claim to being exhaustive. We will not go into any of this here since it would only serve to continue making the same point. Readers interested in more detail on this issue, particularly on the extrabiblical literature, can consult the volumes listed in the bibliography.[12]

- A garden/paradise of God/the gods in the east (*Enki and Ninhursag*;[13] *Gilgamesh*)
- Humans created out of dust/clay to cultivate the land (*Enki and Ninmah* [Sumerian]; *Atrahasis*; *Gilgamesh*)
- Humans infused with the Breath of Life (*Instructions of Merikare* [Egyptian])
- Creation as inchoate, not fully developed (Gen. 2:5; Nippur[14] tradition; *Ewe and Wheat* [Sumerian])
- Streams of water supply irrigation to the garden (*Enki and Ninhursag*)
- Creation of humans as "trial and error"[15] (Gen. 2:18–22; *Atrahasis*)
- A plant that confers immortality and a serpent (*Gilgamesh*; *Enkidu and the Underworld* [Sumerian, Nippur tradition])
- Rivers flowing from a god or holy place (Gen. 2:10; various sources)[16]
- The female made from the male's rib/side (*Enki and Ninhursag* [referring to a goddess])
- From nakedness to a clothed state (*Gilgamesh*; *Ewe and Wheat*)
- Humans becoming like gods (*Gilgamesh*; *Adapa*)[17]
- God/the gods keep immortality from humans (*Adapa*; *Atrahasis*; *Gilgamesh*)
- Garments of skin (*Adapa*)
- Cain and Abel representing pastoralism and agriculture (*Dumizi and Enkimdu*)[18]
- Lengthy lifespan of preflood humans (*Sumerian King List*)

Listing some of the more salient connections between the Adam story and ancient literature adequately underscores that, whatever theological differences there are between Genesis and surrounding literature, Genesis reflects an ancient world, not a modern one. This fact should be fully appreciated when discussing the relationship between the biblical depiction of human origins and modern understandings of evolution.

To put it this way in no way discredits the story or devalues it as God's Word but respects the story on its own terms as it functioned in the world in which those stories were written. When faced with these considerations, insisting that because the biblical creation accounts are God's Word they *must* be historical seems wrongheaded. People have left their faith behind when confronted with such a false choice. If the faith of such readers is to be sustained, they must not cling to the mistaken approaches of the past but find the courage to adjust their expectations to what Genesis is prepared to deliver. Only such a theological reorientation can preserve the integrity of Scripture and engage responsibly the massive amount of scientific and literary knowledge we have.

Reorienting Expectations of Genesis and Human Origins

We have covered a lot of ground in this chapter, although quickly, in looking at the Genesis creation and flood stories in their ancient Near Eastern context. This issue has profoundly affected how modern readers understand the type of literature that Genesis is and therefore what we have the right to expect of it, especially when the topic turns to the relationship between Christianity and evolution. Although there is no absolute scholarly consensus about how to read the creation and flood stories in all their details, the evidence points us clearly in the following direction: the early chapters of Genesis are not a literal or scientific description of historical events but a theological statement in an ancient idiom, a statement about Israel's God and Israel's place in the world as God's people.

The core issue raised by the ancient Near Eastern data has helped calibrate the genre of the biblical creation accounts. I maintain that the failure to appreciate that genre calibration is responsible for much of the tension in the evolution discussion. The tensions among various Christian groups are basically not driven by differences of scientific opinion. Rather, different interpretations of the scientific data are driven by deep theological precommitments, implicit or explicit, that determine the range of options open to Christians. But a literal reading of Genesis is not the firmly settled default position of true faith to which one can "hold firm" or from which one "strays." Literalism is a hermeneutical *decision* (often implicit) stemming from the belief that God's Word requires a literal reading.

These tensions about Genesis are most acute when the topic turns to Adam and human origins. How we read that story will be determined by what we think we have the right to find there. But here especially a reorientation of expectations is sorely needed. For one thing, natural science simply cannot be squared with a literal reading of the biblical description of human origins any more than with the biblical description of the cosmos (a stationary and flat earth, solid dome above, etc.). Genesis 1 speaks of the instantaneous creation of humankind—men and women—on the sixth day. Genesis 2 speaks of the creation of a first couple—without antecedents (although we will see below in chapters 4 and 6 that the traditional interpretation of Adam and Eve as the first humans may not be the best way to handle the biblical evidence). Even though these two creation stories are quite different, they both envision a special act of God in relatively recent history, where one moment there are no humans and the next moment there are. And humans, along with every other form of life, are created "according to its kind"—no development from one species to another. This biblical view cannot in any way be joined to modern scientific models.

I realize that this could invite a strong response: "You are putting science over Scripture." But that is not the right way to frame the issue, for it incorrectly assumes that Genesis speaks to scientific matters. It does not. The various sciences, however, are designed to investigate the natural world and draw conclusions about why things are the way they are and how they came to be. Science is a self-critical, changing entity, and so it should not surprise us to see developments, even paradigm shifts, in the near and distant future. Is the universe ever expanding or oscillating? Are there multiple universes? How many dimensions are there? What about dark matter and dark energy? How many hominids constituted the gene pool from which all alive today have descended? And so forth. But we should not expect science to revert to the kinds of understandable assumptions about the natural world made by ancient Israelites: a flat earth, geocentric solar system, a global flood, or the special and instantaneous creation of earth's species a few thousand years ago. The necessarily self-corrective nature of all true scientific theories does not mean that a literal reading of Genesis is allowed to remain on the table. Further discoveries will take us forward, not backward.

The literary evidence from the ancient Near East that we looked at in this chapter further supports the notion that the creation stories were not written as historical accounts. Our growing knowledge of the cultures, religions, and worldviews of the ancient world in which the Israelites lived, thought, wrote, and worshiped has significantly reoriented our expectation of what Genesis is prepared to deliver. To observe the similarities between the creation and flood stories and the literature of the ancient Near East, and to insist that all of those other writings are clearly ahistorical while Genesis is somehow presenting history—this is not a strong position of faith, but rather a weak one, where Scripture must conform to one's expectations. Genesis cries out to be read as something other than a historical description of events. Resistance to this conclusion rests at least in part on the faulty theological premise that Israel's Scripture, to be truly the Word of God, must be fundamentally different from the kind of literature other ancient Near Eastern cultures produced—and that any similarities between them are merely superficial or incidental and can be safely set to the side. Surely (it is thought) God would not tolerate such nonsense, but give Israel "correct" information.

But to insist that, in order to convey truth, Israel's Scripture must be isolated from the world in which it was written is a violation of basic interpretive practice. It is routinely understood, even by conservative interpreters, that the cultural context of Scripture informs our understanding of Scripture. Responsible biblical interpreters ask themselves, "How would this text have been understood at the time in which it was written?" This principle holds whether we are interpreting Paul, the Gospels, the Prophets, the Psalms, or the Pentateuch—including the creation and flood stories of Genesis. To insist that these stories must be read in isolation from what we know of the ancient world is, ironically, an argument for a noncontextual reading of Genesis, which is something few would tolerate when interpreting other portions of the Bible.

A noncontextual reading of Scripture is not only methodologically arbitrary but also theologically problematic. It fails to grasp in its entirety a foundational principle of theology that informs not only our understanding of the Bible but of all of God's dealing with humanity recorded there, particularly in Jesus himself: *God condescends to where people are, speaks their language, and employs their ways of thinking.* Without God's condescension—seen most clearly in the incarnation—any true knowledge of God would cease to exist.

It is not beneath God to condescend to culturally conditioned human modes of communication. Having such a condescending God is crucial to the very heart of Christianity. True, such a God will allow ancient

Israelites to produce a description of human origins that reflects the ancient ideas and so will not satisfy scientific questions. But if we are going to talk about the Christian God, then this is something we are going to have to get used to. What sets this God apart is his habit of coming down to our level. As Christians confess, God even became one of us. Posing such a condescending and incarnating God as a theological problem to be overcome—which is what a literal reading of Genesis unwittingly requires—creates a far greater and more harmful theological problem than the nonliteral reading of Genesis.

Any real progress in the evolution-Christianity discussion will have to begin with a reorientation of expectations about the type of literature Genesis is and what we therefore can expect to glean from it. Bearing in mind the ancient context in which the creation stories were written is perhaps the most important first step in producing that reorientation. In the next and final chapter of part 1, we will look a bit more at how Israel's stories of origins functioned as statements of self-definition by connecting Israel to primordial time.

4

Israel and Primordial Time

Archaeology has greatly illuminated our understanding of how ancient peoples understood the world around them. Judging by their cultural remains (literature and artifacts), they were occupied with such perennial questions as these: Who are we? Why are we here? Why do we die? What happens afterward? Why is there pain and suffering? Why is there anger and murder? What causes the seasons and the sun, moon, and stars to appear at regular intervals? Why do crops die and bloom? Why is sex such a powerful force? The list goes on. Explanations for why things are the way they are were sought not in laboratories, telescopes, or therapy but ultimately in the activity of the gods in primordial time. Divine activity in the deep past helped explain the world and answered questions of meaning and existence. Stories of the deep past gave . stability and coherence to life.

All ancient Near Eastern religions that we know of believed that these formative primordial divine actions did not just stay in the past but also somehow intersected with the events of history and everyday life. For example, the annual "birth and death" of the crops and seasons were commonly thought to be connected to some divine prototype of a dying-and-rising god. Ancient worship was in effect a celebration of the intersection between divine primordial activity and present earthly reality. Israel's creation stories, as we have seen, inherited many of the themes in stories of their more ancient neighbors. And like them Israel also celebrated the intersection of primordial time and present time. Israel's creation stories were not simply accounts of "how it all began." They were statements about the continuing presence of the God who acted back then. Israel's creation stories rooted their present experiences in the very origins of the cosmos.

Israel and the Cosmic Battle

One way to illustrate the intersection between primordial divine time and present earthly time in Israel's theology is to look beyond Genesis to Exodus and the founding of Israel as a nation. It is widely known that the book of Exodus and the conquest narratives in Joshua and Judges do not give us a journalistic recounting of freed slaves and the beginnings of an independent nation. Actually, as students of Scripture and ancient Near Eastern history know only too well, the historical evidence for Israel's presence in Egypt, the exodus, and the conquest of Canaan is somewhat sparse.

Biblical scholars often acknowledge some sort of historical trigger, however minimal, that gave rise to these stories, but the stories themselves are not blow-by-blow accounts of historical events.[1] Rather, these narratives greatly embellished the events to serve another purpose: they are Israel's declaration that the God of the primordial past was active also in their own formation as a nation. We see this by how the Israelites presented their deliverance from Egypt in terms of primordial cosmic battle themes seen in ancient Near Eastern stories and reflected in Genesis 1.

For example, Psalm 89:5–12 praises Yahweh as creator, which includes a reference to the cosmic battle with Yahweh's crushing Rahab, one of the mythical monsters of the deep (vv. 9–10; see also Pss. 32:6; 87:4). These verses about the cosmic battle are sandwiched by references to God's historical covenant with David (89:1–4 and 14–36). The reference to creation seems to intrude upon the topic of the Davidic covenant, but nothing could be further from the truth. David's line will be established "forever, . . . through all generations" (v. 4). The basis for the psalmist's confidence in David's perpetual line is that David's God is the victor in the cosmic battle in primordial time. Israel's historical enemies are viewed as present-day manifestations of God's primordial enemies, both of which are defeated by God.

Psalm 93 celebrates Yahweh's majesty and strength. His throne, indeed the entire world, was established "from everlasting" (vv. 1–2). In verse 5 the LORD's decrees—Israel's law—also stand firm. The law is as sure and lasting as God's own throne, since God's primordial victory at the sea secures them both. That victory is described in verses 3–4:

> The floods have lifted up, O LORD,
> the floods have lifted up their voice;
> the floods lifted up their roaring.
> More majestic than the thunders of mighty waters,
> more majestic than the waves of the sea,
> majestic on high is the LORD!

This is not about God's being somehow "stronger" than the ocean waves during a bad storm. Rather, the image here is of God's taming the primordial waters into submission—but not simply as a past event. That past event is revisited in the establishment of Israel's law, its national constitution. Israel's status as a nation benefits from Yahweh's primordial victory.

Other passages speak of the exodus specifically as a replay of the primordial battle. We saw in chapter 3 that the plagues and the parting of the sea are described in Exodus in terms of Yahweh's victory in the cosmic battle. Psalm 77 continues this theme, but the distinction between past and present is blurred, as if speaking of the one is also speaking of the other.

The psalm ends with a reference to the exodus and God's making a path through the sea when Israel was led "like a flock by the hand of Moses and Aaron" (vv. 19–20). In verse 16, this sea is described as "writhing" and "convulsing" at the sight of God (cf. NIV). This language is not poetic exaggeration for effect, but bristling with cosmic-battle overtones: the sea is going into a panic attack at the sight of the warrior-Yahweh. Verse 16 alludes to the cosmic victory of Yahweh over the primordial sea, which is *tehom* (the deep) in both verse 16 (17 MT) and Genesis 1:2, the functional equivalent of Tiamat in *Enuma Elish* and Yam (god of the sea) defeated by Baal in Canaanite religion.

Similarly, Psalm 136:1–9, in language reminiscent of Genesis 1, praises Yahweh for creating the cosmos. In verse 10, without missing a beat or indicating that a new topic is introduced, the exodus is in view ("[Yahweh] struck Egypt through their firstborn"). This theme continues through verse 15, and in verse 13 we read that Yahweh "divided the Red Sea in two." A better translation is "cut the Red Sea to pieces," which describes the dividing of the Red Sea in a way that immediately brings to mind Tiamat's fate at the hand of Marduk in *Enuma Elish*. Psalm 74:12–17 uses similar language: God, the King "from of old, . . . divided the sea, . . . broke the heads of the dragons in the waters, . . . [and] crushed the heads of Leviathan."

In Isaiah 40–66, another "exodus," the deliverance from Babylon, is described as an instance of the intersection of primordial time and Israel's history. For example, in Isaiah 48:12–16, the same God who "laid the foundation of the earth" and "spread out the heavens" will now unleash his might to redeem Israel from Babylon (see also 40:12–31; 43:1–7, 16–21). In Isaiah 51:9–11 the prophet sees the imminent deliverance from Babylon as both a second exodus and a second cosmic battle. The prophet speaks of all three in almost the same breath:

> ^{9a}Awake, awake, put on strength,
>   O arm of the LORD
> ^{9b}Awake, *as in days of old,*
>   *the generations of long ago!*
> ^{9c}Was it not you who *cut Rahab in pieces,*
>   who pierced the dragon?
> ^{10a}Was it not you who *dried up the sea,*
>   the waters of the great deep,
> ^{10b}who made *the depths of the sea a way*
>   for the redeemed to cross over?
> ^{11a}*So the ransomed of the LORD shall return,*
>   and come to Zion with singing. (emphasis added)

Here the prophet calls upon God to awake and do again what he had done in "days of old" (v. 9a–b). He moves effortlessly from one bygone event (the cosmic creation battle in v. 9c) to another (the exodus in v. 10a). Notice that if it were not for verse 10b, where the exodus is clearly in view, it would be unclear what verse 10a is referring to. Taken with what comes before, verse 10a refers to creation ("waters of the great deep"), but with verse 10b it signals the exodus ("a way" made in the "depths of the sea"). Verse 10a does double duty as a reference to both battles, the primordial and the exodus. Then, without hesitation, the topic turns to the deliverance from Babylon (v. 11a). All three battles are connected. The deliverance from Babylon is patterned after the exodus, and both merge with the cosmic creation battle.

This is not the place to lay out fully how the Israelites used cosmic language to speak of historical events.[2] They understood God's acts in their national history as continuations of the cosmic battle. However inadequate, confusing, inaccurate, or downright bizarre these stories of primordial time might appear to us, the ancient Israelites spoke this way because they saw in this imagery a point of contact between their own experiences and God's activity. So for all three events—exodus, monarchy, and departure from Babylon—Israel could say to itself, "Look, the God who battled the waters back then is battling for us here too."

This brings us back to the issue of self-definition. Israel's God is (1) the one responsible for the created order and (2) still acting in the here and now to save his people. Yahweh, in other words, is creator and redeemer, and *creation and redemption are not two separate acts*: the latter is an instantiation[3] of the former. That Yahweh was Israel's creator and redeemer is what made him stand out among the crowd of less worthy gods, why their God alone was truly worthy of worship. This vital piece of Old Testament theology will be missed if we obscure the mythic context of Israel's stories of origins or if we fail to see how Israel's creation theology is expressed in the context of their national life. And if we miss this theology, we run the risk of misusing Israel's creation theology by trying to align it with modern science.

Adam and Israel

Another place to see the intersection of primordial time and present time in Israel is the Adam story. Genesis 1–11 as a whole certainly has in view a universal setting. Using ancient categories, Genesis 1 describes how the earth and cosmos came to be. Likewise, the flood story speaks of all life on earth being swept away by the chaotic waters (Gen. 6:7), and the table of nations in chapter 10 recounts how the earth became repopulated.

The Adam story seems to fit into this universal focus, but not entirely so. Some elements of the story suggest that it is not about universal human origins but Israel's origin. This line of interpretation has pre-Christian roots. For example, the book of *Jubilees* (second century BC) presents Adam as a patriarch of the Israelites (3:27–32). Similarly, the apocryphal book Ecclesiasticus (Sirach/Ben Sira, second century BC) presents Adam as an Israelite ancestor (49:16).[4]

I am not suggesting that the Adam story can only be read as a story of Israel's origins. It is, however, a compelling way to read it, for it makes sense out of some well-known interpretive difficulties while also helping along the evolution discussion. If the Adam story is not really a story of the beginning of humanity but of one segment of humanity, at least some of the tensions between Genesis and evolution are lessened—although we would still need to address the issue of Paul's reading of the Adam story, which we will get to in chapter 7.

Table 4.1 Comparison of the Stories of Israel and Adam

Israel		Adam
Creation of Israel at the exodus	→	Creation of Adam out of dust
Commandments (law of Moses)	→	Command (the tree)
Land of Canaan	→	Garden paradise
Disobedience leads to exile/death	→	Disobedience leads to exile/death

The Adam story mirrors Israel's story from exodus to exile. God creates a special person, Adam; places him in a special land, the garden; and gives him law as a stipulation of continued communion with God (not to eat of the tree of the knowledge of good and evil). Adam and Eve disobey the command and as a result are cursed with various curses, but primarily their punishment is death and exile from paradise. So too Israel was "created" at the exodus (as we saw in the cosmic-battle motif above) and brought to the good and spacious land of Canaan, a land "flowing with milk and honey" (e.g., Exod. 3:8, 17; 13:5)—a description of superabundance with rich ancient Near Eastern overtones that evoke images of paradise. Israel also has law to keep, in this case the law given to Moses on Mt. Sinai. But Israel continually disobeys the law, which eventually results in an exile from the land God gave them.

This mirroring can hardly be coincidental. Adam in primordial times plays out Israel's national life. He is proto-Israel—a preview of coming attractions. This does not mean, however, that a historical Adam was a template for Israel's national life. Rather, Israel's drama—its struggles over the land and failure to follow God's law—is placed into primordial time. In doing so, Israel claims that it has been God's special people all along, from the very beginning. But this is no mere triumphalism. Israel is also asserting that (1) its sorry pattern of disobedience and eventual exile has marked their existence since the very beginning; (2) despite this pattern, their creator and savior has always been with them—and remains with them. This message of God's faithfulness would have been especially poignant in the wake of the exile, which is the likely time when these stories were brought into their final form (as we saw earlier).

Understanding Adam as proto-Israel may also help us make sense of a nagging detail or two in the Adam story. First, in Genesis 2:17 God tells Adam that he would die "in the day" that he eats of the fruit. But when he eats of the fruit, he does not die immediately. It is often suggested that the death referred to here is a spiritual death: alienation from God. Certainly that is an understandable conclusion to draw, but spiritual death does not do justice, in my opinion, to the physicality of death pronounced in Genesis 3:19—a return to dust (nor does it do justice to Paul's understanding in Rom. 5:12–21).

More likely the pronouncement of death should be understood in the narrative's logic as the physical death that becomes Adam's inevitable end once he eats of the forbidden fruit. Access to the tree of life, available to them before, is now denied (3:22), and so mortality is introduced. (We will come back to this in chap. 5, when we look at the garden story from yet another angle, that of wisdom.) On one level, the pronouncement of 2:17 is fulfilled in 3:22: immortality could have been theirs, but once access to the tree of life is denied, mortality is introduced.

There is a second level on which Adam's death can be understood that fits perfectly with the parallel with Israel. Note that denial of access to the tree of life (3:22) is followed immediately by exile from the garden (3:23–24). This suggests that Adam's exile from the garden is the "death" sentence pronounced in 2:17. Israel's exile from its land is also a death, as we see in Ezekiel's famous vision of the bones (Ezek. 37). Israel's dry bones are a metaphor for exile, and God promises to revive those bones and bring the Israelites back into the land (see esp. 37:11–14). Exile from the land is death, while presence in the land is life. I am not arguing that a choice necessarily needs to be made between physical and metaphorical death in reading Genesis 3. Adam's physical death can function as a narrative presentation of Israel's metaphorical death as a nation. But death as exile is certainly a viable reading and thus supports the notion that Adam is the proto-Israelite rather than the first human.

A second detail of the Adam story that the parallel with Israel helps clear up is in Genesis 4. There are evidently other human beings assumed to exist outside of the garden, people whom Cain fears will retaliate for his murder of Abel and from whom he picks a wife and settles in the "land of Nod" (Gen. 4:16). If Adam is the first human, how can this be? I do not find conventional explanations helpful here, such as the hypothesis that Adam and Eve actually had many more children—boys and girls not mentioned in the narrative, who apparently procreated with each other and then, for some undisclosed reason, left Eden to settle elsewhere and from whom Cain would have found a wife among his sisters or nieces. If Adam is understood as proto-Israel, however, the presence of other people is no longer an issue.

I recognize that the following is speculative, but I agree with much of contemporary biblical scholarship that the second creation story (Adam) was Israel's original creation story, with some slight universal overtones (still seen, perhaps, in 3:20, where Eve is the "mother of all living"). It was likely modeled after the pattern of *Atrahasis* (creation, population growth, flood), as we glimpsed in the previous chapter. A postexilic writer/writers (perhaps the shapers of the Pentateuch) introduced an alternate account of origins, Genesis 1, modeled after common themes found in *Enuma Elish*, that focused on God's sovereignty and might over his creation, not to mention the rhythm of the week and Sabbath rest (more below). In my opinion, the editors of the Pentateuch subsumed the older story under the newer one so that Genesis 1 became the story of the creation of the cosmos and Genesis 2 became the story of Israel's creation against that universal backdrop. This may be why these two different creation stories are placed next to each other as they are. The editors of the Pentateuch may be expecting their readers to read the two stories sequentially: Genesis 2 presumes the events of Genesis 1 (see also thesis 4 in the conclusion).

The ambiguity of the Hebrew word *'adam* in Genesis 1–3 lends itself to this point. This word does double duty in Genesis. In 1:26–27 *'adam* refers to humanity as a whole. In chapters 2–3 *'adam* refers to the individual man (either as "the man" or as a proper name "Adam") whom God has formed from dust, who would later name the animals, marry Eve, and so forth. Clearly the two uses of *'adam* are meant to be distinguished, but what are we to make of the dual usage? The use of the same word in these stories to designate both humankind and one man is certainly purposeful, not merely an accident of the Hebrew language. (Perhaps Gen. 1 could have avoided the ambiguity by using *'ish* instead of *'adam* to describe humanity.) The editors are clearly saying something significant here, although the significance is not spelled out for us.

In my opinion, the editor might be signaling that the individual man Adam in chapter 2 is a subset of the humanity 'adam in chapter 1. In other words, the individual Adam is that part of the universal 'adam that God is primarily interested in. There is 'adam in the universal sense outside of Eden, but inside Eden, God's garden, there is no 'adam but one Adam—the one human with whom he has a unique relationship, the progenitor of God's chosen people, Israel. The question is whether this Adam will be obedient to God and stay in Eden, or join the other 'adam outside of the garden, in exile.

For ancient Israelites, as well as any other ancient Near Eastern peoples, origin stories are focused on telling their own story, not everyone else's. These stories are about self-definition. It is questionable, therefore, whether the Adam story is even relevant to the modern question of *human* origins. As I mentioned above, if this is the case, much of the tension between Genesis and evolution is relieved. But we still have to address Paul's understanding of Adam, since Paul seems to present Adam as the progenitor of the human race. We will get to that in due course. Here my only focus is on what we can deduce from Genesis about the meaning of the Adam story.

Before we move on, there is at least initially an objection from within Genesis to reading the Adam story as the story of proto-Israel. The story of Noah speaks of the entire earth's population as being wiped out in the flood, leaving only Noah, his wife, their three sons, and their daughters-in-law. So even if Adam is the first Israelite amid the larger world population, that only lasts until Noah, since from Noah's three sons—Shem, Ham, and Japheth—"the whole earth was peopled" (9:19). It seems on the one hand that, however much one people among many may be the point of the Adam story, it quickly becomes a universal story in Genesis 6.

On the other hand, Noah is a descendant of Seth, and so Noah clearly continues Adam's line specifically. As Adam before him, Noah is chosen from among the many to be God's means of continuing the line of Adam. In the genealogies that follow, we see the same pattern of privileging the one among the many that began in the Adam story. Noah's son Shem is singled out from his two brothers to continue that line, and Genesis 10:21 declares Shem to be "the father of all the children of Eber," which is the origin of the name "Hebrew." This line continues to Terah, then Abraham, Isaac, and Jacob, who is renamed Israel.

However we might address all of the ambiguities of the Adam story—which are many regardless of how it is interpreted—and to whatever extent we might be convinced or not of the parallel with Israel, the correspondences between Adam's story and Israel's are striking. Reading Adam as a story of proto-Israel is compelling and worthy of careful attention. It also complements yet another approach to the Adam story we will look at in chapter 5: reading the Adam story as a narrative version of Israel's quest for wisdom in Proverbs. Both of these complementing perspectives support the general point I am making here: Adam is not a story of the origin of humanity in general but of Israel in particular. When seen from this perspective, efforts to reconcile Adam and evolution become unnecessary—at least from the point of view of Genesis. Paul's use of the Adam story, as I have been saying, is another matter.

Creation and Sanctuary

According to Genesis 1, God fashions the cosmos in six days and rests on the seventh. This same six-plus-one pattern is evident in Israel's liturgical life, its weekly rhythm (Exod. 20:11). It is routinely accepted among biblical scholars that presenting creation as a six-day affair reflects Israel's later liturgical life, particularly in the context of the exile. By placing their Sabbath week at the dawn of time, the Israelites express their deep belief that they are uniquely connected to the God of creation. This is the same expression of faith that we have seen above with respect to the cosmic battle and the Adam story: Israel is now and has always been the people of the true God.

The significance of the pattern of seven in Genesis 1 extends beyond Israel's seven-day liturgical week. Medieval rabbis already noticed that creation in Genesis 1 is the primordial preview of Israel's sanctuaries—first the tabernacle in Moses's day and then the temple built by Solomon. Israel's sanctuaries are instantiations of the creation of the cosmos. When the Israelites worshiped God in the sanctuary on the Sabbath, they were declaring that the God who put the cosmos in order and then rested in primordial time was present with them here and now.

The connection between worship and primordial time can be seen in how the tabernacle reflects the cosmic order of creation, especially in the instructions that are given in Exodus 25–31. Both tabernacle and cosmos come to exist through a sixfold creative act culminating in a seventh act of rest. Six times we read, "The LORD said to Moses" (25:1; 30:11, 17, 22, 34; 31:1), which parallels the six creative words of Genesis 1: "And God said . . ." (vv. 3, 6, 9, 14, 20, 22). These six creative acts are followed by the seventh "The LORD said to Moses" in Exod. 31:12, which introduces the Sabbath command. This suggests to many readers, past and present, that building the tabernacle is a microcosm, the re-creation of the cosmos on a smaller scale.[5] Several other elements in Exodus confirm this observation:

- After the tabernacle is constructed, we read in 39:32 that the work was *completed*, using the same Hebrew verb (*kalah*) with which Genesis 2:2 refers to the completion of God's creative work.
- The chief craftsman of the tabernacle is Bezalel, who is filled with the *Spirit of God* (31:3) to do his creative work. In Genesis 1:2 we see the Spirit of God hovering (or sweeping) over the water just before God begins his creative work.
- In 39:43 we read that Moses "inspected the work and *saw*" (NIV) that they had completed the work according to plan. Likewise in Genesis 1 God inspects his creative work and *sees* that it is good.
- Moses *blesses* the people after completing the work (39:43) as God *blesses* his creation in Genesis 1:22, 28; 2:3.
- In 40:33 we read that Moses "*finished* the work," which echoes how God *finished* his work on the seventh day (Gen. 2:2).

Just as the tabernacle instructions are given in seven creative commands, the number seven figures prominently in the construction and dedication of the temple. According to 1 Kings 8 and 2 Chronicles 6–7, the temple, after taking seven years to build (1 Kings 6:38), was dedicated in the seventh month, during the seven-day feast of tabernacles (the "festival" of 1 Kings 8:2). The dedication took place over seven days, followed by the seven-day festival of celebration (8:65; in 2 Chron. 7:9 the altar gets its own seven-day dedication celebration).

Scholars generally agree that this pattern of seven is another example of Israel's transforming the traditions of the ancient Near East for its own theological purposes. This seven-day pattern is known from the Sumerian King Gudea of Lagash (twenty-second century BC), whose temple dedication took seven days. In the Ugaritic Baal story, Baal's temple is built over seven days after his defeat of Yam. The building of that temple is followed by rest for Baal after the exertion of his battle. Unlike the Baal story, however, the Israelites believed that creation itself was a seven-day project. There is no temple in Genesis 1 constructed after creation to celebrate God's victory over chaos; the created world is his temple.

> Thus says the LORD:
> Heaven is my throne and the earth is my footstool;
> What is the house that you would build for me,
>   and what is my resting place?
> All these things my hand has made,
>   and so all these things are mine,
>   says the LORD. (Isa. 66:1–2)

The temple that the Israelites constructed, at God's command, was an instantiation of God's true temple, the heavens and the earth. This is why Israel's sanctuaries are described as minicreations. Psalm 78:69 puts a fine point on it: "He built his sanctuary [the Jerusalem temple] like the high heavens; like the earth, which he has founded forever."

One can also see possible echoes of the creation accounts in three items found in the sanctuaries:

1. The lampstand (Exod. 25:31–40) represents a tree (with seven branches), a common icon in ancient Near Eastern worship. For Israelites, it symbolized the tree of life in Genesis 2–3. The tree from which Israel's first parents were barred is now symbolically available to the Israelites in worship.
2. The curtains of the tabernacle are blue, purple, and scarlet linen with cherubim woven into them (Exod. 26:1), and the temple has floral and arboreal carvings in the posts and latticework (1 Kings 7:13–51). Walking into the tabernacle and looking around is like stepping into creation itself with sky overhead.
3. The temple houses a bronze (or copper) "sea" (*yam*). Sea represents chaos, and Yam is the name of the chaos figure vanquished by Baal in the Ugaritic story. In the temple, the primordial foe is fully tamed, a trophy of the victorious God, on display for all to see.

When we read Genesis 1, therefore, we are not to think simply of a description of cosmic events. The creation story was written with Israel's temple and the Sabbath rhythm in mind. The seven-day pattern of creation in Genesis 1 is not the source of the rhythm of Israel's liturgical week. Rather, as with Adam, Israel's seven-day pattern is brought into primordial time. This is not deception or a failure to be "objective" in writing their story: this is self-definition. By faith, Israel claims that its very purpose is in tune with the created order. The Sabbath is not mere "rest" from work; contemporary blue laws, waning as they are, are a cheap caricature. Sabbath is Israel's weekly participation in God's primordial creation-rest. In *Enuma Elish* and *Atrahasis*, the high gods create lesser beings to do work for them so that *they* can rest—the gods rest at the expense of these lesser beings. Israel's command to "rest" on the Sabbath may seem arbitrary or even harsh for some today, but in the ancient world it was striking: Israel was privileged to share in God's rest after his victory over chaos.

There is no more holy place on earth than the sanctuary and no more holy time than the Sabbath. The sanctuary is the microcosm where Israel participates in Yahweh's cosmic victory. When seen in this light, one can understand why for Israelite theology the destruction of the temple in 586 BC was so utterly devastating. We can also appreciate why so much of Exodus is taken up with the "tedious" details of the tabernacle construction, and why Sabbath observance is so prominent. Reading Genesis 1 as a simple description of cosmic events (mislabeled as "literal") truly devalues the rich theology that the biblical writers put there.

The Gospel and Primordial Time

By employing some of the images we have been looking at, the New Testament describes the final intersection of primordial time and history. For example, we see this in how the Christian Bible ends. The book of Revelation is a highly symbolic, apocalyptic book—not in the Hollywood sense of the word but in the ancient sense: God's reign is about to break into this world and set it right. It does not mean that the world is coming to an end in some catastrophe, with a disembodied heavenly existence waiting on the other side. Rather, the reign of God brings renewal (Rev. 21:5).

Hence, in Revelation 21–22, a new heaven and earth are revealed, a new act of creation that supersedes the heaven and earth of Genesis 1:1. The Christian Bible ends where it begins; thus it is no surprise to see the re-creation of the cosmos described in ways that recall primordial time. In this new creation, "the sea was no more" (21:1), no chaos to tame. Israel's Sabbath celebration of the victory of God over chaos is an anticipation of the eventual complete submission of chaos under God's power. The Israelites captured this belief in the bronze sea in the temple. Revelation claims that the defeat of the sea was accomplished through the victory of the Lamb of God over death—the resurrection is the final defeat of chaos. The enemy is vanquished, and so there is no longer any need for the temple symbolism (21:22). Likewise, part of this new creation is a new Jerusalem, which symbolizes God's immediacy with this creation—the final intersection of the divine plane and the human plane. God's dwelling place is now among the people (21:2–3). God's presence means the ways of the old creation are passing away, including even death and pain (v. 4).

The new creation also includes a new garden where paradise is restored. There is an abundant supply of life-giving river water (22:1), as there was in the original paradise (Gen. 2:10). On each side of this river stands a tree of life (22:2), a double dose of healing that bears its fruit all year long, to which the inhabitants of the re-created cosmos now once again have unlimited access. The "healing of the nations" (v. 2) has begun, and there is no longer "any curse" (v. 3). Even the lights created in Genesis 1:14–19 will no longer be needed, for God himself will give light (Rev. 22:5, alluding to Gen. 1:3; see also Isa. 60:19 and Zech. 14:6–7 for a similar theme). One might say that God's goal all along has been to bring humanity and all of creation back to the paradisiacal state of Genesis. That which was lost is now regained through Christ's resurrection, God's final act of chaos-taming, where, through the overcoming of sin, the ultimate and universal enemy, death, is actually (not symbolically) brought to its knees.

In the New Testament, Jesus is the final and unsurpassed intersection of primordial time in history. The opening line of John's Gospel captures this well: "In the beginning was the Word. . . ." The echo of Genesis 1:1 is intentional and unmistakable. Jesus brings with him a new beginning, a new creation. Primordial time meets present time in as full an expression as possible, the ultimate instantiation: the incarnation of God. Jesus is the Word, who was with God at the very beginning, through whom all things were made. This ancient Word is now walking among humankind as redeemer (John 1:1–5). Those who know him participate in this new creation. They are no longer born only of earthly parents but are also "born of God" (vv. 12–13), "born from above" (3:3). We see a similar chord struck in Colossians 1:15–20. All things were created through and for Jesus, but not so he could sit back and admire a job well done. The primordial one is also the head of the church (v. 16). Through his resurrection he has become "the beginning, the firstborn from the dead" (v. 18). All those who believe in Jesus are part of this new start, this new beginning inaugurated by Jesus the creator/redeemer.

John's Gospel also says that Jesus is God's sanctuary. In John 1:14 we read that the Word became flesh and "lived" among the people— better, he "pitched his tent" or "tabernacled" among them. (The Greek verb here [*skēnoō*] is used throughout the Greek Old Testament, the Septuagint, to refer to the tabernacle.) Likewise, in John 2:19–21 Jesus claims to be the temple. This is typically understood to mean that God "came down" from heaven and is embodied in Jesus, and for good reason, but this does not exhaust the symbolism. As we have seen, the sanctuary is the nexus not just between heaven and earth, between "there and here." It is also the place where the creator of primordial time takes up residence in earthly time; the tabernacle is the meeting place of "then and now." Jesus as sanctuary is an instantiation of primordial time.

In the Old Testament, Israel transforms the traditions common to the ancient Near East into vehicles for expressing who their God is and who they are as a people bound to him. Likewise, the New Testament transforms Israel's own traditions to address the climactic turn of events in the gospel. How Israel articulates the intersection of primordial time and history is no longer adequate. Israel's self-definition is not abandoned, but it is transformed to account for the climactic act of God. In the resurrection of the Son of God, the people of God now see more deeply what the Israelites have expressed in their own way. Some of their articulations remain as vibrant as ever, while others are exposed as mere shadows, awaiting the clearer word that is in Jesus (Heb. 1:1–4; 8:5–6).

It remains for Christians today to continue thinking through this unavoidable issue of continuity and discontinuity between Israel's Scripture and the gospel, which in some respects is the very stuff of Christian biblical theology. A proper Christian understanding of the creation narratives will follow the lead of the New Testament writers in seeing the gospel as the culmination of the ancient message. Christians should not search through the creation stories for scientific information they believe it is important to see there. They should read it, as the New Testament writers did, as ancient stories transformed in Christ.

More so than any other New Testament writer, Paul presents Jesus as the final and crowning intersection of primordial time and history. His resurrection is a new beginning, a new creation, not only for him but also for all those who believe. As Paul puts it, "So if anyone is in Christ, there is a new creation" (2 Cor. 5:17). For Paul, being "in Christ" means starting over, not in a generic sense of being given a second chance; one actually participates in a renewed creation, which began at the resurrection of Jesus and is symbolically represented in the final chapters of Revelation. In his resurrection, Jesus is, according to Paul, Adam revisited, although new and much improved. He has come in real time to undo the curse of primordial time (Rom. 5:12–21). He is the "second man," born not of dust, as was the first man, but "from heaven" (1 Cor. 15:47–48). To borrow C. S. Lewis's memorable phrase, in Jesus of Nazareth "myth has become fact."[6] However we phrase it, Adam plays a role in Paul's explication of the gospel, and this has posed the most formidable obstacle to Christians for accepting evolution. How Paul understands Adam is the topic of part 2.

PART TWO

UNDERSTANDING
PAUL'S ADAM

5

Paul's Adam and the
Old Testament

Doesn't Paul Settle the Matter?

A literal reading of the Genesis creation stories does not fit with what we know of the past. The scientific data do not allow it, and modern biblical scholarship places Genesis in its ancient Near Eastern cultural context, one where ancient peoples were asking questions of self-definition and expressing those convictions in the idiom of their time. These factors have calibrated for us the genre of Genesis; they alert us to what we have the right to expect from these biblical texts with respect to their historical and scientific value.

But Genesis is not the only portion of the Bible that Christians have to consider, and with this we come to the topic of part 2. The conversation between Christianity and evolution would be far less stressful for some if it were not for the prominent role that Adam plays in two of Paul's Letters, specifically in Romans 5:12–21 and 1 Corinthians 15:20–58. In these passages, Paul seems to regard Adam as the first human being and ancestor of everyone who ever lived. This is a particularly vital point in Romans, where Paul regards Adam's disobedience as the cause of universal sin and death from which humanity is redeemed through the obedience of Christ. Many Christians, however creative they might be willing to be about interpreting Genesis, stop dead in their tracks when they see how Paul handles Adam.

It is understandable why, for a good number of Christians, the matter of a historical Adam is absolutely settled, and the scientific and archaeological data—however convincing and significant they might be otherwise—are either dismissed or reframed to be compatible with Paul's understanding of human origins. For many other Christians, the matter is not so black and white, but the overall sense remains that it is theologically necessary for there to be some sort of Adam somewhere in human history who is personally responsible for alienating humanity from God.

For all Christians, what Paul says about Adam and Christ is a vital point of Christian theology, and I wholeheartedly agree. Clearly, what Paul says cannot be ignored but must be addressed with complete integrity. But giving an account of Paul's thoughts on Adam is not as straightforward as is sometimes assumed. Many times in my own experience, I have heard: "Well, I may not know what all the scientific and archaeological data are, but I can read English and I *know* what Paul says. That is obvious, and any other piece of information—like science or archaeology—has to fall into line." Again, for all those who look to Scripture as the final authority on theological matters, this reaction is understandable. But a bit of probing into Paul's view of Adam will show that the matter is more involved than "Paul says it; that settles it." Numerous factors, to be addressed here in part 2, come into play in gaining a broader understanding of what Paul is saying and why he says it.

With that in mind, allow me to lay out where part 2 of this book is headed. Beginning in this chapter, we will consider the role that Adam plays (and does not play) in the Old Testament. This brief survey will help show that Paul's Adam is not a result of a "straight" reading of Genesis or the Old Testament, but stems from other factors (to be addressed in the following chapters). In this chapter I also suggest that reading the Adam story as a wisdom story, as others have done, is compelling in its own right.[1] Such a reading also overlaps nicely with the Adam–Israel parallel we saw in chapter 4 and is a very attractive option for those wishing to find some resolution for the evolution discussion.

In chapter 6 we will look at Paul's ancient setting and how that setting might have influenced what Paul says about Adam. As a first-century Jew, Paul, along with his contemporaries, assumed various ways of thinking about the world; these almost certainly include the issue of cosmic and human origins. Also, as a trained Jewish interpreter of his Scripture, Paul's handling of Adam must be seen against the backdrop of the variety of ancient Jewish interpretations of Adam, all of which grapple with the significance of this story for their time and place. Paul's Adam is one example among many in the ancient world.

In this chapter we also take a closer look at how Paul uses the Old Testament in general. Paul's handling of his Scripture is marked throughout by a creative engagement of his tradition. That creativity stems from two factors: (1) the Jewish climate of his day, likewise marked by imaginative ways of handling Scripture; and (2) Paul's uncompromising Christ-centered focus. In other words, Paul's understanding of the Adam story is influenced both by the interpretive conventions of Second Temple Judaism in general and by his wholly reorienting experience of the risen Christ. Paul is not doing "straight exegesis" of the Adam story. Rather, he subordinates that story to the present, higher reality of the risen Son of God, expressing himself within the hermeneutical conventions of the time.

With these factors in mind, in chapter 7 we will turn to a closer look at Paul's Adam, particularly in Romans 5:12–21. This is a huge area, and we will take only a brief glimpse from 30,000 feet into what scholars have been debating for ages, and particularly in recent decades of renewed attention. Romans is often understood by Christians as a summary document of Christian theology, and not without reason. In this letter Paul addresses many of the vital theological issues of the Christian faith, which is at least part of the reason why there is reluctance to give much ground on what Paul says about Adam in Romans 5:12–21. But, along with other contemporary readers of Paul, I do not think that Romans is a primer for systematic theology, so to speak. Rather, I see a dominant theme in Romans to be Paul's case that Jews and gentiles together make up one people of God. If we revisit Paul's arguments from the viewpoint of the social and religious tensions that existed at the beginnings of Christianity, we will gain a greater appreciation for the rhetorical reason for why Paul calls upon Adam the way he does.

With respect to Romans 5:12–21 specifically, let me summarize my conclusion here at the outset. The role that Paul assigns to Adam in this vital passage is largely unique to Paul in the ancient world, and it moves well beyond what Genesis and the Old Testament have to say. As I see it, Paul's motivation for using Adam the way he does is to explain how Christ's crucifixion and resurrection put all of humanity on the same footing. Specifically, Paul argues that Jews and gentiles are equally subject to the same universal dilemma, sin and death, and so both equally require the same Savior. This is a point that Paul began arguing in chapter 1 of Romans and that reaches its climax in chapter 5, where Adam is brought into the argument.

In making his case, Paul does not *begin* with Adam and move *to* Christ. Rather, the reality of the risen Christ drives Paul to mine Scripture for ways of explicating the wholly unexpected in-breaking of the age to come in the crucifixion and resurrection of the Son of God. Adam, read as "the first human," *supports* Paul's argument about the universal plight and remedy of humanity, but it is not a *necessary* component for that argument. In other words, attributing the cause of universal sin and death to a historical Adam is not necessary for the gospel of Jesus Christ to be a fully historical solution to that problem. To put it positively, as Paul says, we all need the Savior to deliver us from sin and death. That core Christian truth, as I see it, is unaffected by this entire discussion.

I hope it is crystal clear that my intention in looking at Paul's argument in this way is not to undermine Paul or complicate Paul unnecessarily simply to make room for evolution. Without question, evolution requires us to revisit how the Bible thinks of human origins. But many will immediately recognize the complex and unavoidable network of issues before us in addressing what Paul says about Adam, why he says it, and what we should take away from it—wholly irrespective of evolution. My motive is to allow some of those issues to come into play as we look at the specific problem of what to do about Paul in light of evolution. Further, although I feel strongly enough about my own thoughts to write a book like this, I make absolutely no claim to have found the best path forward in this complex set of issues. Rather, I remain now, as I stated at the beginning, committed to offering some perspective for interested readers to begin exploring Paul's theology on their own in light of the reality of evolution.

Not Paul's Adam

As important as Adam is for Christian theology—elevated as he is to that status by Paul—it may be surprising to see how relatively absent explicit reference to Adam is in the Old Testament. While in one sense "Adam" is a dominant theological motif in the Old Testament,[2] what is missing from the Old Testament is any indication that Adam's disobedience is the cause of universal sin, death, and condemnation, as Paul seems to argue. In fact, even though death is mentioned as a consequence in Genesis 2:17 and 3:19, the Old Testament nowhere returns to this scene, though there is ample opportunity. If Adam's disobedience lies at the root of universal sin and death, why does the Old Testament never once refer to Adam in this way? This is a matter worth looking at more closely.

The name "Adam" does not appear in the Old Testament after the account of his death at the age of 930 years in Genesis 5:3, save the lone reference in 1 Chronicles 1:1, where Adam is the first name in a postexilic genealogy that strives to connect the returnees from exile to Israel's primordial beginnings. As we saw in chapter 2, Chronicles argues that Israel is still God's special people despite the crisis of the exile—the Israelites have an unbroken pedigree back to the beginning, back to Adam, Israel's first ancestor. But this tells us little of how these postexilic Israelites understood Adam, other than placing him at the beginning of Israel's time line. (There seems to be some difference in perspective between how Chronicles views Adam and how Paul does. As Israel's first ancestor, Adam in Chronicles seems to be a positive figure, the first of many, not the cause of sin and death, although I admit that this is more an argument from silence in Chronicles.)

There are two other references to an "Adam" in the Old Testament, but they are irrelevant, since they refer to geographic locations.[3] One is Joshua 3:16, where Adam is clearly the name of a town near Zarethan, where the waters of the Jordan "stood still, rising up in a single heap." The other is Hosea 6:7. Because this verse mentions Adam and the transgressing of a covenant, it is sometimes cited in support of an Old Testament foundation for Paul's reading of Adam. But that reading is impossible when we look at the larger context. Verses 6–9 read as follows:

> [6]For I desire steadfast love and not sacrifice,
>   the knowledge of God rather than burnt offerings.
> [7]But *at Adam* they transgressed the covenant;
>   *there* they dealt faithlessly with me.
> [8]*Gilead* is a city of evildoers,
>   tracked with blood.
> [9]As robbers lie in wait for someone,
>   so the priests are banded together;
> they murder on the road to *Shechem*,
>   they commit a monstrous crime. (emphasis added)

The NRSV treats Adam in verse 7 as a place name, and this is certainly correct. Even though the Hebrew phrase *ke-'adam* could mean "like [the man] Adam," the context does not support that. Perhaps Adam could refer to humanity in general (as in Job 31:33), but this too seems out of place in Hosea 6:7. Hosea is not concerned with the sin of humanity in general, but with Israel's failure to repent (which begins at 6:1).

The "Adam" in Hosea 6:7 is neither the Adam of Genesis nor humanity in general, but certainly a geographic location. Adam is the first of three place names where Israel's unrepentant state has been displayed, the other two being Gilead and Shechem in verses 8–9. The key is the adverb "there" (Hebrew *sham*) in the second half of verse 7, referring back to Adam in the first half. All three are names of places where something bad has happened: bloodshed, ambush, murder. Verse 6 is also important. Hosea says that Israel has failed to show "steadfast love" and "knowledge of God." This is hardly a reference to the original sin of Adam but a condemnation, so common in the prophetic literature, of Israel's perfunctory maintenance of ritual while forgetting mercy. To see in verse 7, therefore, a reference to the Adam of Genesis, let alone Pauline Adam theology, is rather forced.[4]

One might object that there is no indication—either in verse 7 or anywhere in the Old Testament—of any covenant transgression occurring at a place called Adam. True, but the events said to have transpired in Gilead and Shechem are also imprecise. Hosea seems to have some problem with Gilead (see 12:11), but what event or events is he referring to specifically? Perhaps it is the massacre of Ephraimites by Gileadites in Judges 12:1–6. But that seems rather remote—and irrelevant—for Hosea. Likewise, the ambush and murder on the road to Shechem in Hosea 6:9 is not specifically identified. Whatever events, attitudes, or reputations are referred to in these verses are ambiguous. We must also entertain the possibility that Hosea may have had in mind traditions that are not even recorded in the Old Testament. Places like Gilead or the "road to Shechem" may have come to be associated with violence, and so his reference is symbolic.

Those are interesting options to ponder, but my general point is less ambitious: Hosea 6:7 is not a brief allusion to the Adam of Genesis disobeying God in the garden. None other than John Calvin shows no patience for reading verse 7 as a reference to the Adam of Genesis. He considers that reading "frigid and diluted" and "vapid," not worthy even of refutation.[5]

So, after Genesis 5, aside from 1 Chronicles 1:1 Adam makes no explicit appearance in the Old Testament. Further, the Adam of Paul's theology—as the explicit cause of human sinfulness and death—does not seem to be found in the Old Testament either. The Old Testament portrays humanity in general and Israel in particular as out of harmony with God, but the root cause of this condition is nowhere laid at Adam's feet.[6]

We see a list of curses in Genesis 3:14–19, which, to be sure, have lasting consequences for Adam and Eve's offspring. Eve's disobedience means pain in childbearing and being ruled by her husband—although the language seems restricted to Eve, the implication is that this curse will be for all women. Adam's curse is twofold. The ground is cursed, which means difficulty in harvesting (3:17–18), and it appears that this curse likewise has lasting consequences, but may implicitly affect only men. The promise of death in 3:19, however, in the logic of the story, applies to men and women from here on out.

Among all of these consequences, however, we do not read that hereafter all humans will be born into a state of sinfulness from which all efforts to eradicate oneself are in vain. Leaving Paul to the side for the time being, this is not what Genesis says, which is the only point I am interested in here. This omission may be surprising to some, since being born in a state of sin and condemnation as the central consequence of Adam's disobedience is often seen as the entire point of the garden story. But if this is what the garden story is trying to get across, why is it entirely silent on this important matter?

We can see the force of this question by looking at the two episodes that follow Genesis 3. First, think of what happens in the Cain and Abel story (Gen. 4:1–16). This story is notoriously devoid of details, and so it is tempting to fill in the gaps. But we must be careful what we put there. Does this story imply that Cain's murder of his brother, Abel, is a consequence of being born in a state of sin due to his father's transgression? Or should Cain's sin be understood, like the sin of his parents, as his own responsibility, his own decision to disobey?

In other words, "like father, like son" certainly seems to be at work here, but that may simply mean that *both* make the same crucial error of failing to follow God's command. We do not read that Adam's disobedience is somehow causally linked to Cain's act. God's warning to Cain in 4:7 seems to imply that the choice—whether to give in to his anger or "master" it—is entirely his own. Cain's choice seems to be that either he can take hold of ("master") his anger or follow in his parents' footsteps. Cain dismisses the warning, as did his father, and falls into disobedience. The picture drawn for us is that Cain is fully capable of making a different choice, not that his sin is due to an inescapable sinful inheritance.

To be clear, my comments above are not be taken as suggesting that Cain—or any of us—is capable of living a sinless life. My point is that such a question goes beyond the parameters of the story. I am merely pointing out that the story of Cain does not attribute his act to his father, nor does the story seem to be concerned about what "made" Cain do what he did. The focus of the story is on the very same choice that confronts all of us, as it confronts Israel throughout the Old Testament: will you obey and receive blessing, or disobey and suffer consequences? The story does not seem to be concerned with *why* Cain does what he does. It focuses on Cain's *act*, that he does what he should not do although he has the capability of resisting his impulses. Adam's disobedience is not presented as having any causal link to Cain's. Rather, the two acts are presented as two successive examples of the same problematic pattern: command given, disobedience, consequence.

The same issue comes up in the flood story. We saw in chapter 3 that the cause of the flood is twofold: the intermarriage of divine beings and human women (6:1–4) and then the general condition of "wickedness" that permeates all of humanity (6:5). But notice that apparently one man, Noah, seems to have escaped this description. He is "a righteous man, blameless in his generation" (6:9; cf. 7:1). The phrase "in his generation" does not soften the description, as if to say, "Noah isn't *really* righteous or blameless, just 'good enough' compared to the extreme wickedness on earth at the time." Rather, Noah alone is found to be worthy to escape the otherwise universal punishment of death in the flood and thus will be the one through whom all of humanity will get a fresh start. If Adam were the cause of universal sinfulness, the description of Noah is puzzling. Further, if Adam's disobedience is the ultimate cause of this (near) universal wickedness, one can only wonder why, at this crucial juncture in the story, that is not spelled out or at least hinted at.[7]

Here too my point is not that sin is anything other than an inescapable and universal human reality, as Paul says. Rather, I am saying that these Old Testament stories have at best a submerged interest in the question of "why we do what we do." I am further suggesting, already here, that Paul's use of Genesis is clearly rooted in something other than a simple reading of that story. There is more at work in Paul's thinking than simply repeating the plain sense of Genesis.

What we see in the stories of Cain and Noah also holds for the Old Testament as a whole. The Old Testament does not seem to be interested in the causal question, why do Israelites or others do what they do? And it certainly does not explain the sinful choices of others by appealing to Adam. If Adam's causal role were such a central teaching of the Old Testament, we wonder why the Old Testament writers do not return to this point again and again, given Israel's profound capacity to disobey.

Rather than attribute to Adam a causal role, however, the recurring focus in the Old Testament is on Israel's choice whether or not to obey God's law—the very choice given to both Adam and Cain. Rather than explaining what it is about the human condition that answers why Israel continues to disobey God, the Old Testament restricts its gaze to God's commands to Israel and the clear expectation that obedience is not only required but also easily within Israel's grasp—if only this people would leave its stubborn ways. This seems to be the very point of such passages as the curses and blessings in Deuteronomy 27:9–28:68, where the choice to obey is expected, or 30:11–14, where following God's commands is simply a matter of choosing what is easily accessible.

> Surely, this commandment that I am commanding you today [obedience to the commands and decrees of Deuteronomy, see v. 10] is not too hard for you, nor is it too far away. It is not in heaven, that you should say, "Who will go up to heaven for us, and get it for us so that we may hear it and observe it?" Neither is it beyond the sea, that you should say, "Who will cross to the other side of the sea for us, and get it for us so that we may hear it and observe it?" No, the word is very near you; it is in your mouth and in your heart for you to observe.[8]

The choice offered to Adam and Cain is the same choice later offered to Israel: obedience yields blessing and disobedience yields cursing. What does not seem to be of interest in the Old Testament is tying Israel's disobedience—or that of humanity at large—to Adam's one act of disobedience.

To be sure, Christians may say that Paul's view provides us with the proper understanding of the garden episode, regardless of what that story seems to say or how the rest of the Old Testament takes it. In one sense, this is true because Paul is reading Genesis in light of God's final authoritative act in Christ (see chap. 7 below). But that is precisely my point: Paul's reading of Genesis is driven by factors external to Genesis. Paul's use of the Old Testament, here or elsewhere, does not determine how that passage functions in its original setting. (And, as we will see in chap. 6 below, Paul's handling of his Scripture is notoriously creative and complex, not simple and straightforward.) Paul's view of the depth of universal, inescapable human alienation from God is completely true, but it is also beyond what is articulated in the Old Testament in general or Genesis specifically.[9]

To admit as much is not to cast aspersions on Scripture. Rather, *allowing Paul's distinctive voice to surface will help us come to terms with the impact that Christ's death and resurrection has on how Israel's theology is to be understood in fresh ways.* Paul's theology (a point to which we will return in the next two chapters) exemplifies such a fresh reworking of the Old Testament.

Adam and Wisdom

In chapter 4 we looked at a way of reading the Adam story as an Israel-centered story: Adam is a proto-Israelite. Here I'd like to return to this idea from a different but wholly complementary angle, one that puts Paul's reading in sharper relief.

Paul's understanding of Adam's role in the human drama has had a very influential interpreter, at least for Western Christianity—Augustine (354–430). Augustine is one of the most brilliant thinkers in the history of the church, and like most brilliant thinkers, his ideas can hardly be packaged quickly—and this includes his view of Adam. Still, in its bare outlines, Augustine understood that in Adam and Eve's transgression, the state of humanity was transformed. From then on, the depraved and guilty nature of the first couple was transmitted through sexual union to their offspring and consequently to all humanity. Augustine even goes so far as to say that all of humanity was present in some sense in Adam's transgression, and so all humanity shares in Adam's guilt. My point here is not to engage Augustine's position but to offer it as a baseline that most Protestant Christians at least presume as the biblical teaching.

Nevertheless another view, although not strictly contradictory, approaches the Adam story from another angle. This view was advanced by second-century apologists such as Theophilus of Antioch and Irenaeus of Lyons, and it continues to be advocated by the Orthodox Church. According to this view, the garden story is not about a descent from a pristine, untainted original state of humanity (which is how the Adam story is popularly understood). Rather, it tells the story of naïveté and immaturity on the part of Adam and Eve and the loss of childlike innocence in an illicit move to grasp at a good thing, wisdom, represented by the tree of the knowledge of good and evil. Adam and Eve are like children placed in a paradise, where they are to *learn* to serve God and grow in wisdom and maturity, to move toward spiritual perfection.[10]

According to this view, Adam's first lesson in moving toward spiritual maturity is the command to keep away from the tree of the knowledge of good and evil (Gen. 2:15–17). The command not to eat of that tree is not a random test of faith to see if Adam is worthy—to see if this untainted creature might fall from his perch, so to speak. It is about *how* such knowledge is to be pursued. Knowing the difference between good and evil, right and wrong, is desirable; it is the wish of every parent for their children, the very goal of what it means to be a mature, faithful, covenant-keeping Israelite. This quest to know right from wrong is articulated in Israel's Wisdom literature, namely Proverbs. Having such wisdom is not "bad" in either Genesis or Proverbs; it is the very picture of what God wants for his people. The issue at stake in the garden narrative is how humans are to obtain such knowledge: in God's way or in some other way.

Reading the garden story side by side with Proverbs will help us see more clearly the wisdom dimension of the garden story. The serpent is described as more *cunning* (*'arum*) than any other creature (3:1). The serpent tempts Eve by outwitting her. In Proverbs 1:4, one of the benefits of wisdom is to give "*shrewdness* ['*ormah*] to the simple": the same Hebrew root, '*rm*, underlies both Genesis 3:1 and Proverbs 1:4. To the simple (naive), wisdom gives cunning/shrewdness to make godly choices so they will not be fooled into traveling down an ungodly path. Eve therefore is not stubbornly disobedient but a naive, childlike creature whose cunning cannot match the serpent's. Eve lacks wisdom and so is not shrewd enough to see what the serpent, with his cunning, is up to. Her mistake is trusting her ability to fend off the serpent by her own attempt at cunning rather than trusting God and what God has said. (Notice that Eve adds words to God's command in Gen. 3:3: she says they may not even *touch* the fruit of the tree.)

The serpent's words to Eve are a half-truth: "When you eat of it, . . . you will be like God" (3:5). Often this is read as an indication that the eating of the fruit represents an illicit attempt to become like God, in other words, to be proud. But this is not the case. Becoming like God *in knowing good and evil* is precisely what God wants for Adam and Eve. The issue is not that knowledge should be avoided lest one claim to be like God, and Eve's observation that the tree "was to be desired to make one wise" (Gen. 3:6) is exactly correct. The problem is the illicit way in which Eve tries to attain wisdom—quickly, prematurely, impatiently.

As in Proverbs, God wants his people to be like him *eventually*, to grow *through training* to have a godlike knowledge of things—to have wisdom. But such wisdom has to be attained in God's way. In the language of Proverbs, "The fear of the LORD is the beginning of wisdom" (9:10; cf. 1:7). All of Proverbs is aimed at training the son, the young man, the simpleton, to learn to follow wisdom's voice and thus gain a true knowledge of good and evil, and in doing so attain life (e.g., 1:19; 2:19; 3:22; 4:22; 6:23; 8:35). Elsewhere in Proverbs we read that deferring one's impulse and listening to instruction is a source of life (13:12–14). Adam and Eve give in to their childish impulses, listen to the cunning serpent rather than their Father, and choose the path of foolishness, which leads to death, rather than the path of wisdom, which leads to life. Adam and Eve's disobedience is a failure to fear God.

Following the path of wisdom yields life. The Adam story depicts this as maintaining access to the tree of life. Likewise, in Proverbs wisdom leads to life, and wisdom is referred to as "a tree of life to those who lay hold of her" (3:18; cf. 11:30). This is why Adam and Eve, when they take their own path toward wisdom and eat the forbidden fruit, are barred from eating of the tree of life. Life can only be gained through wisdom, and wisdom is rooted in the fear of God—which in the garden story means obeying God's command. When Adam and Eve depart from the true path, they lose life—they are barred from eating of the tree of life, to which they had been given free access previously.[11]

The contrast between these two paths is succinctly and beautifully personified in Proverbs 9:1–18. The simple, the naive (9:4, a different Hebrew word *peti*), are called by Wisdom to enter Wisdom's house, partake of a banquet, and thus gain long life (vv. 5–6, 11). Verse 4 reads, "You that are simple, turn in here!" Beginning in verse 16, repeating exactly verse 4, Folly calls out to the simple and naive (as does the serpent). Folly mimics Wisdom's call but tempts the naive one to partake of stolen food taken in secret (vv. 16–17). Folly's mimicking of Wisdom's words parallels the snake's enticement of Eve to eat: "Did God say . . . ?" (Gen. 3:1). But listening to Folly leads only to death, Sheol itself (Prov. 9:18), just as listening to the serpent leads to death. The only hope one has to see past the superficial similarities between the calls of Wisdom and Folly is to adopt a posture of fear and obedience toward God, which Adam and Eve do not do. Proverbs calls its readers not to follow in Adam and Eve's footsteps.

Seeing the story of Adam and Eve as a wisdom story nicely complements reading it as a story of Israel's exile (chap. 4 above): both are Israel-centered rather than universal. Reading the Adam story as the story of Israel's disobedience and eventual exile from the land parallels Israel's *narrative* tradition in the Old Testament. Reading it as a wisdom story parallels Israel's *wisdom* tradition. And both readings make the same general point but from two different angles: failure of God's people to follow God's path has disastrous consequences.

Let's tie this in with the story of Cain. According to a wisdom reading of the garden story, Cain is seen to continue his parent's unwise pattern. His decision to act on his anger and kill his brother, despite God's stern warning in Genesis 4:7, betrays an unwise, immature decision to follow the path of foolishness, just as his parents have done. It is perhaps no coincidence that the first trespass between people recorded in the Bible is murder and that the first warning the son receives in Proverbs is not "to lie in wait for [someone's] blood" (1:11). This seems to be a rather random way of beginning Proverbs until we read it in conjunction with the story of Cain. The taking of an innocent life captures well the ultimate outcome of an unwise life, for which every human is directly responsible.

It is compelling to read the Adam story as a wisdom text—a narrative version of Israel's failure to follow Proverbs' path of wisdom. Whom will you follow, wisdom (God) or folly (your own path)? The Adam story speaks to each and every Israelite—and to others through the centuries—that they too have a choice to make every day, whether to follow and trust or to go astray and doubt. Will you live in harmony with the Creator, whose path is wisdom? Or will you choose the path of foolishness and come to ruin?

In suggesting this way of reading the Adam story, I want to restate the concern I raised above, anticipating an understandable but ultimately irrelevant objection. I am not trying to advocate some form of Pelagianism. Pelagius (354–420/440) argued that Adam was literally the *first human* but was nevertheless only responsible for his own sin. Adam was simply a bad example, which humans may or may not choose to follow, and so humans can theoretically live sinless lives. I, however, read the Adam story not as a universal story to explain human sinfulness at all but as a proto-Israel story. A wisdom reading of the garden story does not address, and so in no way negates, the universal and inescapable *reality* of sin and death and the *need* for a Savior to die and rise. I arrive at this conclusion, however, not from reading the garden story but on the basis of Paul's Christology, which (as we will see in the next two chapters) is what drove Paul to read Adam as he did.

But even so, the story of Cain illustrates how easy it is, at the very outset of Israel's story, to follow the wrong path. The fact that Cain simply slides into the same foolish, unwise behavior as his parents already hints at the depth of the problem—the true depth of which can only be truly perceived when God reveals his final resolution. Wisdom is God's path to life, but as Paul says, ultimately even that wisdom is an act of grace: "He is the source of your life in Christ Jesus, who became for us wisdom from God" (1 Cor. 1:30). Elusive wisdom is now embodied in the crucified and risen second Adam.

Any way you look at it, the garden story is difficult to interpret. There are too many gaps, ambiguities, and unanswered questions that have occupied interpreters for over two thousand years to cling too rigidly to any one approach. But I am hardly alone in handling the story as one of wisdom and lost innocence. It maintains the flow of the story, sensitive to context, and fits well with how the Old Testament portrays Israel's covenant relationship with God. The closest Genesis comes to the idea of Adam's handing down something to his offspring is Genesis 5:3, where Seth is said to be in Adam's image and likeness. But surely this is not a comment on Seth's inherited sinfulness. If anything, 5:3 stresses Seth's privileged role as continuing Adam's line in view of Abel's death and Cain's banishment. Again, the cause and transmission of sin are not the topic.

There is a seemingly endless line of questions to be explored here and throughout the Adam story, but these would take us too far afield. The bottom line for our restricted purpose is this: what Genesis says about Adam and the consequences of his actions does not seem to line up with the universal picture that Paul paints in Romans and 1 Corinthians—or at least the way in which many Christians have understood Paul after Augustine. At this point it might seem logical for some to conclude that Paul was "wrong," but the matter is far too rich and interesting to jump to this conclusion—and Paul is far too skilled a thinker. "Right" and "wrong" are false choices. Paul's subtle and creative theological appropriation of the Adam story deserves its own patient and respectful hearing, something that we can only touch on below. But as I hope to show, I do not think the gospel stands on whether we can read Paul's Adam in the pages of Genesis.

Toward that end, the next two chapters are centered on why Paul comes to use the Adam story the way he does (particularly in Rom. 5:12–21)—in a way that is distinct from that story's meaning in Genesis and how the Adam story is used in the Old Testament and even elsewhere in the New Testament. To understand better Paul's reasons for so employing the Adam story, in the next chapter we will look at Paul's reading of it in the larger context of the Judaism of his time. This will set the stage for looking specifically at Paul's Adam in the final chapter, especially as he is found in the all-important passage—Romans 5:12–21.

6

Paul as an Ancient Interpreter
of the Old Testament

Paul as an Ancient Man

Paul's gospel was fresh, radical, and counterintuitive to Jew and gentile alike. He claimed that Israel's messiah had been crucified and raised from the dead, and in doing so God had broken into history once and for all to restore all people to a true relationship with him. This was a scandalous and absurd notion, both to his fellow Jews and to the gentiles (1 Cor. 1:23). Nevertheless, as unique as Paul's gospel was, he wrote as an ancient man and naturally held widely accepted views on a good number of things. However much he was guided by the Spirit of God to proclaim his gospel, as Christians confess, he was guided by the Spirit not as an empty vessel but as a first-century Jew. To admit as much is to state the obvious. Paul had a cultural context like every other human being.

For example, along with other ancient people, Paul understood the cosmos to be made up of levels, a three-tiered cosmos: heaven above, the earth, and beneath the earth (Phil. 2:10–11). In 2 Corinthians 12:2, he speaks of being "caught up to the third heaven," something he unfortunately does not explain, and his own lack of certainty about whether this was physical or spiritual (vv. 2–3) does not help the matter. We do know, however, that the Judaism of Paul's day spoke of heaven as having various levels, as few as three, more often seven, and as many as ten (and even seventy-two in one Christian text written around AD 200, *1 Apocalypse of James*). The threefold heavenly realm seems to find some precedent in 1 Kings 8:27; 2 Chronicles 2:6; 6:18; Nehemiah 9:6; and Psalm 148:4, which speak of "the highest heaven." The fact that biblical authors wrote these things down does not mean they are accurate descriptions of physical reality. Rather, they simply reflect ancient ways of thinking. Paul's conception of what is above him reflects his intellectual world.

I am quick to add that what we prize today as knowledge of physical reality does not exhaust all things that are worth knowing. I am not a materialist, nor have I bowed the knee to the false god that natural science is sometimes made to be. My aim is simply to observe that Paul (and other biblical writers) shared assumptions about physical reality with his fellow ancient Hellenistic Jews. We can safely add other examples: Paul's world did not include the Western hemisphere or the arctic poles; reproductive barrenness is solely the woman's fault; the world was created by discreet acts of God in relatively recent history, not through an evolutionary process over millions and billions of years. (Paul would not have a category for the astronomical numbers we casually toss about.) Most important, this would also include Paul's understanding of humanity as created by God in a discrete act, not by a lengthy process that involved common descent. We are fully warranted in concluding that Paul shared with his contemporaries certain assumptions about the nature of physical reality, assumptions that we now know are no longer accurate. The real issue before us is not whether Paul shared those assumptions, but what the implications are for how we read Paul, especially his view of Adam.

For some, inspiration implies that Paul could not articulate mistaken views of any aspect of the physical world. Admittedly, this is a fairly extreme position to take, and others understand that what Paul thought about physical reality does not necessarily conform to what we understand to be the case today. Many Christian readers will conclude, correctly, that a doctrine of inspiration does not require "guarding" the biblical authors from saying things that reflect a faulty ancient cosmology. If we begin with assumptions about what inspiration "must mean," we are creating a false dilemma and will wind up needing to make tortuous arguments to line up Paul and other biblical writers with modes of thinking that would never have occurred to them. But when we allow the Bible to lead us in our thinking on inspiration, we are compelled to leave room for the ancient writers to reflect and even incorporate their ancient, mistaken cosmologies into their scriptural reflections.

It is my experience that Christians by and large have little trouble with what I am saying here in principle, but all bets are off when this logic is applied to Paul's understanding of human origins—which is where his take on Adam in Romans 5 and 1 Corinthians 15 comes into the picture. Paul certainly appeals to Adam to make a profound point about the human condition. But does this mean that Paul's assumption about this one aspect of physical reality—human origins—necessarily displays a unique level of scientific accuracy? Just as with any other of his assumptions and views of physical reality, the inspired status of Paul's writings does not mean that his view on human origins determines what is allowable for contemporary Christians to conclude. Few would try to make that argument about the other issues listed above, and we should not try here.

Some will balk, however, insisting that the gospel is at stake with respect to Adam in a way that it is not at stake with a three-tiered universe and other matters, and that Christian orthodoxy requires us not to entertain such a theologically harmful notion, regardless of what "science says." I understand and respect the motivation to preserve the gospel that lies behind this sentiment. I do not grant, however, that the gospel is actually at stake in the question of whether what Paul assumed about Adam as the progenitor of humanity is scientifically true. That is the very assumption we need to examine, and we will look at this more closely, beginning in this chapter.

We start below by looking at how Paul read and understood his own Bible. Paul was a first-century Jew, and his approach to biblical interpretation reflects the assumptions and conventions held by other Jewish interpreters at that time. The purpose of this chapter is to explore what we have the right to expect from Paul when he interprets his Bible (our Old Testament). Paul engaged his Scripture against the backdrop of hermeneutical conventions of his day, not ours, and we must understand Paul in that context. In other words, in the same way that we must calibrate the genre of Genesis by looking at the surrounding culture, we must also understand Paul's interpretation of the Old Testament within his ancient world. That is a courtesy we owe any writer, especially a biblical one.

Interpreting the Bible after the Exile

In chapter 2, I mentioned that Christians too commonly undervalue the impact of the centuries after Israel's return from Babylonian exile, the Second Temple period, as it is typically called. Israel's story had come to a stuttering halt with the exile and the occupation of the promised land by the Persian, then Greeks, and finally the Romans. But this period was not marked by spiritual inactivity. In response to the specific cultural and religious pressures placed upon them by their captors, Judaism began to reflect diligently on what it means to be the people of God in a land not their own—whether in exile in Babylon or in their own homeland under foreign rule. Judaism is the postexilic transformation of Israel's preexilic faith as it answered one fundamental question of national identity: "How can we be connected to our past and be God's people here and now when things are so different?"

It was during this time of political and religious turmoil that Israel's Scripture was formed as a marker of their national identity, as we discussed in part 1. This turmoil also prompted something that for us is just as important when the topic turns to Paul: the beginnings of the *interpretation* of that sacred text. Israel's monarchy and temple worship ceased in exile, as would the prophetic word eventually. Engaging their past became Israel's main means of connecting with God. The decline of temple observance after its destruction in 586 BC gave rise to the synagogue, the meeting place where learned men of Israel could plumb the depths of what God said in the past and how that pertains to the present. The stories of the past became the vehicle through which Israel could continue hearing the Word of God. This focus on the written Word of God prompted a learned class of teachers and scribes to rise to the challenge of what we today call "exegesis."

By the time Jesus came on the scene, Jews had already been steeped in several hundred years of careful reflection on their own now sacred and inscripturated story. This process already began within the pages of the Old Testament itself, a phenomenon sometimes referred to as "inner-biblical interpretation," where Israel's later literature shows evidence of transforming its older texts in view of changing circumstances.[1] A clear example is the book of Chronicles, where postexilic Israel rethought its own history in light of the crisis of exile, as we have seen.

To maintain Israel's connection to the past, Israel's exegetes transformed that past to speak to new times. Evidence for such creative engagement with the past in later Judaism is not hard to find. Perhaps the most widely known example of such ancient interpretive activity is the Dead Sea Scrolls. There Israel's story is reinterpreted in view of what this sect thought was the end of the age and the beginning of the new age of Torah obedience and purity under the leadership of someone they called "The Righteous Teacher." The discovery of these scrolls, beginning in 1947, led to a renewed interest in early Jewish biblical interpretation, and scholars continue to see much overlap between how this community creatively handled their Bible and how the New Testament authors approached biblical interpretation.

Less well known in popular circles but no less important are the major translations of the Old Testament. The Aramaic translations, or targumim (plural of "targum," Aramaic for "interpretation"), were first among them. Aramaic is a sister language to Hebrew and became the dominant language of Israel sometime during the postexilic period. Targumim may have begun orally not long after the return from exile.[2] Along the way unclear passages were explained or elaborated on—not in footnotes as you might find in a modern study Bible but right in the middle of the biblical text. These elaborations and explanations reflect the work of this class of biblical interpreters whose job it was to make sure not only that the text was translated properly but also that its meaning would not be lost. Likewise, once Greek culture began to dominate, the Hebrew Old Testament was translated into Greek (Septuagint), sometime between the middle of the third and the second century BC. No translation is "pure," and the Septuagint regularly shows how its translators struggled to interpret Hebrew words, concepts, and idioms for an audience that thought in an entirely different language system—Greek.

In addition to these translations, there are whole bodies of literature originally written in Hebrew and Greek devoted to interacting with Israel's sacred story. A significant example is a collection of texts referred to as the Pseudepigrapha. These texts date more or less from after the Greek conquests under Alexander the Great in 332 BC to the first century or two of the Christian era. Authorship was often attributed to some famous biblical or divine figure, hence "pseudepigrapha," literally, "false writing," although it is not certain that the writers were actually trying to fool anyone. Instead, claiming the authorship of a famous biblical or divine figure was a way of getting a message across, and people back then likely understood that. Included among these writings are such important texts as *Jubilees*, the books of *Enoch*, *Book of Biblical Antiquities* (= *Pseudo-Philo*), and *Testament of the Twelve Patriarchs*.[3] These are not commentaries on the biblical text as we might understand commentaries today, but include creative "retellings" of biblical episodes, thus following the example of Chronicles.

The Apocrypha ("hidden things") is a collection of books included in the Roman Catholic and Orthodox canons but not in the Protestant canon. The reason is that Protestants consciously adopted the books of the Jewish canon (although not the Jewish order). These apocryphal books were written roughly over the same period of time as the Pseudepigrapha and contain such books as Ecclesiasticus (Sirach/Ben Sira), Wisdom of Solomon, Tobit, Judith, and the four books of Maccabees. The authors were utterly dependent on the Jewish Scriptures as they worked to bring that tradition to bear on their own current circumstances. The result is often a fresh and creative interaction with the Bible.

More could be said about this period of intense interpretive activity, but that would take us far afield. My purpose in skimming this topic is to show that there was a tremendous literary output by faithful Jews in trying to come to grips with how their Scripture and their own current story intersected. The New Testament was written amid this flurry of interpretive output and so likewise engaged Israel's Scripture with almost relentless energy (about 365 citations and well over 1,000 allusions). The New Testament message was unique in its world, but the manner in which the New Testament writers handled the Old Testament was not. So once again, just as we calibrate the genre of Genesis by looking to the surrounding religious cultures, we can calibrate the interpretative approach of Paul and any New Testament writer by paying close attention to the *interpretive culture* surrounding them.

Both in terms of specific content and general interpretive approach, the handling of Scripture by the New Testament authors fits nicely into the Jewish world of the time. That is why understanding something of the interpretive milieu of Judaism is indispensable to having a well-rounded understanding of how the New Testament authors handled their Scriptures—which is no small factor in coming to terms with how Paul handled Scripture, including the story of Adam.

With respect to the Adam story, Paul was hardly the first Jewish interpreter to try to come to terms with it, and there was considerable diversity in how the story was read. The garden story is, after all, not only of central importance but also notoriously ambiguous, and so energetic and creative interpreters of antiquity were bound to see things differently. When viewed in the context of the larger Jewish world of which Paul was a part, his interpretation is one among several, with nothing to commend it as being necessarily more faithful to the original.

To gain a broader perspective on Paul's Adam, it is helpful to glimpse briefly how other Jewish interpreters of the same general time period understood the Adam story. We will turn to that topic now, followed by a look at Paul's use of the Old Testament in general before moving to Paul's use of the Adam story in chapter 7.

Various Adams of Jewish Interpreters

How did Jewish interpreters around the time of Paul understand Adam? In various ways, which reflects the flexibility of the story itself. For example, the Wisdom of Solomon (Apocrypha, late first century BC to early first century AD) refers to Adam as one who was "delivered from his transgressions" (10:1). This should make those familiar with Paul's Adam pause for a moment. Wasn't Adam punished? Apparently this Jewish interpreter has read the Adam story as a rescue mission.

Adam was created to be master over all things (Wis. 10:2), yet he transgressed God's command. But it seems that this interpreter doesn't place much of the blame on Adam himself. He even portrays Adam as somewhat of a victim. According to 2:23–24, death entered the world "through the devil's envy," not through Adam's disobedience. (Equating the serpent with the devil is itself an interpretive move, since in Genesis the serpent is simply a cunning creature.) This is hardly explicit in the biblical story, so what does it mean for the devil to be envious? The Wisdom of Solomon does not explain this, but according to another ancient tradition, the devil is envious of the elevated status that God has given to Adam in creating him in God's image (*Life of Adam and Eve*, 13:1–14:3, made famous in Milton's *Paradise Lost*). As the image of God, the angels are even commanded by the angel Michael to worship Adam. Rather than worship a creature made of mere dust, the devil leads a rebellion and is cast to earth. This prompts an angelic rebellion led by the devil. For the author of the Wisdom of Solomon, Adam is a victim, certainly not the originator of human sin. (Cain's "unrighteousness" in 10:3 is not in any way connected to his father.) Adam was made by God "for incorruption" (2:23), but the devil succeeds in bringing Adam and Eve down to size. God, however, will not allow his plan to be thwarted, and so he "delivered" Adam from total destruction (10:1).

Ecclesiasticus (Sirach/Ben Sira, second century BC, in the Apocrypha) talks about Adam being formed from the dust, but there is no mention of a fall or sinful nature inherited by his offspring (17:1–14; 33:10). This author portrays Adam not as a victim or the font of human misery but the most exalted figure in all of creation, yet as one who also lacks wisdom, is mortal, comes from the earth, and returns there. Sirach places no blame on Adam for the misery of humanity. Rather, this author blames Eve for death: "From a woman sin had its beginning, and because of her we all die" (25:24). First Timothy 2:14 expresses the same point of view: "Adam was not deceived, but the woman was deceived and became a transgressor." Elsewhere, Sirach puts sole responsibility for choosing life or death in the hands of each individual (15:14-17).

In the book of *Jubilees* (second century BC, in the Pseudepigrapha), Adam is a priestly figure who actually offers sacrifices for his own transgression. This author leaves out Genesis 3:8–13, where Adam and Eve are found out. The first couple, rather than being expelled from the garden, simply "go forth" rather innocently, at which point Adam offers incense to God. This author's retelling of the garden story reflects his theological agenda: in seed form the garden story contains the historical basis for Israel's cultic life, all of which is already recorded in the "heavenly tablets" narrated to Moses on Mount Sinai by an angel.

One can chide this author for playing fast and loose with the text to fit his own agenda, but one of the lessons to be learned from these early interpreters is that they all read selectively and with an end goal in mind, to support what one knows to be the case. The author of *Jubilees* assumed that he and his community were the true continuance of faithful Israel. Paul may not make Adam into a priestly figure, but he too is driven in his exegesis by what he has experienced as fundamental to the new phase in God's plan: God's purposes are now fully revealed in the crucified and risen Messiah. Paul's point is central to Christianity, but that does not mean his use of Adam stands alone as a straight reading of the story. Ancient interpreters were not neutral observers of the text—which is often considered to be a model of biblical interpretation in the modern world. Rather, they read selectively, capitalized on ambiguities in the text, and brought it all to bear on some pressing concerns of their community. It is most certainly true that, by observing these early interpreters at work, we are learning at least as much about them as we are about the biblical passage they cite.

The well-known Alexandrian Jewish philosopher Philo (ca. 20 BC to ca. AD 50) was known for his allegorical interpretation of the Bible. In his work *On the Creation of the World*, Philo understands Adam to have been made perfect and immortal, fully possessing the image of God (134–35). The further the human race extends from Adam, the less of the image of God they possess (141). There is no "fall" for Philo, however, but more of a decline that is instigated by his wife. As long as he was single, Adam enjoyed an intimate connection with God. But once again Eve is to blame. When she was introduced into Adam's life, the desire for pleasure meant exchanging immortality for mortality (151–52). Elsewhere (*Questions and Answers on Genesis*) Philo is clear that Cain's sins are his own, not the result of Adam's sin, and that Seth continues to bear the image of his father Adam (81; see Gen. 5:3). No state of sin is handed down from Adam to all subsequent humans.

Thus far we have seen Adam as victim, exalted human, priest, and innocent bystander to Eve's shenanigans; in no case is Adam responsible for human sinfulness, which is what Paul says. Other interpreters, however, are somewhat closer to Paul's meaning. Second Esdras is an apocryphal book written not long after the destruction of the temple in AD 70. (Chapters 3–14 are also referred to as *4 Ezra*, but I will retain the alternate title since it appears in most printed versions.) This book addresses the present and future status of Israel by explaining the predicament they find themselves in presently: subject to the Romans, with the Jerusalem temple lying in ruins. The answer is found in what happened to the first man, Adam. His transgression affected all of humanity by introducing death, although individuals are still responsible for their own moral path (3:4–27). Among all the nations, this author tells his readers, God has chosen Israel eventually to reestablish the dominion that would have been conferred on all humanity if Adam had not transgressed (6:53–59). Israel is true humanity.

In 2 Esdras 3:7 the author speaks of Adam's transgression as leading to "death for him and for his descendants" (cf. 7:48).[4] This clearly follows the gist of Genesis 2:17 and 3:19 and is quite similar to what Paul says in Romans 5:12. Some have even raised the possibility that Paul might have been influenced by 2 Esdras, although the direction of influence—or any influence at all—is typically hard to determine. What is clear for the author of 2 Esdras, though, is that Adam's transgression does not result in a "sinful state" handed down to his offspring—only death. In this sense, the author remains tied closely to the narrative in Genesis.

In 2 Esdras 3:20–22, Adam has an "evil heart" that led him to transgress God's law. All those who came after Adam likewise transgressed and were "overcome," but nowhere is it implied that Adam's disobedience was anything more than a pattern of conduct that subsequent generations followed. An evil root took hold and God chose not to prevent that from happening. This passage describes an inclination to evil present in humanity that was already present in Adam, but it does not suggest a causal link from Adam to his descendents. Second Esdras 4:30 adds that "a grain of evil seed was sown in Adam's heart from the beginning, and how much ungodliness it has produced until now." We are not told who sowed this seed, but it seems that Adam was inclined to sin all along. Among other things, this writer seems to be concerned with the difficult question of why Adam sinned at all, and he does not imply that the sinful behavior of subsequent humans was inherited from Adam.

Second Baruch is another Jewish work written to make sense of the fall of Jerusalem in AD 70. This author sees Adam as the cause of everyone's "corruption" (= death; 23:4; 48:42–43), but Adam is not the cause of anyone else's sin. Humans imitate Adam when they sin and so have personal moral responsibility to decide whether to follow in Adam's footsteps. As we read in 54:15, "For, although Adam sinned first and has brought death upon all who were not yet in his own time, yet each of them who has been born from him has prepared for himself the coming torment. And further, each of them has chosen for himself the coming glory."[5] Adam's disobedience leads to universal death, but our sin is our own—which is a good reflection of the biblical story. That each person controls one's own destiny spoke volumes to post–AD 70 Jews: they will not be held responsible for the past sins that resulted in the destruction of the temple, which is the same message that we see in Chronicles. Some have suggested that 54:15 is also reflected in Romans 5:12, where Paul says that "death spread to all *because all have sinned*" (emphasis added). Death may have entered the world through Adam, but we personally die *because we* sin, not because Adam did.

What happened to Adam in the garden received its due attention in ancient Judaism. It clearly was important theologically, but the story was also ambiguous or silent on key points, and biblical interpreters approached these factors differently. Paul's Adam is one example of this rich interpretive activity, where Adam was called upon to address various theological concerns. Some might quickly say, "I don't care what these other interpreters said. I'm with Paul. He gets it right." I agree on one level. Paul gets it right, but the "it" he gets right is the gospel; Paul's Adam is a vehicle by which he articulates the gospel message, but his Adam is still the product of a creative handling of the story. In that sense, Paul's handling of Adam is *hermeneutically* no different from what others were doing at the time: appropriating an ancient story to address pressing concerns of the moment. That has no bearing whatsoever on the truth of the gospel.

What makes Paul stand out is not his exegetical fidelity to the Old Testament context but how the authority of the risen Christ drives him to read the Old Testament in fresh ways. How Paul does that can be seen more clearly by looking at some examples of how Paul generally handles the Old Testament as bearing witness to Christ.

Paul and His Bible

Paul cites the Old Testament often and for various purposes,[6] and little is gained by making sweeping generalizations. But one point is virtually uncontested: Paul does not feel bound by the original meaning of the Old Testament passage he is citing, especially as he seeks to make a vital theological point about the gospel. Even casual readers of Paul, who have taken the time to turn back to look at the Old Testament context of the passage Paul cites, have asked, "How does Paul get *that* out of *this* Old Testament text?" Paul's use of the Old Testament is not marked by the so-called balance and objectivity of modern exegesis. Paul was an ancient interpreter, schooled in the ways of Second Temple Judaism (Phil. 3:4–6; Acts 22:3). How he handles his Bible is a reflection of the interpretive conventions of *his* day. We will never understand Paul's use of the Old Testament until we come to terms with this fact.

To admit as much is simply to point out what we have seen throughout part 1: the authors of Scripture are not inspired by God to speak from a safe distance from their culture. Rather, God works in and through writers from within their time and place in human history. Reading Paul's use of the Old Testament is another exercise in allowing the analogy of the incarnation to inform our conclusions. (See the introduction and thesis 7 in the conclusion.) The cultural trappings of the biblical authors are not obstacles to be overcome in order to get to the "real" point of Scripture. Rather, by being alert to the writer's contextual influences we can gain a deeper understanding of their intended meaning. As we look at specific examples below of Paul's use of the Old Testament, we will do well to keep this principle in mind.

Paul's use of the Old Testament is also driven by his conviction that now, in the risen Messiah, God has spoken the final word in his plan to save humanity. This final word in Christ is understood by Paul as the necessary concluding chapter to Israel's story. Conversely, the gospel is also the lens through which Israel's story is now to be read in a fresh way. That is the hermeneutical tension that runs throughout Paul's Letters (and the New Testament as a whole): the gospel is presented simultaneously as the expected completion of Israel's story and as an unexpected transformation of that story. That transformative dimension is seen wherever Paul interprets the Old Testament in a fresh way in light of the death and resurrection of Christ, God's climactic redemptive act.

The five examples that follow are intended to illustrate this point. They are certainly not exhaustive and are presented in no particular order.

2 Corinthians 6:2 and Isaiah 49:8

The principle that Paul's interpretation of the Old Testament is driven by his prior conviction of the lordship of the risen Jesus can be plainly seen in his use of Isaiah 49:8. In that portion of Isaiah, the topic is Israel's release from Babylonian captivity. The Lord says through the prophet,

> In a time of favor I have answered you,
> on a day of salvation I have helped you.

The verb tense in the Hebrew is somewhat ambiguous, and so this passage is either referring to Israel's recent release from captivity or to its imminent release. Some translate the verbs in the present tense to let the ambiguity stand. Regardless, at the right time and day, "salvation" happens: return from Babylon.

Toward the end of 2 Corinthians 5, Paul tells the church at Corinth that they are ambassadors for Christ, meaning that God is making his appeal through them, offering redemption to the world (5:20). They are, therefore, in an exalted and privileged position in God's redemptive work and so are urged "not to accept the grace of God in vain" (6:1). Paul cites Isaiah 49:8 in support of this.

> As we work together with him [God], we urge you not to accept the grace of God in vain. For he says,
>
> > "At an acceptable time I have listened to you,
> > and on a day of salvation I have helped you."
>
> See, now is the acceptable time; see, now is the day of salvation! (2 Cor 6:1–2)

Paul's "day of salvation" refers to the period of time inaugurated by the death and resurrection of Christ, not the release from Babylonian captivity. Neither is Paul referring here to the individual's "now," the moment they become followers of Christ. The "now" in Paul's purview is the larger picture of what God is doing now in history through the crucified and risen Son of God. This act of grace, this climactic moment in the history of God's people, which Paul and his readers have seen with their own eyes, what they are privileged to experience, is something they should not receive "in vain."

It is self-evident that Paul's reading of Isaiah's words is not bound by its original meaning. Rather, Isaiah's words are transformed to speak to a new situation. And this transformation is much more than an "application" of Isaiah's words; it is a revelation of what those words—which are God's words—ultimately refer to. There is no doubt that Paul knows perfectly well what Isaiah's words meant to his original audience. But there is likewise no doubt that Isaiah's intention does not dictate to Paul what he sees there in the light of Christ. Rather, because the same God who spoke through Isaiah is now speaking climactically in Christ, Isaiah's words must be expanded to account for what God is doing now, for, "See, now is the acceptable time; see, now is the day of salvation."

One might ask why Paul complicates his gospel-driven point by bringing in a passage in need of such drastic transformation, but that question misses the point. Paul sees what Isaiah did not, that all of God's saving activity through history is ultimately embodied somehow in the death and resurrection of Christ. Paul expresses that conviction by fostering a deep theological connection between the two events of deliverance from Babylon and deliverance through Christ. But since the latter now has theological and hermeneutical priority, Paul is obligated to use Isaiah's words in a way that was not at all in Isaiah's purview.

Paul's theological conviction drives his interpretation of Isaiah 49:8 and recasts that passage to explain the significance of Christ's coming. In essence, that is the point that is illustrated in one way or another in the examples to follow.

Abraham's "Seed" in Galatians 3:16, 29

In this passage Paul employs an interpretive technique that is well documented in both Second Temple texts and later rabbinic works: exploiting grammatical flexibility to make a theological point.[7] In Galatians 3:15–29 Paul argues that one is truly Abraham's heir by promise,

not by adherence to the law (see also Rom. 4). Since the promises spoken
to Abraham were made 430 years before the law was even put into effect
(Gal. 3:17), Paul concludes that those who are truly Abraham's heirs
are those who likewise are children of promise, not of law.

There is much in this rich passage that has occupied New Testament
scholars, but we will focus only on one aspect of Paul's argument,
where he plays off of the grammatical ambiguity of the word "seed"
(v. 16, often translated "offspring" in English).

> Now the promises were made to Abraham and to his *offspring* [*seed*];
> it does not say "And to *offsprings* [*seeds*]," as of many; but it says,
> "And to your *offspring* [*seed*]," that is, to one person, who is Christ.
> (emphasis added)

Like the English word "seed," both the Greek *sperma* and the Hebrew
zera' are collective nouns: singular in form but either singular or plural
in meaning depending on the context. It is not exactly clear what specific
Old Testament passage, if any, Paul is referring to, but he is certainly
alluding to the promise to Abraham in such passages as Genesis 13:14–17
(cf. 12:7; 24:7), where Abraham is promised offspring (seed) numbering
more than the dust of the earth (or the stars in the sky, 15:5).

The entire point of the promise is that the offspring will be many,
not one. Paul, however, exploits the singular *form* of seed to argue that
the promise to Abraham was for one son, not many, and that that son
was Christ. Paul's theological point is not surprising given the Christ-
centered theology throughout his writing—in Jesus, Israel's story finds
its completion, its end point. Paul seems to come to Genesis with the
expectation that Jesus is its ultimate subject, which is something any
Christian should affirm along with Paul. But this is not what Genesis
means, despite the grammatical flexibility of "seed."

Paul certainly knows his Greek and Hebrew and so understands
that "seed" is a collective noun. Verse 29 even makes it clear that Paul
is well aware of what he is doing. When his topic moves to the church,
Paul shifts to the plural meaning of "seed."

> In Christ Jesus *you are all* children of God through faith. *As many of
> you* as were baptized into Christ have clothed yourselves with Christ.
> There is no longer Jew or Greek, there is no longer slave or free, there
> is no longer male and female; for *all of you* are one in Christ Jesus.
> *And if* you *belong to Christ, then* you *are* Abraham's offspring [*seed*],
> *heirs according to the promise.* (vv. 26–29, emphasis added)

Verse 29 is the climax of Paul's argument that *all* come to be children of God (v. 26) through Christ. What have been causes for division (being Jew or Greek, slave or free, male and female) now count for nothing. Being Abraham's offspring is now determined by whether or not one belongs to Christ. In other words, Christians (plural) are Abraham's seed (read collectively in v. 29), but only insofar as they "belong to Christ," *the* seed (read singularly in v. 16). Christians participate in the promise to Abraham, but only insofar as they belong to Christ first.

Paul does not derive this notion *from* reading the Old Testament. Rather, he begins with his conviction that Christ is God's final word; then he reads Old Testament seed theology in light of that fact, even if that means claiming that "seed" means "one" when the immediate context of Genesis calls for the plural. For Paul, whatever meaning the Old Testament had in this regard now has a deeper meaning in light of Christ's coming. As we shall see, this is an extremely important point for our understanding of how Paul handles the Adam story.

Galatians 3:11 and Habakkuk 2:4

In Galatians, Paul argues that Christians are justified before God by faith, not through observance of the law. Human effort does not bring the Spirit to us, but believing in the gospel does (3:1–5). There are Jewish Christians in Galatia, however, who insist that gentiles first need to become Jews—be circumcised—in order to be justified before God in Christ. This is not an unreasonable expectation given what we see in the Old Testament (see Gen. 17:11–14; Exod. 12:48). For Paul, however, such a requirement is a false "gospel" and therefore worthy of condemnation (1:8). Circumcision, that physical sign of covenant obedience in the Old Testament, now actually is a "yoke of slavery" (5:1), a desertion from true faith in God (1:6), an undoing of the benefits of Christ's death and resurrection (5:2).

Paul's view of the relationship between Old Testament law and the Christian life is complicated, to say the least, and we cannot and need not delve into it all here. In Galatians, however, Paul is clearly drawing a contrast between the freedom that is in Christ, working itself out in the fruit of the Spirit (5:16–26), and any thought that law/circumcision justifies one before God. Taken at face value, such a view of the law is in tension with the Old Testament's view, where law is a "lamp to light one's path" (cf. Pss. 18:28 and 119:105; all 176 verses of Psalm 119 praise God for his decrees, laws, and statutes). Yet

Paul, as always, seeks ways to anchor the gospel, which brings freedom from the burden of the law, in the Old Testament. This conviction to connect the gospel and Israel's story is a recurring issue in Paul's Letters and often leads Paul to a creative interaction with the Old Testament. Habakkuk 2:4 is one celebrated example. Habakkuk 2:4 is cited in Galatians 3:11 (cf. Rom. 1:17) to make the case that righteousness is by faith, not by the individual's effort in keeping the law. True faith follows the model of Abraham (Gal. 3:6–9; see also Rom. 4), who believed God before the law was given and even had the gospel declared to him in advance (the good news being the inclusion of the gentiles: Gal. 3:8; Gen. 12:3). In making his case, however, Paul calls upon Habakkuk 2:4 in a way that does not seem to reflect the prophet's purposes.

Habakkuk 2:4 is conventionally translated "the (one who is) righteous will live by/through faith." The Hebrew of Habakkuk 2:4 is ambiguous at one or two points, but grammatical fine-tuning is not necessary for us to appreciate the problem. From the context of Habakkuk 2:4, one can see that the prophet is lamenting the injustice perpetrated by Israel's leaders (1:1–4). That is why God is about to "do something in your [Habakkuk's] days that you would not believe, even if you were told": God will raise up the Babylonians to teach Israel a lesson (1:5–6).

Habakkuk finds this objectionable and asks God to reconsider (1:12–2:1). God responds by telling Habakkuk in essence, "Don't worry: the Babylonians will get what they deserve too." That begins in 2:2. Paul cites part of 2:4, but the entire verse reads as follows:

> Look at the proud [Babylonians]!
> Their spirit is not right in them,
> but the righteous will live by their faith.

In the first two lines, Habakkuk is speaking of the Babylonians,[8] whom he calls proud (v. 4). Verse 5 continues the themes by saying that their wealth is treacherous and they are arrogant and as greedy as death itself. In short, God knows all about the Babylonians, and that Habakkuk should not mistake God's use of them to teach Israel a lesson as a sign of approval of their wickedness.

When we read verses 4 and 5 together, we see that Habakkuk contrasts the Babylonians' behavior with that of the righteous, who live "by their faith." Understandably, when many Christians read "faith," they may think immediately of a disposition of the will, a heartfelt surrender to God and his grace as opposed to one's efforts. But the Hebrew word is *'emunah*, which means steadfast faithfulness in one's actions. In other words, Habakkuk is saying that those who are righteous are those who live *faithfully*—not like the arrogant and proud Babylonians, but by God's standard, the law, which Israel's leaders are perverting through violence and injustice (1:2–4). In 2:4, which in the context reads like an aside (the NIV even sets it off with dashes), Habakkuk is saying that neither the perversion of the law by Israel's leaders nor Babylonian lawlessness are the standard of conduct. To be righteous is now, as it always has been, a matter of "faithfulness" to God's standard of justice, to his law: righteousness comes from behaving faithfully.

In Galatians, Paul makes the case for a very different point. He argues that it is only faith[9] that justifies one before God, not adherence to the law—and certainly not circumcision. Of course, no Christian will dispute this point, but what leaves lingering questions for us is this: Paul calls upon Habakkuk 2:4 to make his point, a passage that, in its Old Testament context, does not have much to contribute to Paul's argument—in fact it seems to make the opposite point. Habakkuk 2:4 commends as righteous those who keep the law. Paul, however, uses Habakkuk 2:4 to take law-keeping out of the equation entirely.

Paul also seems to understand "righteous" differently from Habakkuk. For Paul it is an inner state that is conferred upon the individual by virtue of faith (whether Christ's or the individual's; see previous note), where one's sinful state is no longer counted against one. In the Old Testament, God is certainly concerned with one's heart (among other places, see Deut. 10:16, which speaks of the circumcision of the heart). But in the Old Testament, "righteous" (and other words derived from the Hebrew root *tsdq*) refers to doing what is right, faithful obedience to God's commands.

A thorough study of Paul's use of Habakkuk would involve addressing numerous other issues, but the general point is clear enough: for Paul, Habakkuk's words are transformed in light of the gospel. The latter drives his reading of the former. Habakkuk's words now serve Christ, just as Paul does.

Romans 11:26–27 and Isaiah 59:20

The final two examples come from the book of Romans and lead us to a discussion of Adam in Romans 5, in the next chapter. These certainly are not the only examples in Romans, but they illustrate and reinforce the point made thus far.[10]

Toward the end of a robustly debated section in Romans (chaps. 9–11), Paul declares that "*all* Israel will be saved" (11:26), a comment that has generated its share of disagreement concerning God's plan for Israel. Leaving that issue aside, Paul supports his assertion by citing Isaiah 59:20 (plus):[11]

And so all Israel will be saved, as it is written:

"*Out of Zion* will come the Deliverer;
he will banish godlessness *from Jacob.*"
"And this is my covenant with them when I take away their
sins." (emphasis added)

Paul's point is that all Israel will at some point in time be saved through Christ, the deliverer, who comes to them "out of Zion."

As we saw in our first example above, Isaiah 59:20 refers to Israel's release from Babylonian captivity. God is coming like a "pent-up stream" (59:19), ready to burst onto the scene and bring his people home. This is how Isaiah 59:20 puts it:

And he will come *to Zion* as Redeemer,
to those in Jacob who turn from their transgression, says
the LORD. (emphasis added)

Notice how Isaiah 59:20 promises that God will come *to Zion*, to redeem the penitent. (Zion and Jacob are simply ways of referring to the people of Israel.) The Hebrew and Septuagint clearly say that Zion is the redeemer's destination.[12] Paul, however, says "*out of* Zion."

For Paul, Zion is not the redeemer's destination but his point of origin. One could suggest that Paul had access to a different version of Isaiah, unknown to us, that read "out of Zion," although that is pure guesswork. Paul's creative citation of Isaiah, however, has ample precedent in the ancient world, where texts were mined and adjusted in order to allow alternate meanings of the text to emerge. What Paul does here would not have raised an eyebrow in his day.

By citing the text this way, Paul may have intended to draw attention to Christ as one who came from among his own people: he is a Jew. I think that is likely the proper understanding, mainly because it fits well with the context of this section of Romans, where Paul argues that gentiles are branches grafted onto the Jewish root. Even though Israel needs the same redeemer as the gentiles, that redeemer is from among them, out of Zion. Alternatively, Zion could refer to a "heavenly Jerusalem," such as we see in Galatians 4:26 ("Jerusalem above"). This reading may be based on the notion of a heavenly tabernacle, which is the pattern of the earthly one (Exod. 25:9; cf. Heb. 8:5; Rev. 21:2), or in such passages as Jeremiah 3:17, where Yahweh's throne and Jerusalem are synonymous. A similar notion is also a common theme in later Jewish literature, after the destruction of the temple in AD 70. In that case, Paul's "out of Zion" could be referring to Jesus's divine origin.

Both options make sense contextually and theologically. Nevertheless, the relevant point is that Paul's "out of Zion" is not simply an interesting twist but an alteration designed to produce a fresh meaning. Whatever the text meant originally, it now serves the proclamation of the gospel.

Romans 4 and Genesis 15:6

In Romans 4, Paul gives a detailed and challenging argument for seeing Abraham as the father of all those who have faith. Abraham himself, Paul argues, was righteous by his faith, not by works of the law (v. 13). In other words, Paul dissociates Abraham's faith from law keeping—a startling move in Paul's Jewish context, which he has already made in his reading of Habakkuk 2:4 mentioned above. In making his case, Paul returns three times to Genesis 15:6, which he presents as an anchor for his understanding of Abraham: "And he believed the LORD, and he [LORD] reckoned it to him as righteousness" (Gen. 15:6; Rom. 4:3, 9, 22; cf. Gal. 3:6, where Paul makes the same point).

The problem, however, is that here too Paul's use of an Old Testament passage does not rise naturally from the context. Paul calls upon Genesis 15:6 to help create a rather significant reinterpretation of Abraham, one that will occupy him in this chapter (and feeds into his discussion of Adam in Rom. 5, as we will see in the next chapter). One can glimpse Paul's unique take on Abraham in Romans 4:19–20, where he claims that Abraham "did not weaken in faith" and "no distrust made him waver" when promised a child in his old age. It is hard to square this view with what we read in Genesis 17:17, where Abraham "fell on his face and laughed" at the news. In fact, the very name of his son, Isaac, is a pun on the Hebrew verb "to laugh" (tsakhaq).

In context, Genesis 15:6 does not refer to that act of faith that makes one righteous before God. First, Genesis 15 is not the point of Abraham's initial act of trust, which changes him from a typical Mesopotamian to a follower of God. That conversionlike experience (if we can even use that term) happened in Genesis 12:1, when he was called by God to leave Haran. Second, Abraham's act of faith (better, "trust") has a concrete focus. It concerns the promise of children, and for Paul to extrapolate from that some general sense of a sinner being justified before God apart from the law does not seem to be consistent with the context. Abraham is simply saying that he trusts God to deliver on his promise of offspring, and God counts that as an act of righteousness toward him.

This connects to the third example above, Paul's use of Habakkuk 2:4. As we saw there, "righteousness" in the Old Testament is not someone's inner status before God; instead, it refers to specific right actions that please God, often adherence to the law or (as here) a prelaw act of covenant fidelity. In fact, God himself is referred to as "righteous" when he acts faithfully toward his people (e.g., Ps. 4:1 NIV; NRSV "God of my right"). Here, God says to Abraham, "I promise I will give you children." Abraham responds, "I trust you to do that." God says, "In this act of trust, you have done well [you are righteous]." This seems to be the heart of the exchange; if it were not for Paul, readers would pass this verse with hardly a pause.

Finally, any notion of a dramatic turn in 15:6 is nullified in verse 8. Abraham may have trusted God in verse 6 to give him offspring, but not the land in verse 7. When Abraham says in verse 8, "O Lord God, how am I to know that I shall possess it?" he is asking for some concrete assurance that God will do as he promises—which God proceeds to give him in verses 9–21 in the form of covenant ceremony where a number of animals are cut in two and the halves are laid out opposite each other. This ceremony is a contract between God and Abraham, initiated by God to assure Abraham that God will fulfill his obligation. God will walk between the pieces in the form of "a smoking pot and a flaming torch" (v. 17). The significance of the details of this ceremony is not entirely clear, but it seems this passage is reporting a self-imprecatory oath, where God in essence says to Abraham, "May I be like these pieces if I do not come through on my promise" (see Jer. 34:18). So in verse 8, rather than simply trusting God, Abraham says in effect, "Can I have that in writing?" And God is not in the least put off by that request. He does not say: "But Abraham, you just said you believe me! So much for being justified by faith."

Once again, Paul knows exactly what he is doing. He certainly understands the contours and details of the Abraham narrative. Yet true to his conviction that Israel's story must now be rethought in view of the death and resurrection of Christ, Paul proceeds to reread Genesis to support those convictions. One might object that such a forced reading would work against Paul, for who would be convinced by such shoddy use of Scripture? But that is a modern way of thinking. Such creative handling of the biblical text was not simply common in Paul's time but also seems to have been part of Israelite and Jewish conviction of how Scripture is to be handled.

As we saw concerning Chronicles in chapter 2, the Old Testament already does in principle what Paul is doing here: reworking the past to speak to the present. That interpretive conviction is seen time and time again throughout Second Temple Jewish literature where the past needs to be rethought in view of the present. This can be counterintuitive for modern readers: it is the very act of *altering* the past to address present circumstances that ensures its *continuation* as the active and abiding Word of God, not a relic of a bygone era. That is why the Chronicler does what he does with Samuel–Kings, and it is why Paul does what he does with the Abraham story. The text is not the master: it serves a goal. For Paul, that goal is the absolute and uncompromised centrality of what God has done here and now in the crucified and risen Christ.

Paul's handling of the Old Testament may raise questions in our minds about the nature of Scripture. As we observe Paul's behavior, however, I think it is important not to feel as if we need to defend or detract from what he is doing—and certainly not to obscure what he is doing in an effort to protect our theologies. These larger theological issues can and should be worked through, but without losing a sense of Paul's handling of his Scripture. Paul's use of the Old Testament is a creative, Christ-driven exercise. Likewise, we can expect from Paul a similar Christ-driven creativity in his handling of the Adam story (see next chapter).

Paul and His Interpreted Bible

Paul's relationship to his Scripture can be viewed from another angle. At times how Paul understood the Old Testament was affected by interpretive traditions that were older than Paul but that shaped his thinking more subtly.

A modern parallel might help illustrate this. Anyone who has grown up familiar with the story of Jesus's birth will be able to recount the story with ease. Mary rides into Bethlehem on a donkey, led by Joseph. She is about to give birth, but they are turned away by one insensitive innkeeper after another. They make their way to a stable, and after Jesus is born, the three wise men come and present him with gifts. This is the general gist of the story known to any child who has ever been in a Christmas pageant (and any parent dedicated enough to sit through them). The problem, though, is that what I have just recounted is not actually in the Bible but is part of common tradition that over time has grown up around it. Read the Gospel accounts; there is no donkey, no mean innkeepers, and no three wise men (the number is not given, let alone the traditional names of Melchior, Caspar, and Balthasar).

The images that come to our minds about Jesus's birth have been influenced by tradition, and examples could be multiplied. It is not uncommon to hear a similar phenomenon in sermons. Several years ago, my pastor at the time was preaching on Exodus 17:10–13, that odd incident where the Israelites were able to hold the Amalekites at bay as long as Moses's hands remained raised. The pastor casually remarked, again and again, how Moses's hands were raised "in prayer," but the text does not say this. It is silent on what the raised hands signified, and it is that very silence that has motivated interpreters over time to fill in the gap. So some Christian interpreters mused that Moses's outstretched arms anticipated Jesus's on the cross (Justin Martyr, Tertullian), while others said, as my pastor, that Moses's hands were raised in prayer (Targum Neofiti). My pastor was not aware that his casual comment was extrabiblical, an ancient tradition designed to explain a puzzling element in the biblical story.

This phenomenon is sometimes referred to as the "interpreted Bible." What earnest Bible readers think the Bible says is sometimes a merging of what is there in black and white and how one's faith tradition has come to understand it. And that merger is often seamless, so much so that most readers are not even aware of it.

Biblical writers were not immune to this phenomenon. For example, in 2 Timothy 3:8 we see a casual reference to the magicians in Pharaoh's court of Moses's day as Jannes and Jambres. Where did these names come from? No names are given in the Old Testament. Nor are they the product of special revelation, for they simply come up in the flow of the argument with no fanfare, no indication that the writer is now privy to some special or long-lost (and irrelevant) piece of information. If we want to understand the source of this information, it is in the interpretive traditions of his Second Temple world. The name Jannes is found among the Dead Sea Scrolls (*Damascus Covenant* 5.17–19), and both names are found in a targum (Targum Pseudo-Jonathan to Exod. 1:15). During the Second Temple period it was common to "concretize" biblical episodes by giving names to otherwise anonymous biblical figures, and "Jannes and Jambres" is an example of that. These names then became part of a larger cultural conviction about the biblical story (like the names of the three wise men), and 2 Timothy 3:8 is an instance of that process.

Likewise, in Galatians 3:19 Paul makes a casual reference to something not found in the Old Testament. He says that the law given to Moses was "ordained [put into effect] through angels." The same thought is expressed in Acts 7:53 and Hebrews 2:2. Angelic involvement in the giving of the law is not an Old Testament idea but finds its way into the New Testament. Again, this is not presented by these three New Testament writers as some new piece of information given by a special act of inspiration. The point that Paul and the others make requires that it be a common bit of knowledge. Paul is contrasting the law mediated by angels to the grace of God in Christ. The force of that contrast is lost if angelic mediation is some new idea that came to him. Where and when this conviction arose is not clear. (The second-century-BC book of *Jubilees* has an angel mediating God's word to Moses on Mount Sinai, so perhaps this reflects the same idea.) Deciding on this point, however, is not important. Galatians 3:19 does not reflect an Old Testament idea but one that, as 2 Timothy 3:8, was part of tradition, a bit of common knowledge that required no explanation or defense.

One final example is found in 1 Corinthians 10. Paul is warning his readers to stand firm during temptation (v. 12) and uses Israel's exodus and desert experience as a teaching point. He comments that the food (manna) and water (from the rock) the Israelites had in their desert wandering was nothing less than spiritual food, which is Christ himself (vv. 3–4). In this way, Paul is encouraging his readers to persevere, knowing that the same power is at work in them as was working with the Israelites—Christ himself. At the end of this encouraging word, Paul adds a curious clause: "For they [Israelites] drank from the spiritual rock *that followed them*" (v. 4, emphasis added).

The rock refers to the incidents of Exodus 17 and Numbers 20, where Israel is twice given a miraculous provision of water. But a "following" rock—apparently moving about with the Israelites in the desert—is not found in the Old Testament. What Paul is saying here remains a mystery until we see that other ancient writers made a similar point about a moving rock or some other source of water that accompanied the Israelites in the desert. For example, the *Book of Biblical Antiquities*, written sometime in the latter half of the first century AD, recounts the episode this way:

> Now he [Moses] led his people out into the wilderness; for forty years he rained down for them bread from heaven and brought quail to them from the sea and brought forth *a well of water to follow them.* (10:7, emphasis added)[13]

A few other ancient texts say something similar (e.g., Targum Onqelos to Num. 21:16–20). There is no moving rock in the Old Testament, but it is possible that this interpretive tradition is an attempt to account for a curious detail in the Pentateuch. The Israelites get water from a rock in Exodus 17, at the beginning of the wilderness wandering, and then again in Numbers 20, near the end. Ancient interpretive imagination being what it is, it didn't take long before someone concluded, "Maybe they are the same rock, following the Israelites around for forty years." Again, however we account specifically for the tradition is speculation. We only need to notice that Paul's understanding of the water-giving rock in the Old Testament is shaped by interpretive activity independent of him and that formed his view of the biblical narrative. Paul had an interpreted Bible.

We could draw other examples from Paul's writings, but there is no need for our purpose. It is clear to biblical scholars that Paul's understanding of the Old Testament reflects his Jewish cultural context. What makes Paul so interesting, and sometimes difficult to read, is that his use of the Old Testament is informed both by the ancient conventions we are looking at here *and* his conviction that the crucified and risen Jesus requires Israel's story to be reinterpreted. Rather than a modern academic giving a neutral interpretation of the Old Testament, when we read Paul we must learn to expect from him an interpretive challenge. Our task as modern Christian readers is to understand Paul's ways.

Nowhere is this lesson more valuable to keep in mind than when we turn to Paul's use of the Adam story. When we read Paul and then turn back to Genesis, expecting that what Paul says will be found there plain and simple, we have not understood Paul, his world, or his theology. Simply put, we cannot and should not assume that what Paul says about Adam is necessarily what Genesis was written to convey—any more than we should assume that what Paul says about Isaiah or Habakkuk is exactly what those authors had in mind, or that Jannes and Jambres actually were the names of Pharaoh's magicians, or that a rock followed the Israelites through the desert. If we fail to grasp that point and assume that Paul is an objective interpreter of Genesis, we will paint ourselves into a corner where we will expect to find something in Genesis that Genesis is not prepared to deliver. I wish to be very clear that admitting this much is not to denigrate Paul in any way whatsoever: it is to understand Paul.

When we keep in mind some of what we have seen thus far—the ambiguous nature of the Adam story in Genesis, Adam's functional absence in the Old Testament, the creative energy invested into the Adam story by other ancient interpreters, and Paul's creative use of the Old Testament in general—we will approach Paul's use of the Adam story with the expectation of finding there not a plain reading of Genesis but a transformation of Genesis. We will see that, whatever Paul says of Adam, that does not settle what Adam means in Genesis itself, and most certainly not the question of human origins as debated in the modern world. Paul was an ancient man with ancient thoughts, inspired though he was. Respecting the Bible as God's Word entails embracing the text in context.

With that in mind, we now turn to Paul's engagement of the Adam story. This is the major source of concern for Christians who wish to bring evolution and Christianity together. This impasse is partly due to false expectations about Paul's use of the Old Testament, as we have just seen. Another contributing factor may be a faulty understanding of what Paul is trying to accomplish in his use of the Adam story, which is the topic of the next chapter.

7

Paul's Adam

Paul's Adam: The Historical First Man, Responsible for Universal Sin and Death

If Adam had stayed within the confines of Genesis 2–5, there would be far less difficulty in synthesizing evolution and Christianity—a "historical Adam" would likely be no more crucial to Christian faith than a literal talking snake or a literal garden paradise. The symbolic nature of the garden story would be even clearer if we see Adam as a proto-Israel figure, not the first human, as discussed in chapter 4. Paul, however, presents Adam as the first human and responsible for the problem of universal sin and death that Jesus came to eradicate. This is why the question of a historical Adam is understandably so important for many Christians and why digressing from a historical Adam can generate great concern.

Paul's view of Adam is articulated in Romans 5:12–21 and 1 Corinthians 15:21–22, 44–49, although not in entirely the same way in both places. It is primarily in Romans 5 that Paul lays out Adam's role in bringing death (v. 12) and condemnation (v. 18) to all and "making" many into sinners (v. 19). In 1 Corinthians 15, without contradicting Romans 5, Paul's focus is elsewhere. There he is defending the reality of the future resurrection of believers; the heart of his argument is in verses 44–49, where he contrasts two types of bodies, represented by Adam (physical) and Christ (spiritual). Precisely what Paul means by that distinction is a thorny issue and will not detain us. Our focus is on Paul's understanding of Adam as having a determinative role for introducing sin and death to the human condition. Both passages share this understanding, but I believe the most pressing interpretive issues are in Romans 5, and so my comments will largely be focused there.

At the outset we should admit that Adam is a vital theological and *historical* figure for Paul. Without question, Adam plays a significant theological role for Paul. But Adam's theological significance cannot be distanced from Paul's assumption that Adam was the first man created by God. To be sure, Adam is *more* than merely a historical figure for Paul, but one of penetrating theological significance. For example, he is a "type" of Christ in Romans 5:14. In 1 Corinthians 15:44–49, Adam seems to represent humanity—all those whose existence is marked by a "natural" body (v. 44 NIV). Some read Paul's struggle with sin in Romans 7:7–25 as the garden drama being played out in each of us. In each of these instances, Adam's significance for Paul is somewhat symbolic and clearly more than historical. But Adam's theological importance does not exist for Paul independent of Adam's historical position as the first man, from whom the human race descended and from whom all inherited sin and death—at least according to common Christian understanding. In other words, it is Adam *as first man* that makes him such a vital theological figure.

We do not reflect Paul's thinking when we say, for example, that Adam need not be the first created human but can be understood as a representative "head" of humanity. Such a head could have been a hominid chosen by God somewhere in the evolutionary process, whose actions were taken by God as representative of all other hominids living at the time and would ever come to exist. In other words, the act of this "Adam" has affected the entire human race not because all humans are necessarily descended from him but because God chose to hold all humans accountable for this one act. But this would hardly have occurred to Paul, and posing such an "Adam" does not preserve Paul's theology.

Having said that, it is within the realm of possibility that Paul's depiction of Adam does not reveal what Paul might actually have thought about human origins. Perhaps he entertained some other notion that he chose not to write about. Or it may be possible that Paul understands Adam to be a symbolic character and knowingly only presents him as a literal man to advance a theological point.[1] These are intriguing possibilities, and if either one could be reasonably defended, I admit it would go far in reconciling evolution and

Christianity. Nevertheless, I believe this introduces a vain hope of finding behind Paul's words something other than what he says. But there are other ways to address Paul's view of Adam and the conversation with evolution, which we will get to below.

At any rate, simply deciding whether or not Paul's Adam is a historical figure would hardly put to rest the discussion of how Paul used the Adam story. In the previous chapter, we saw a number of complicating factors, such as Paul's intellectual world—his assumptions about human origins as mediated to him through his Jewish cultural heritage, how his Jewish contemporaries handled the Bible in general and Adam in particular—and Paul's own creative handling of the Old Testament. We only glimpsed those issues in the previous chapter, but even that glimpse is enough to show that wrapping our arms around Paul's thinking is more involved than appealing to the "plain meaning" of Paul's words.

In addition to these extrabiblical factors, Paul is challenging to understand in many other well-known respects, which should be kept in the back of our minds as we proceed. First, Paul's Letters already presume a context of which he and his recipients are aware but which sometimes eludes contemporary readers. To repeat the famous quip, when we read Paul, we are reading someone else's mail, and it is not always easy to know how well we are grasping that conversation or when we are imposing upon it. Second, there are many grammatical challenges to reading Paul's Letters. Sometimes his meaning seems to hinge on subtleties of even the smallest parts of speech in the Greek language, to which beginning students of Greek can attest with despair and scholars regularly debate.

Third, Paul's thoughts tend to come with such a flurry of energy and passion that his pen (or that of his secretary; see Rom. 16:22; 1 Cor. 16:21; Gal. 6:11) can hardly keep up with his head and heart. Paul is not the logical, systematic, clinical thinker he is sometimes made out to be. He is known to begin a thought, only to insert a lengthy digression, and then come back to the original thought later (e.g., Eph. 3:2–13 "interrupts" the connection between 3:1 and 14; likewise, the thought of Rom. 5:12 is not resumed again until v. 18). N. T. Wright puts it well, "Like an artist in a hurry, Paul paints with a few large, sweeping strokes on a giant canvas, creating an overall picture without many details."[2] It is clear that when he wrote, Paul did not have in mind nonnative speakers two thousand years removed from his moment in time, hanging on his every syllable.

These types of interpretive challenges arise in Romans 5 and 1 Corinthians 15 as much as any other of Paul's Letters. It is good for us to be reminded that learning what Paul has to say—including his view of Adam—should not be taken lightly. I am aware that we cannot begin to adequately address every issue that arises from these passages, but I also trust that the ground we are covering here in part 2 will open doors of further exploration and perhaps put some readers on new paths of discovery.

Bearing in mind all of these factors, let me summarize my understanding of Paul's use of the Adam story before we move on. However much Paul's view of Adam intersects at points with what we see in Genesis, the Old Testament, and early Judaism, Paul's Adam stands out. Adam's primordial act of disobedience invariably brought all subsequent humanity to be enslaved to the power of death *and* sin. The reason behind Paul's distinct portrayal of Adam reflects his Christ-centered handling of the Old Testament in general, as we saw in the previous chapter. Israel's story, including Adam, is now to be read in light of its climax in the death and resurrection of Christ. In other words, Paul's understanding of Adam is shaped by Jesus, not the other way around.

But if we lose Paul's understanding of Adam as the historical first human, do we not also lose all that Paul connects to this first man? What do we make of the universal grip of sin and death that, as Paul says, Adam personally introduced to humanity and that a real historical Jesus came to conquer? That, I feel, is the pressing question for many. I want to suggest, however—and this is hardly a novel thought—that the uncompromising reality of who Jesus is and what he did to conquer the objectively true realities of sin and death do not *depend* on Paul's understanding of Adam as a historical person.

Certainly we are dealing with difficult and important matters, and thinking Paul's thoughts after him means entering a discussion that has occupied many of the greatest thinkers in the history of Christianity. Above all, it is important to maintain a conversational posture about how all this fits together, and I do not think for one moment that my thoughts on the matter are the final word. Still, as I see it, the scientific evidence we have for human origins and the literary evidence we have for the nature of ancient stories of origins are so overwhelmingly persuasive that belief in a first human, such as Paul understood him, is not a viable option. The way forward, I believe, is to recognize the profound historical (not simply symbolic) truths in Paul's words that remain despite his view of human origins.

Sin and Death without Adam?

In Romans in particular, Paul has his sights on a problem that has been the topic of world literature for millennia before Paul, Genesis, and the Israelites: death. On some level all cultures have grappled with the question of why everyone and everything dies. Evidence of such grappling is seen both in the literature (by which I also mean things like art, cave drawings, and monuments) those cultures have produced and the religious rituals to which the archaeological evidence bears witness. Paul also sees death as the universal reality—and domineering enemy—of the human drama (cf. Rom. 5:14). As a child of Israel's traditions, Paul uses the theological vocabulary available to him and so names the root *cause* of that universal dilemma as Adam and his disobedience.

By saying that Paul's Adam is not the historical first man, we are leaving behind Paul's understanding of the *cause* of the universal plight of sin and death. But this is the burden of anyone who wishes to bring evolution and Christianity together—the only question is how that will be done. I have already mentioned attempts to preserve an "Adam" who is not the first human as Paul has it but is the first "spiritual" hominid (or group of hominids) endowed with a soul and so forth, who acts as a "representative head" of humanity. But in my view any such a creature is as foreign to Paul as any other solution that is trying to bring Paul and evolution into conversation. It may well be that the human drama began when some hominids were endowed with spiritual awareness, but that does not satisfy the requirements of Paul's Adam. So, although my suggestion here leaves behind the truly historical Adam of Paul's thinking, so do any other attempts—except those of strict biblical literalists, who reject the evolutionary account of human origins.

Admitting the historical and scientific problems with Paul's Adam does not mean in the least that the gospel message is therefore undermined. A literal Adam may not be the first man and cause of sin and death, as Paul understood it, but what remains of Paul's theology are three core elements of the gospel:

1. The universal and self-evident problem of death
2. The universal and self-evident problem of sin
3. The historical event of the death and resurrection of Christ

These three remain; what is lost is Paul's *culturally assumed* explanation for what a *primordial* man had to do with *causing* the reign of death and sin in the world. Paul's understanding of Adam as the cause reflects his time and place. Although Paul interprets this story in his own distinct way and for his own distinct purposes, the Israelite tradition handed to him still provides the theological vocabulary by which he can express his unique theology. There is no hint of modern arrogance (or heresy) whatsoever in a modern reader's making that observation.

The reality of sin, death, and the resurrection, however, belong to a different category entirely. Even without a first man, death and sin are still the universal realities that mark the human condition. Everyone dies, and this hardly needs further elaboration. And what the Judeo-Christian tradition calls sin is likewise as clear and present as the sky above—and one does not have to appeal to a Hitler, Pol Pot, or the Enron scandal to make the point.

People find it tremendously difficult to live in true peace with each other, yet they discover a correspondingly tremendous capacity to harm and manipulate strangers, friends, and family alike. People carry around the dysfunction of their families of origin and pass down their inherited toxicity to their own children, try as they might to be "good" parents. And Christians need only glance at the teachings of Jesus—such as dying to oneself, losing one's life, laying down our lives for others, loving not just those who wish us well but also those who are intent on harming us—to see how distant we are from the human ideal that Jesus models. Moreover, few are truly at peace even with themselves. The neurochemical and environmental contributors to the common list of emotional struggles we face betray a deep sense of the inevitable disquiet in our own hearts. We are all sinners. We have all fallen short of the mark; we fail to do what we know we should; we bear the burdens of the harm we cause to ourselves and others. Whatever words we want to use to describe it, this self-evident reality of repeated, relentless sin remains an unalterable and existential fact of human existence.

For understanding this state of sin, it is helpful to keep in mind the crucial theological distinction expressed succinctly by Lutheran theologian George L. Murphy. This distinction is between "original sin" and "sin of origin."[3] The former, as bequeathed to us through Augustine, refers to an event at the beginning of history and requires a historical Adam as the first human to sin and transmit that sin to all subsequent humans. The latter affirms the absolute inevitability of sin that affects every human being from *their* beginnings, from birth. In other words,

Murphy and others counsel that we must remain open on the ultimate origins of *why* all humans are born in sin (original sin) while resting content in the observation *that* all humans are born in sin (sin of origin). Furthermore, as we have seen already in chapter 5, the notion of "original sin," where Adam's disobedience is the cause of a universal state of sin, does not find clear—if any—biblical support. "Sin of origin," however, seems to be a veritable undercurrent of the biblical witness, and becomes explicit in such passages as Psalm 51:1–5 ("Indeed, I was born guilty, a sinner when my mother conceived me" [v. 5]) and Job 14:1–4 ("Who can bring a clean thing out of an unclean? No one can" [v. 4]). Maintaining this distinction between "original sin" and "sin of origin" respects Scripture by remaining silent on the former, as Scripture is silent, but affirming the latter, as Scripture does. And this distinction has the added value of relieving some of the pressure created by evolution for Christian theology.

So, even without attributing their cause to Adam, sin and death are with us, and we cannot free ourselves from them. They remain the foes vanquished by Christ's death and resurrection. The fact that Paul draws an analogy between Adam and Christ, however, does not mean that we are required to consider them as characters of equal historical standing. Unlike Adam, Christ was not a primordial, prehistorical man known only through hundreds and hundreds of years of cultural transmission. The resurrection of Christ was a present reality for Paul, an event that had happened in Jerusalem about twenty-five years before he wrote Romans.

Yet for many scholars of Christianity and ancient religions in general, the resurrection of Christ is every bit as mythical as Adam, given the commonality of resurrection stories in the ancient world—not only in Paul's time but also in other religions throughout antiquity. No student of early Christianity can afford to brush this aside, but it is actually beside the more modest point I am making here. For Paul, the resurrection of Christ is the central and climactic *present-day event* in the Jewish drama—and of the world. One could say that Paul was wrong, deluded, stupid, creative, whatever; nevertheless, the resurrection is something that Paul believed to have happened in his time, not primordial time.

This historical resurrection is the singular focus of Paul's writings and missionary activity,[4] God's climactic statement of his love for and presence in the world. It is the recent event that Paul claims to bear witness to along with more than five hundred others who saw the resurrected

Christ (1 Cor. 15:3–8). It is the event to which Paul applies his conscious theological acumen and without which nothing he says makes any sense at all. In other words, the resurrection is not a *cultural* assumption that Paul makes about *primordial* time, as he does with Adam. It is for Paul a *present*-time reality, an actual *historical event*.

I am not trying to offer a cheap apologetic for the resurrection of Christ; accepting the resurrection of Christ is truly a matter of faith. I am simply pointing out that Adam as disobedient primordial first man and Christ as obedient and raised-from-the-dead historical last man are not of the same historical category, even if Paul's historical Adam represents an unquestioned historical reality *for him*. It is commonly argued that, as goes the historicity of Adam, so goes the historicity of Christ. I disagree and suggest that we need to move beyond that obstacle. Locating the problem in Adam is Paul's way of explaining the objective human dilemma of sin and death in a way that reflects his intellectual world and the theological vocabulary available to him.

One last point before we move on. I am aware that this explanation will understandably raise an extremely important issue that I leave unaddressed: if Adam is not the cause of sin and death for all humanity, *why* then do humans sin and die? As we have seen, "why" (original sin) does not seem to be a question that Scripture is prepared to answer, and so seeking an answer for "why" in the Adam story may be off the mark to begin with. Still, this philosophical and theological issue of what makes us deeply flawed humans marching inexorably toward death is a vital issue to work through. For many people, Adam has been a powerful explanation for addressing the question of human existence: what makes us who we are; why we do what we do; why our time on earth is short, with pain and suffering always at our side. Providing explanations other than the one act of a primordial man for these questions, proposing answers that respect both Scripture and evolution, is one of the more pressing and inevitable philosophical and theological issues before us.

My own thinking reflected above is focused solely on hermeneutical issues—the purpose of this book—and so I make no claim to answer the many intellectual issues that the Christianity/evolution discussion raises. But the fact that the "why" question remains does not dismiss the hermeneutical observations; failure to provide at once an adequate counterproposal to a historical Adam for "why" does not mean that the scientific and archaeological data that raised the problem in the first place can be set to the side. The hermeneutical factors discussed concerning Genesis and Paul are here to stay, and they bring to the front and center the tremendously important work of Christian philosophers and theologians sorting out the implications of hermeneutics. I will be among the many who listen in on those discussions and try to discern the best way forward.

As we pursue these questions, even though we may not be able to point to the Adam of Christian tradition, we can still point to Christ, the Alpha and Omega, the one whom Christians confess was from the foundation of the world—before Adam, before hominids. Even if we cannot point to Adam as Paul does, we can, with Paul, begin with Christ and allow that reality to continue to reorient our thinking as well.

The One People of God

Although the presence of a historical Adam in Paul's thinking reflects his cultural setting, the reason he appeals to this Adam is due to more than a simple matter of availability. In Romans, the very fact that he appeals to Adam at all reflects a larger and pressing theological concern about the unity of the body of Christ, made up of Jew and gentile alike. Paul's goal is to show that what binds these two utterly distinct groups together is their equal participation in a universal humanity marked by sin and death and their shared need of the same universally offered redemption. Paul's Adam serves that goal.

To understand Paul's purpose for calling upon Adam the way he does, it will help to take a step back and look at Paul's theology, especially in Romans, from a broader—and, for some, perhaps new—vantage point. Since the 1970s, there has been a growing movement among New Testament scholars to rethink some (not all) aspects of Paul's theology. This movement is often referred to as the New Perspective on Paul, which is an unfortunate term, since its focus is not innovation but the recovery of Paul's theology within the thought world of first-century Palestinian Judaism. Much of what has driven this movement is renewed attention to the literature of Second Temple Judaism, inspired in part by the discovery of the Dead Sea Scrolls, which began in 1947.

Scholars working within this perspective have argued that Paul's theology had too long been refracted through the lens of medieval theological debates, which erupted in the Protestant Reformation, especially with Martin Luther. Luther was plagued by a guilty conscience due to his inability to live up to God's standard and famously found the remedy, while reading Romans 1:17, in the grace of God in Christ ("For in it [the gospel] the righteousness of God is revealed through faith for faith"). As the argument goes, this focus on one's personal inner state has spawned the well-known Protestant focus on making a "personal decision" for Christ, and this template has been placed over Paul himself—he too must have been burdened with a guilty conscience of being unable to live up to God's law and finally found relief for his personal plight in Christ. To put it in contemporary jargon, Paul confessed his sin and inability to save himself and accepted Jesus as his Savior, and led others to do likewise.[5]

Reading Paul in the context of his Jewish thought world began to yield a perspective on Paul's theology different from that of the Reformers—and subsequent Protestantism. Paul's gospel is certainly one where the grace of God reigns supreme. There is no other means of reconciliation to God, not even through keeping the law. Instead, God freely justifies those who put their faith in Christ. That is straightforward enough, but here is where the New Perspective comes in and where it has generated some controversy, especially among conservative Protestants. In books like Romans and Galatians, when one reads Paul's trenchant criticism of the Judaism of his day, it seems that Paul is indeed making the point Luther made: Jews teach works but the gospel teaches grace, and the two are opposed to each other. Jews believed they were "saved by works"—the burden of Luther's guilty conscience—and the gospel provides the opposite message: "saved by grace through faith." Paul seems to be saying that Judaism is a religion of works, and Christianity a religion of grace.

In his landmark 1977 book, *Paul and Palestinian Judaism*,[6] E. P. Sanders begins to turn this assumption on its head by arguing that such a "works-versus-grace" dichotomy in first-century Judaism is a caricature. The Protestant reading of Paul reflects medieval theological debates, not Paul or the Judaism of his time. Instead, Sanders argues for a concept he calls "covenantal nomism." This means that Jews did not think of themselves as earning their way to God's favor through the scrupulous observation of the law (Greek *nomos*)—they were not "saved by works." Rather, they understood themselves already to be part of the people of God by grace; God formed a covenant people, from Abraham on down. The function of the law is not to "get in," to *become* God's people. It is about "staying in" for those in the covenant *already*.

Arguably, this same pattern of "covenantal nomism" describes what we see in the Old Testament. The Israelites are not God's covenant people because they keep the law, but the opposite; they are given the law because they are God's covenant people, which begins with the call of Abraham (Gen. 12:1–3). Yahweh delivers the Israelites from Egypt to keep a promise to Abraham (see Exod. 2:24–25). Only afterward is the law introduced—law follows grace; the law is a gift to a people already chosen. As God's people they are expected to keep the law, and there are consequences if they do not—most notably the eventual exile to Babylon after Israel's long-standing history of covenant unfaithfulness. But Israel's status as Israel does not depend on keeping the law—even the exile eventfully comes to an end, with God's bringing the Israelites back to the land. Keeping the law, rather, determines whether they are in God's favor or not. If you will excuse the homey analogy, a child's status as child in the home is not determined by how well he obeys his parents. He is their child regardless, although disobedience will have clear consequences that affect the *nature* of that status.

Sanders and others[7] since have argued that "covenantal nomism" describes the Judaism of Paul's day. Regardless of what individual Jews might have thought, Judaism did not teach that one was saved by keeping the law. But if that is true, if Judaism was not a religion of works to please God and to gain entrance into the kingdom, what do we make of Paul's repeated arguments to his readers that they should avoid the influence of those Jewish Christians who were telling them to rely on the law to be justified before God (e.g., Gal. 3:14)? Are these New Perspective scholars so bold as to suggest that not only did Luther and all of Protestantism misread the Bible, but also that Paul misread his own moment in time or perhaps even intentionally caricatured his opponents?

The New Perspective does not argue that Paul was wrong about Judaism but that Paul's post-Lutheran interpreters were wrong not to read him against the backdrop of his cultural context. For neither Paul nor the Jews of his time was the law seen as the entryway into God's covenant. For both Christian and Jew, entry was by God's grace. The crucial (and obvious) difference, however, is that Christians saw God's grace in the cross and resurrection of Christ; Jews saw grace in their election in Abraham and subsequent ethnic and national identity—and circumcision was a sign of that identity. So, with respect to the churches in Galatia, these were made up of two different ethnic groups, Jew and gentile. The struggle Paul was addressing was not that these Jewish Christians were advocating "salvation by works" as opposed to grace. Rather, they were telling the gentiles among them that they had to take on the mark of Judaism, circumcision, in order to have access to Christ.

With this we come closer to how all of this relates to the question of Paul's Adam. On one level, one can hardly blame these Jewish Christians for insisting that gentiles be circumcised. They were simply following what their own Scripture required of them (Gen. 17:9–14). But the gospel that Paul preached was radical and led to such a deep rift between Jewish and gentile Christians that much of the New Testament either hints at this division or deals with it explicitly. Paul's gospel insists that there is only one people of God, made up of Jew and gentile on equal footing. However central the Jew/gentile distinction may have been under the old covenant, it is no longer valid under the new. *The resurrection of the Son of God is a game changer*: gentiles can now be part of the family of God *as gentiles*—which for faithful, biblically knowledgeable Jews was nothing less than turning the Old Testament on its head, if not dismissing it entirely. Any attempt to retain the old distinctions was met by Paul with his full arsenal of rhetorical skill, passionate personality, and theological insight.

This is precisely where Paul's Adam comes into the picture, especially in Romans. Romans is often read within Protestantism as a tract for how an individual can get saved: we are justified by grace through faith, not by works. But we must keep in mind that Paul was writing to a Roman church that was already Christian, although consisting of Jews and gentiles. "Getting saved" may be part of the application of Romans, but if one makes it the whole message, much of Paul's argument will be missed. Instead, the focus of Romans is that the death and resurrection of Christ put Jew and gentile on an even footing. They reveal the heretofore unrealized fact that together Jew and gentile make up one people of God because they are both saved from the same plight (sin and death) by the same solution (Jesus's death and resurrection).

This may sound anticlimactic for some, but that may be because we are not used to reading Paul in his cultural context. The church in Rome was primarily gentile but with a significant Jewish population. The question of how gentiles would be included in the family of the Jewish God without first becoming Jewish was a virtual preoccupation in the early church, and the New Testament lets us in on the controversy with some of Jesus's encounters with Jewish exclusivism (e.g., Luke 4:24–30; 10:25–37; 14:15–24; John 4:1–42), much of the book of Acts (esp. chap. 15), the entire book of Galatians, and much of what undergirds Romans. Paul's vision for the church is that God "has broken down the dividing wall, that is, the hostility between us," meaning Jew and gentile (Eph. 2:14). Once we grasp how important is the issue of the one people of God, it jumps out at us throughout the New Testament.

This brings us to our central question: what does Paul's focus on the "one people of God" tell us about his use of the Adam story?

The Solution Reveals the Plight

What drove Paul to see that Jew and gentile now constitute one people of God was not his own imagination or sense of social justice, and it certainly was not his "straight" reading of his Bible. If anything, putting Jew and non-Jew on the same level cuts against the Old Testament grain. What drove Paul to this revolutionary, countercultural conclusion was the reality of the resurrection of Christ.

As Sanders and others have argued, Paul's theology—in Romans 5:12–21 and everywhere else—began with the reorienting reality of the risen Christ. That was his point of departure, the center around which everything else now revolved—the hermeneutical focal point around which Paul's own Scripture was now to be reinterpreted, as we glimpsed in chapter 6.

The crucified and risen Son of God was God's climactic, fundamentally drastic, and unexpected act of salvation. For God to have provided a "solution" of such earth-shattering significance, there must have been a corresponding "problem" it was designed to address. God's solution through the death and resurrection of Jesus exposed the true plight of humanity. Because of the nature of the solution, Paul came to understand that the human plight was far deeper and more widespread than his own Jewish worldview thought. The real problem is not that Jews have failed to keep the law. The real problem is that all sin and all die—Jew as well as gentile. That is the true plight of all humanity, and the resurrection of Christ has brought that to light. Paul now began a process of reunderstanding Israel's national story in light of this unexpected universal ending, which accounts for much of how Paul interpreted the Old Testament.

Seeing the true, universal scope of things, Paul placed Adam front and center in a way that had not been done before. If God's solution was Christ's dying and rising from the dead, the root problem must be death—and for Paul the cause of death can be traced to the trespass of Adam, understood as the first man. The resurrection brought Paul to see the full depth of the problem, which until the resurrection could not have been seen, and in fact was not seen as clearly and deeply as now—neither in Judaism nor in the Old Testament. Paul pressed Adam into new service in view of the reality of the empty tomb.

Skimming the content of Romans leading up to chapter 5 helps us see how Paul has been preparing his readers for his discussion of Adam and the universal nature of the problem and solution. In 1:14 he announces his universal focus when he states his obligation to both Greeks and non-Greeks (v. 14), claiming that the gospel is for the Jew first, but then also for the gentile (v. 16). This is not just a polite way to begin a letter, but an announcement of the letter's focus: one gospel for two heretofore distinct peoples.

At 1:16 Paul begins a sustained argument that Jew and gentile benefit equally from the grace of God, the reason being that both are equally deserving of God's wrath and judgment (v. 18). All are without excuse, for they suppress the truth that creation itself speaks to them (vv. 18–20). Jews have no room to brag simply because they possess Torah, especially since they fail to do what it says. Simply having the law as an ethnic possession means nothing at all, nor does circumcision (2:17–29). Paul begins to reach the crescendo of his argument in 3:9: "both Jews and Greeks are under the power of sin." The law won't solve the problem, for the law makes no one righteous; it simply makes those under the law more conscious of sin (3:19–20), a view that is difficult, to say the least, to find in the Old Testament.

Having announced the universal nature of the problem, Paul continues in 3:21–22 by saying that a righteousness of God has been revealed that comes through faith in Christ. *All* have sinned and fall short of God's glory (v. 23). "All" does not refer to an indiscriminant "everyone." "All" in the context of Paul's argument means Jews and gentiles together (to feel the force of the point, replace "all" with "both"). There is no room for boasting by either group, even the group that happens to have the law as their possession (3:27). God's salvation is for gentiles too, and both Jews and gentiles will now be justified before God by the same faith in the crucified and risen one (v. 30).

This leads Paul to retell the Abraham story (chap. 4) in such a way that emphasizes his status before God as dependent on faith, not on law. Paul's Abraham is not the father of Torah-centered Israel but the father of many nations (4:17; citing Gen. 17:5), of all those who are righteous by faith *apart* from the law (Rom. 4:13–15).[8] It is hard for Christians today to sense how explosive such a statement would have

been in Paul's day, given the well-documented tensions between Jews
and gentiles. We need to appreciate clearly that Paul's interpretation
of Abraham as the father of Jews and gentiles by faith is rooted in
the dominant, reorienting reality of the resurrection. This brings us
to Romans 5. Jews and gentiles are equally culpable before God, as
can be seen in that both groups are sinful and are subject to death.
The solution that God offers to address this universal problem is the
death and resurrection of Christ (5:1–11). All humanity is powerless
to take the first step toward God, to escape sin and death, and so
Christ's death is an act of grace, pure and simple (v. 6).

Romans 5:12–21 continues in this vein, although now for the
first time Paul locates the cause of this universal plight in Adam
(although some argue that Paul alludes to Adam in 1:18–25 and
3:23). Earlier Paul was content to point out the obvious nature of
human depravity throughout the human drama of history (1:18–32).
Here, however, Paul anchors the universal nature of the problem in
Adam. Sin and death came into the world through this first man
(v. 12), which preceded the law (vv. 13–14). Adam's trespass was the
introduction of death for "many" (v. 15), the dominion of death
(v. 17), that "led to condemnation for all" (v. 18) and through which
"many were made sinners" (v. 19).

Paul lays much at Adam's feet, more than a straightforward reading
of Genesis dictates. Genesis focuses on death as the central, universal
consequence of Adam's disobedience, which Paul picks up on, but
Paul also says more. Not only did Adam's trespass lead to his death
and ours, but also Adam's trespass somehow is responsible for putting all of humanity under the power of sin. We see this most clearly
in verses 18 and 19:

> Therefore just as one man's trespass *led to* condemnation for all, so
> one man's act of righteousness leads to justice and life for all. For
> just as by the one man's disobedience the many were *made* sinners,
> so by the one man's obedience the many will be made righteous.
> (emphasis added)

Adam's trespass brought condemnation for "all" and made "many"
sinners.

Neither Genesis nor the Old Testament speaks of Adam's trespass
as having such power, but Paul seems to be connecting some dots that
had not been connected in quite the same way before. Paul seems to
reason that, since Adam's trespass resulted in both *his* death and the

death of *all* humans, his trespass, the cause of death, was handed on as well somehow. Hence, if Adam's death is ours, so is his trespass. Just as each subsequent person born after Adam invariably faces death, so too does everyone invariably face sin. There is a logic behind this, even if this logic is not laid out in Genesis or the Old Testament. But the impetus for Paul to connect the dots in this innovative way was not an isolated decision to take a closer look at Genesis on its own terms. Rather, it was the death and resurrection of Christ that drove Paul to go back to Genesis and engage that text in a fresh way.

I realize that my rather speedy run through Romans 5:12–21 leaves unaddressed some of the interpretive challenges of that passage, those places where commentators tend to pause at length.[9] Ferreting out the broad and complex range of interpretive issues is entirely beside the point here, since our central concern would not be affected in any substantial way: Paul's Adam as first human, who introduced universal sin and death, supports his contention that Jew and gentile are on the same footing and in need of the same Savior.

This is hardly a view that one could expect Paul's fellow Jews to embrace with open arms. The Jewish hope in Paul's day, as it has been ever since Israel's exile, is that the people and king's fidelity to the law of Moses would restore their glory and usher in the messianic age of divine favor and Jewish dominance over their enemies. From the perspective of the Jews, the problem that needs to be addressed is Israel's continued "exile" in its own land so long as it is under foreign rule. Once the Romans are gone, Israel would be saved yet again, and the new golden age would begin. Failure to keep Torah is Israel's problem; fidelity to Torah is the solution.

Paul's argument takes an entirely different turn: the law of Moses is not central. Failure to obey it is not the true source of Israel's woes, nor does obedience to it secure future blessing. The Messiah, as it turns out, did not solve the problem of Roman occupation of Palestine as God's response to Jewish transgression of the law. Torah was only *part* of the problem: it came in and simply made worse a bad situation brought on by Adam (Rom. 5:20–21). Rather, this Messiah was crucified and rose from the dead. The resurrection of Christ showed that the real problem was Adam and the universal problem of the reigning power of sin and its nefarious partner, death. These were at work long before the law (Rom. 5:12–14), and so Christ's resurrection—death's reversal—was clearly a solution to a much deeper problem than the law.

To say that the law is neither the real problem nor the solution is in effect saying that Israel's story is not God's sole focus. The main drama began with the first Adam and ended with the last Adam. That is why being a Jew or gentile is no longer the primary distinction among humans, but rather being or not being "in Christ" is. The heart of Jewish identity is therefore marginalized, and the God of Israel and his salvation are denationalized. Jews and gentiles share the same plight, and Jesus came to solve it. And all of this stems from Paul's rereading of his Scripture in light of the central and prior conviction that God raised Jesus from the dead. (Israel's role is much more positive in Rom. 9–11, but that is beyond our focus.)

Explaining Paul's Adam this way may seem to some to be a low view of Scripture, but I think Paul would disagree. It shows, rather, a high view of Christ—so high that even Israel's story, specifically Adam, must be recast to account for Christ. Paul invests Adam with capital he does not have either in the Genesis story, the Old Testament as a whole, or the interpretations of his contemporary Jews. His reading of the Old Testament in general is creative, driven both by hermeneutical conventions of the time and—most importantly—by his experience of the risen Christ.

Hence, Christians who take Paul's *theology* with utmost seriousness are not also bound to accept Paul's view of Adam *historically*. How we today explain the origin and development of human life does not affect our acceptance of the reality of the human plight of sin and death or of God's unexpected, universal solution.

Conclusion

ADAM TODAY: NINE THESES

How are Christians—those who value Scripture as God's Word and who also accept evolution as the correct model for human origins—to think of Adam today? That is the question we began with at the beginning of the book, and the question for everyone to work through on their own. I hope the thoughts I have outlined thus far may be of some help. Toward that end, I think it is appropriate to conclude this book by outlining in nine theses the core issues before us, retracing some of the steps we have taken throughout this book while also adding a point or two.

Thesis 1: Literalism is not an option.

Much of part 1 addresses this issue in one way or another. One cannot read Genesis literally—meaning as a literally accurate description of physical, historical reality—in view of the state of scientific knowledge today and our knowledge of ancient Near Eastern stories of origins. Those who read Genesis literally must either ignore evidence completely or present alternate "theories" in order to maintain spiritual stability. Unfortunately, advocates of alternate scientific theories sometimes keep themselves free of the burden of tainted peer review. Such professional isolation can encourage casually sweeping aside generations and even centuries of accumulated knowledge.

Literalism is designed to protect the Bible but in reality subjects the Bible and its literalist interpreters to ridicule. As we saw in chapter 2, Augustine made this point more than one and a half millennia ago concerning the cosmology of Genesis 1:

> It is a disgraceful and dangerous thing for an infidel to hear a Christian, presumably giving the meaning of Holy Scripture, talking nonsense on these [cosmological] topics, and we should take all means to prevent such an embarrassing situation, in which people show up vast ignorance in a Christian and laugh it to scorn.[1]

As this quote indicates, literalism can lead thoughtful, informed people to reject any semblance of the Christian faith. This is more my concern than anything else. Literalism is not just an outdated curiosity or an object of jesting. It can be dangerous. A responsible view of the biblical stories must *account* for the scientific and archaeological facts, not dismiss them, ignore them, or—as in some cases—manipulate them.

Thesis 2: Scientific and biblical models of human origins are, strictly speaking, incompatible because they speak a different "language." They cannot be reconciled, and there is no "Adam" to be found in an evolutionary scheme.

Although we should not take the Genesis creation accounts literally, Adam is nevertheless a key theological figure. Hence, some understandably seek to merge evolution with Adam in an attempt to preserve what they perceive as the heart of Paul's teaching on Adam, yet without dismissing natural science. In other words, evolution is fine so long as an "Adam" can be identified somehow, somewhere. So, for example, it is sometimes argued that Adam and Eve were two hominids or symbolic of a group of hominids with whom, at some point in evolutionary development, God entered into a relationship. At this point God endowed them with his image, thus making them conscious of God and thereby entering into a covenant relationship with them. Such a scenario is thought to preserve at least the general story of Genesis.

I support the effort to take seriously both the theological heart of the Adam story and natural science, and to be willing to rethink the biblical Adam in the process. But as well intentioned as this approach is—and many thoughtful people envision such a scenario— I see several problems.

First and foremost, it is ironic that in trying to hold on to biblical teaching a scenario is proposed that the Bible does not recognize: gradual evolution over millions of years rather than the sudden and recent creation of humanity as the Bible has it. Now I will say it is *possible* that, tens of thousands of years ago, God took two hominid representatives (or a group of hominids) and with them began the human story where creatures could have a consciousness of God, learn to be moral, and so forth. But that is an alternate and wholly ad hoc account of the first humans, not the biblical one. One cannot pose such a scenario and say, "Here is your Adam and Eve; the Bible and science are thus reconciled." Whatever those creatures were, they were not what the biblical authors presumed to be true. They may have been the first beings somehow conscious of God, but we overstep our bounds if we claim that these creatures satisfy the requirements of being "Adam and Eve."

Second, another problem with this scenario, though not as central, is that it presses "image of God" (Gen. 1:26) into service beyond its limits. In the Old Testament "image of God" refers to humanity's role as ruler over creation, as God's earthly representatives. Ancient kings were considered to be living images of the gods, ruling on the gods' behalf. Ancient kings also placed statues (images) of themselves in the far corners of their kingdom to proclaim, "This is mine." Humans were God's images to represent to all creatures God's rule over the earth. Consciousness of God, heightened moral sense, and so forth are not the topic. Again, it is possible that at some point in the evolutionary process, God endowed hominids with an awareness of himself, and so began the human religious drama; but "image of God" cannot be appealed to, for it gives the false impression that this ad hoc scenario is biblically grounded.

Third, searching for ways to align modern-scientific and ancient-biblical models of creation—no matter how minimal—runs the risk of obscuring the theology of the biblical texts in question. The creation stories are ancient and should be understood on that level. Rather than merge the two creation stories—the scientific and the biblical—we should respect that they each speak a different language. The fact that Paul considered Adam to be the progenitor of the human race does not mean that we need to find some way to maintain his view within an evolutionary scheme. Rather, we should gladly acknowledge his ancient view of cosmic and human origins and see in that very scenario the face of a God who seems far less reluctant to accommodate to ancient points of view than we are sometimes comfortable with.

Thesis 3: The Adam story in Genesis reflects its ancient Near Eastern setting and should be read that way.

Following on the previous thesis, the Adam story must be understood first and foremost as an ancient story that addresses ancient Israelite questions in ancient ways. This is hardly a radical statement but simply asserts a principle of biblical interpretation that would be readily acknowledged if it were not for the controversial nature of this topic. This principle is often referred to as grammatical-historical interpretation, which stresses that the Bible's meaning is rooted somehow in what would have been understood at the time.

Personally, I think a grammatical-historical approach to reading Scripture has its limits, partly because it does not account for how Paul handled his own Bible (see chap. 6 above). But when we are asking what Genesis meant to those who wrote it, this principle is our first order of business. We do not approach these texts properly by assuming that embedded therein is some secret knowledge that corresponds to modern science, which could not have been understood until recently. Further, following on thesis 1 above, I don't think we can proceed in isolation from the comparative literary evidence we have from the ancient Near East.

A grammatical-historical approach has always fed off of our growing knowledge of the biblical world, the result being a clearer understanding of what the text is trying to get across. Placing the Bible in its historical contexts is the principle that lies behind every commentary on our shelves and the notes and maps that make up our study Bibles. The fact that the scientific and archaeological evidence concerning Genesis can be somewhat challenging does not permit us to abandon this principle.

Thesis 4: There are two creation stories in Genesis; the Adam story is probably the older and was subsumed under Genesis 1 after the exile in order to tell Israel's story.

What follows is speculative but hardly random. Here is how I see the relationship between the two creation stories, Genesis 1:1–2:3, and Genesis 2:4–3:24. The second of these is older, perhaps stemming from the first quarter of the first millennium BC (early in Israel's existence as a nation). The story may have originated orally and remained so for generations before being written down, or it may have originated in written form and was handed down that way, or perhaps some combination of both processes. I am not concerned to settle the matter. But the Adam story was the older of the two stories and, together with the flood story,[2] reflects common ancient Near Eastern themes and may be modeled after the *Atrahasis Epic*.

The Adam story functioned as Israel's creation story and was probably rethought and retold along the way as Israel grew and developed in its self-understanding. In exile, faced with this national crisis and asking themselves basic questions of self-definition, their relationship with God, and so forth, Israel's theologians added another creation story, Genesis 1, modeled more along the lines of the stories of their captors, the Babylonians, with perhaps *Enuma Elish* exerting an indirect influence. I am not suggesting that Genesis 1 was "written" at this point out of whole cloth, especially since the themes are not necessarily strictly Babylonian, and Israel was hardly immune to Babylonian influence before the exile. But what became Genesis 1:1–2:3 seems to fit best in the context of national struggle. The story stresses the sovereignty of Israel's God over all of creation, who alone made all that is, and this set Israel's God apart from the gods of Israel's captors and of every other nation. Hence, what we call Genesis 1 was put at the head of Israel's national story, a collection of writings either composed or brought together in what eventually came to be called the Bible.

What had earlier been Israel's sole creation story, the Adam story, was now subsumed under this newer story. I am noncommittal as to whether the Adam story ever functioned for Israel as a story of universal human origins, although referring to Eve as "the mother of all living" (Gen. 3:20) suggests as much. Perhaps the Adam story always functioned primarily as a story of Israel, with the world stage as the backdrop. But however it functioned originally, when it was subsumed under the universal story of origins in Genesis 1, the Adam story took on, it seems to me, a clearer Israelite-centered focus. As we saw in chapter 4, the Adam story seems to be a preview of Israel's history, from exodus to exile. Genesis 1 tells the story of the sovereign God over all of creation, but from the outset Genesis 2 focuses on what for Israel was the heart of the matter, that this universal sovereign God is also their God, and that they had been his elect people, among all other peoples, since the very beginning.

This same idea seems to be at work in the only other mention of Adam in the entire Old Testament, 1 Chronicles 1:1: Adam is the first name in the nine-chapter genealogy that establishes Israel's unwavering status as God's people from the very beginning. The postexilic community, wishing to affirm its national and religious identity, traced its lineage back to Adam—not the universal first man, but the first man in the chosen line, the first Israelite.

In my view, reading the Adam story as it was intended to be understood by those who shaped the Bible—primarily as a story of Israel within the larger stage of universal world history—is the most fruitful approach. The Adam story is not an obligatory nod on the part of ancient Israelites to account for how humanity came to be. The primary question Israel was asking was not, "Where do people come from?" (a scientific curiosity), but "Where do we come from?" (a matter of national identity).

Thesis 5: The Israel-centered focus of the Adam story can also be seen in its similarity to Proverbs: the story of Adam is about failure to fear God and attain wise maturity.

When read in light of Proverbs, the Adam story is about failing to follow the path of wisdom and reach maturity and not about a fall from perfection. Adam and Eve were innocent, childlike creatures in need of maturation. When naive Adam and Eve chose to listen to the cunning (the opposite of naive) serpent and follow another path to wisdom, they veered off God's path. The tree that they had had access to, the tree of life, was now off limits. As Proverbs puts it, in a clear echo of the garden story, "She [Wisdom] is a tree of life to those who lay hold of her" (Prov. 3:18).

When read as a wisdom story, the story of Adam becomes a story for "every Israelite," those who are daily in a position of having to choose which path they will take: the path of wisdom or the path of foolishness. Paul himself does not develop this metaphor in his proclamation of the good news in Romans 5. As we have seen, he presents Adam as the first human who introduced sin and death to all. Nevertheless, there is a way in which Paul's reading of the Adam story and the wisdom reading may inform each other. As Paul says in 1 Corinthians 1:30, part of the redemption in Christ is that Christ "became for us wisdom from God." In other words, the wisdom that Adam and Eve lacked and that sent them veering off course is restored, like everything else, by an act of God (cf. Col. 2:3, which says that "all the treasures of wisdom and knowledge" are hidden in Christ). A wisdom reading of Adam does not diminish Paul's gospel but complements it by means of a different metaphor.

Thesis 6: God's solution through the resurrection of Christ reveals the deep, foundational plight of the human condition, and Paul expresses that fact in the biblical idiom available to him.

As discussed in chapter 7, Paul's reading of the Adam story was conditioned by his experience of the risen Christ. As Paul does so often in his use of the Old Testament in general, he interprets it in such a way as to highlight the work of Christ and the equality of Jew and gentile.

The death and resurrection of the Son of God was a surprise ending to Israel's story. No one familiar with the Old Testament messianic hope was prepared for a crucified—and risen!—messiah. This jarring climax to Israel's story, according to Paul, served to relativize Israel's story: faithful Torah obedience was no longer the necessary preparation to usher in the messianic age (understood as Jewish political and religious freedom). Torah was actually part of the problem: it merely exacerbated and made plain a much deeper truth about the human condition—that we are broken and alienated people, in need of rescue (Rom. 5:20).

The solution that God gave in the death and resurrection of Christ served not only to show the depth of God's love for his creation but also revealed—for the first time clearly—the extent to which that creation was in need of deliverance (Rom. 8:19–23). Paul, as a first-century Jew, bore witness to God's act in Christ in the only way that he could have been expected to do so, through ancient idioms and categories known to him and his religious tradition for century upon century. One can believe that Paul is correct theologically and historically about the problem of sin and death and the solution that God provides in Christ without also needing to believe that his assumptions about human origins are accurate. The need for a savior does not require a historical Adam.

Thesis 7: A proper view of inspiration will embrace the fact that God speaks by means of the cultural idiom of the authors—whether it be the author of Genesis in describing origins or how Paul would later come to understand Genesis. Both reflect the setting and limitations of the cultural moment.

Following on thesis 6, even the expression of deep and ultimate truth does not escape the limitations of the cultures in which that truth is expressed. Unfortunately, this is not always fully appreciated. A barrier to the evolution-Christianity discussion is a view of the Bible where God's accommodating himself to the views of the time—whether in Genesis or Romans—is assumed to be somewhat unworthy of God. Some seem to expect the Bible to be a document that fundamentally transcends its setting. It is true that the Bible tells a grand narrative that is not merely restricted to its cultural moments, but we do the Bible a great disservice when we minimize the settings in which the texts were written, as if they are an unfortunate impediment of some sort.

A central tenet of Christianity is the mystery summarized in Philippians 2:6–8, that although Christ "was in the form of God, [he] did not regard equality with God something to be exploited, but emptied himself, taking the form of a slave, being born in human likeness. And being found in human form, he humbled himself and became obedient to the point of death—even death on a cross." This is a fitting metaphor for the Bible, where God condescends to speak, empty of all beauty and perfection, more like a humble servant subject to the lowest status.

Understanding the nature of the Bible as analogous to the mystery of the incarnation helps us to adjust our expectations of what the Bible is prepared to deliver. The entire matter is beautifully put by the Dutch theologian Herman Bavinck (1854–1921), and I cannot resist quoting him at length:

> Scripture . . . is the working out and application of the central fact of revelation: the incarnation of the Word. The Word (*logos*) has become flesh (*sarx*), and the word has become Scripture; *these two facts do not only run parallel but are most intimately connected*. Christ became flesh, a servant, without form or comeliness, the most despised of human beings; he descended to the nethermost parts of the earth and became obedient even to death on the cross. So also the word, the revelation of God, entered the world of creatureliness, the life and history of humanity, in all the human forms of dream and vision, of investigation and reflection, *right down into that which is humanly weak and despised and ignoble*. . . . All this took place in order that the excellency of the power . . . of Scripture may be God's and not ours.[3]

There is a reason why Scripture looks the way it does, so human, so much a part of its world: it looks this way to exalt God's power, not our power, according to Bavinck. The Bible reflects the ancient contexts in which it was written, and this very fact proclaims the glory of God. The "creatureliness" of Scripture is not an obstacle to be overcome so that God may finally be seen. Rather, just as Christians proclaim concerning Christ, it is through creatureliness that God can be seen. We can only see God truly because of the limited, human form he has chosen as a means of revelation, and if we try to look past it, we will miss everything. And this humanity, as Bavinck puts it, whether of Christ or of Scripture, is "weak and despised and ignoble." We see God through the humiliation. To marginalize, minimize, or somehow get behind the Bible's "creatureliness" to the "real" Word of God is, for Bavinck, to strip God of his glory (not to mention being quasi gnostic).

When we read the Bible, whether the creation accounts of Genesis or Paul's reading of them, we are not to look past the "unfortunate" human encumbrances to catch a glimpse of the divine. We are to see the divine in and through the human words of the writers. When we read Genesis and see the clear and undeniable overlap with Mesopotamian myths, that is not a reason for offense—as if God would not do such a thing. This actually is the only thing he does do: take on humanity when he speaks. And when we see Paul rereading the Adam story from the vantage point of his Second Temple and postresurrection setting, thereby engaging the text creatively and not being bound to the original authors' intentions, we do not conclude that this "ignominy" is somehow unworthy of God. Quite the opposite: incarnation is God's business.

For many, it is important for the future viability of faith, let alone the evolution-Christianity discussion, that we recognize and embrace the fact that the Bible is a thoroughly enculturated product. But it is not enough merely to say so and press on, with a quaint nod or an embarrassed shuffling of the feet. It is important for future generations of Christians to have a view of the Bible where its rootedness in ancient ways of thinking is embraced as a theological positive, not a problem to be overcome.[4] At present there is a lot of fear about the implications of bringing evolution and Christianity together, and this fear needs to be addressed head-on. Many fear that we are on a slippery slope, to use the hackneyed expression. Perhaps the way forward is not to resist the slide so much as to stop struggling, look around, and realize that we may have been on the wrong hill altogether.

What makes some uncomfortable is that such a view of the Bible can open the door for all sorts of uncertainty, and most of all to questioning familiar ways of talking about God, the Bible, and much else. And with this we get to a key and even central barrier to the debate.

Thesis 8: The root of the conflict for many Christians is not scientific or even theological, but group identity and fear of losing what it offers.
The Christian faith is invariably tied to its sacred book, where God speaks. Any challenge to how that book has been understood—and evolution requires some significant adjustment for many—is bound to be threatening and so elicit strong reactions. Saying that the Adam story in Genesis is not a historical account, even though it seems to be understood that way by Paul—no matter how gently one puts it—presents a real threat to some because it is believed to undermine the trustworthiness of the Bible.

The reason why this tension is felt so acutely—particularly among evangelicals and fundamentalists—is because of the central role that the Bible plays in those traditions. Although they express their commitments differently, both of these groups share a commitment to the supreme authority of the Bible in all theological matters, which typically (or at least historically) has included a commitment to the historical accuracy of the Bible. When challenges to this "boundary marker" arise, tensions naturally increase.

The roots of this commitment to the Protestant evangelical and fundamentalist consciousness are varied, but certainly one significant historical factor is the Reformation concept of *sola Scriptura*: the Bible alone is the church's final authority on all matters pertaining to faith and life. Though by no means a necessary conclusion, *sola Scriptura*— according to some in our present moment—does not leave much room for reinterpreting the Bible in view of extrabiblical information, be it science or Mesopotamian creation texts. These external forces introduce ambiguity into the otherwise clear meaning of the Bible and are seen to relativize its teachings as cultural expressions. Evolution requires Christians to rethink theology, yet some believe accepting this challenge calls into question their core Protestant identity. For some Christians, therefore, evidence from natural science or archaeology, no matter how compelling, is simply inadmissible. Too much is at stake.

As sociologists will be quick to tell us, movement from one's social group takes tremendous effort and often occurs only at the prompting of some significant personal crisis or upheaval. We all tend to resist having our life narrative rewritten, particularly when those narratives include familiar notions of ultimate significance, such as the nature of the universe and our place in it, God, eternal life, and so forth. For some, that personal narrative also includes a denominational history of strong resistance toward perceived "attacks" on the gospel by such "modernist" forces as natural science or biblical scholarship. Adopting a more conversational posture toward new ideas can be seen as an act of infidelity toward the tradition, and therefore toward God himself.

Rewriting one's narrative is always a threat, but until new narratives are written, where openness to change when warranted is valued as part of the journey of faith rather than feared, conflict will continue. Creating ecclesiastical and academic cultures where at the very least the nature of biblical authority can be seriously discussed, if not conceived of differently, is central to moving beyond the uneasy and hostile relationship between evolution and some examples of Christianity.

Thesis 9: A true rapprochement between evolution and Christianity requires a synthesis, not simply adding evolution to existing theological formulations.

Evolution is a serious challenge to how Christians have traditionally understood at least three central issues of the faith: the origin of humanity, of sin, and of death. Although, as we saw in chapter 7, sin and death are universal realities, the Christian tradition has generally attributed the cause to Adam. But evolution removes that cause as Paul understood it and thus leaves open the questions of where sin and death have come from. More than that, the very nature of what sin is and why people die is turned on its head. Some characteristics that Christians have thought of as sinful—for example, in an evolutionary scheme the aggression and dominance associated with "survival of the fittest" and sexual promiscuity to perpetuate one's gene pool—are understood as means of ensuring survival. Likewise, death is not the enemy to be defeated. It may be feared, it may be ritualized, it may be addressed in epic myths and sagas; but death is not the unnatural state introduced by a disobedient couple in a primordial garden. Actually, it is the means that promotes the continued evolution of life on this planet and even ensures workable population numbers. Death may hurt, but it is evolution's ally.

Evolution, therefore, cannot simply be grafted onto evangelical Christian faith. As similar as Galileo's moment might be to the present paradigm shift, it is much easier to adapt a vast, heliocentric cosmos to traditional Christian theology than to adapt evolution to Christian thought. (At least this is true in retrospect, since Galileo's telescope revealed an unimaginable expanse of outer space that relegated the earth to relatively unimportant status and raised the question of where, exactly, God resides in the heavens.) Evolution is not an add-on to Christianity: it demands synthesis because it forces serious intellectual engagement with some important issues. Such a synthesis requires a willingness to rethink one's own convictions in light of new data, and that is typically a very hard thing to do (thesis 8). The cognitive dissonance created by evolution is considerable, and I understand why a piecemeal approach to bringing it and Christianity together might be attractive. But in the long run, the price we pay for not doing the hard and necessary synthetic work is high indeed.

Often Christians focus on the need to be faithful to the past, to make sure that present belief matches that of previous generations. I support the sentiment in general, but we must be just as burdened to be faithful to the future, to ensure that we are doing all we can to deliver a viable faith to future generations. That too is a high calling—even if it is unsettling, destabilizing, perhaps frightening. Nevertheless, it is a journey that must be taken, for the alternatives are not pleasant. Christians can turn away, but the current scientific explanation of cosmic and biological origins is not going away, nor is our growing understanding of the nature of Israelite faith in its ancient Near Eastern context. I do not believe that God means for his children to live in a state of denial or hand-wringing.

Likewise, abandoning all faith in view of our current state of knowledge is hardly an attractive—or compelling—option. Despite the New Atheist protestations of the bankruptcy of any faith in God in the face of science, most world citizens are not ready to toss away what has been the central element of the human drama since the beginning of recorded civilization. Neither am I, not because I refuse to see the light, but because the light of science does not shine with equal brightness in every corner. There is mystery. There is transcendence. By faith I believe that the Christian story has deep access to a reality that materialism cannot provide and cannot be expected to know. That is a confession of faith, I readily admit, but when it comes to accessing ultimate reality, we are all in the same boat, materialistic atheists included: at some point we must trust in something or someone beyond logic and evidence, even if it is to declare that there is nothing beyond what we see.

As for Christians, perhaps evolution will eventually wind up being more of a help than a hindrance. Perhaps it will lead Christians to see that our theologies are provisional; when we forget that fact, we run the risk of equating what we think of God with God himself. That is a recurring danger, and the history of Christianity is replete with sad and horrific stories of how theology is used to grasp at and maintain power over others. It may be that evolution, and the challenges it presents, will remind us that we are called to trust God, which means we need to restructure and even abandon the "god" that we have created in our own image. Working through the implications of evolution may remind Christians that trusting God's goodness is a daily decision, a spiritually fulfilling act of recommitment to surrender to God no matter what. That is not easy. But if we have learned anything from the saints of the past, it is that surrendering to God each day, whatever we are facing, is not meant to be easy. Taking up that same journey now will add our witness for the benefit of future generations.

Notes

Introduction

1. For example, violence and death drive forward natural selection and survival of the fittest. Any attempt to align the Christian faith and evolution will have to address how evolution affects our understanding of the nature of God and the "unnaturalness" of death, as both Genesis and the apostle Paul presume.

2. Peter Enns, *Inspiration and Incarnation: Evangelicals and the Problem of the Old Testament* (Grand Rapids: Baker Academic, 2005).

3. There are so many helpful books for the nonspecialist that I hardly know where to begin, but see the books by Collins, Giberson, Glover, Polkinghorne, and Poole in the bibliography. Those treatments are as good a place to begin as any, and all are clearly written and spiritually sensitive while also pulling few punches with respect to the challenges of science.

4. See David Adam, "The Flat Earth? What Planet Is He On?" February 23, 2010, www.guardian.co.uk/global/2010/feb/23/flat-earth-society. The URL for the Flat Earth Society is www.theflatearthsociety.net/. See also FAQ at http://theflatearthsociety.net/talk/viewtopic.php?f=3&t=69.

5. Answers in Genesis, www.answersingenesis.org.

6. Albert Mohler, president of Southern Baptist Seminary, expressed this view the summer of 2010. The video can be found at www.christianity.com/ligonier/?speaker=mohler2; a transcript of the talk can be accessed at www.biologos.org/resources/albert-mohler-why-does-the-universe-look-so-old.

7. Here too there are many fine books one can read with great profit, such as works by Collins, Falk, Haarsma, and Harrell in the bibliography. These books focus on evolution but do not address the biblical issues in depth, if at all.

8. The ancient world in which the Israelites arose is referred to among biblical scholars as the "ancient Near East" (often abbreviated ANE). This term corresponds roughly to how we use "Middle East" today. Another term, "Mesopotamia," designates the area that roughly corresponds to modern Iraq.

9. Bible passages are from the NRSV unless otherwise noted: NIV means NIV ©
2011; AT means the author's translation; MT means versification of the Masoretic Text.

10. After Gen. 5:3, Adam is mentioned by name elsewhere in the Old Testament
only as the first name in the genealogy in 1 Chron. 1:1 (see discussion in chap. 5).
In the New Testament, Adam appears in two genealogies (Luke 3:38 and Jude 14),
which will not be considered here, since our New Testament focus is Paul, and the
issues raised by these genealogies add little to the conversation. Only Paul deals
with Adam in detail, specifically in Rom. 5:12–21 and 1 Cor. 15:20–58. (In 1 Tim.
2:13–14, Adam and Eve are mentioned with respect to female authority in church,
but this brief comment adds nothing of importance to the topic that is the focus
of this book.) The importance that Paul places on Adam relative to the apparent
lack of emphasis elsewhere, especially in the Old Testament, seems a matter worth
considering seriously, which we will do in part 2.

11. Recently three helpful books have been published that deal with the biblical
and theological issues raised by evolution: two books by Lamoureux and one by
Carlson and Longman (see bibliography). Lamoureaux and Longman both have
doctoral degrees in biblical studies and have firsthand considerable experience in
these matters; Carlson is a physicist.

12. "Second Temple Judaism" is the preferred way of referring to the centuries
following Israel's rebuilding of their temple in 515 BC and it destruction in AD 70
(although, technically, the temple that was destroyed in AD 70 had been significantly
expanded by Herod in 19 BC, and so might be thought of as a "third" temple). Commonly Christians refer to that same general period as the "intertestamental period,"
but that term is falling into disuse. Apart from the obvious Christian bias, a number
of biblical books were clearly written well into the fifth century BC and perhaps even
later. "Second Temple" is also preferred because it gives due acknowledgment to the
profound affect Israel's exilic experience had in later developments in Judaism. We
will come back to this below.

Chapter 1: Genesis and the Challenges of the Nineteenth Century

1. Genesis and the Pentateuch are a package deal in modern Old Testament
scholarship; the same issues come up throughout these five books. So even though
we will be focusing on Genesis, we cannot do that well without also mentioning the
Pentateuch in the same breath.

Chapter 2: When Was Genesis Written?

1. It is widely understood that Genesis contains two creation stories: creation of
the cosmos in six days in Gen. 1 and the story of Adam and Eve in Gen. 2. This is not
seriously debated, although how to relate the two has been the concern of both modern
and ancient biblical interpreters, some of which we will see later.

2. Two excellent places to begin surveying the early history of Jewish interpretation
of the Bible are James Kugel's *The Bible As It Was* (Cambridge, MA: Belknap, 1999) and
Traditions of the Bible (Cambridge, MA: Harvard University Press, 1998). The latter is
a bit more detailed and technical, although both are eminently readable.

3. Augustine, *The Literal Meaning of Genesis*, trans. J. H. Taylor, 2 vols. (New York:
Paulist Press, 1982), 1:42–43.

4. Even though there is a division in Gen. 2:4, for convenience's sake I will refer to the two creation stories as Gen. 1 and Gen. 2. Also, I make the division between the two stories at the beginning of 2:4, not in the middle of 2:4, as many scholars do. There is no need to be adamant about this, but Gen. 2:4 begins, "These are the generations of the heaven and the earth when they were created." Since it seems that the other instances of "these are the generations of" in Genesis introduce what follows, I end the first creation story at 2:3. See Bill T. Arnold, *Genesis*, New Cambridge Bible Commentary (Cambridge: Cambridge University Press, 2010), 3–4.

5. Throughout much history there has been some discussion about the meaning of the first couple of Hebrew words in Deut. 34:6. The Hebrew text literally reads, somewhat cryptically, "He buried him [Moses]." Some claim that "he" refers to God, so it was God who personally buried Moses in "Moab, in the valley opposite Beth-peor," presumably in secret. However, God is not mentioned explicitly, as one might expect if such an unusual event were actually the topic. Also, the Hebrew can be translated in the passive voice in English, hence, "He was buried."

6. For the point I am making here, there is no need to take the next step and look at the implications of the beginning and end of Deuteronomy for the date of the remainder of the book. Briefly stated, however, the beginning and end tell us a great deal about the whole. The beginning and end are not just a late "frame" for what Moses wrote. Moses's speeches begin in 1:6 and continue through 31:29, followed by a song (32:1–43) and a blessing to the tribes (33:2–29). These are all first-person accounts, but they are woven together by third-person narrative connecting phrases like "Moses convened all Israel, and said to them" (5:1; cf. 27:1 and 29:1, among several others). The entire structure of the book is post-Mosaic. Further, we should be wary of assuming that a first-person speech was written by that person. Jesus certainly did not write the Sermon on the Mount even though it reports his speech.

7. "We must certainly understand 'this day' (Deut. 34:6) as meaning the time of the composition of the history, whether one prefers the view that Moses was the author of the Pentateuch or that Ezra reedited it. In either case I make no objection." The comment and its context can be found in "The Principal Works of Jerome," in Series 2 of *Nicene and Post-Nicene Fathers of the Church*, vol. 6, *Letters and Select Works*, trans. W. H. Fremantle (repr., Edinburgh: T&T Clark, 1989), 337–38.

8. Abraham Ben Meir Ibn Ezra, *Ibn Ezra's Commentary on the Pentateuch*, vol. 1, *Genesis (Bereshit)*, trans. H. Norman Strickman and Arthur M. Silver (New York: Menorah, 1988), 151. Ibn Ezra holds the same opinion about Gen. 13:7 ("At that time the Canaanites and the Perizzites lived in the land").

9. Spinoza argued that biblical interpretation belongs to everyone, not just the ruling elite, and that one needs nothing more than the natural light of reason to do so. There is no room for any external authority, either the church or God. Spinoza had political motives for this. He wanted to challenge the ecclesiastical power structures of his native Holland, which were tied to the political structures. Undermining the Bible was a necessary first step for undermining the government. Casting off the shackles of ecclesiastical authority had also been the theme of the Protestant Reformation one hundred years earlier.

10. This quote is from the version appearing in Benedict Spinoza, *Theologico-Political Treatise*, ed. Jonathan Israel, trans. Michael Silverstone and Jonathan Israel, Cambridge Texts in the History of Philosophy (Cambridge: Cambridge University Press, 2007), 122. The entire discussion begins at 118 and continues to 125. Thomas

Hobbes (1588–1679) actually preceded Spinoza by several years in publishing his view that Moses did not write the entire Pentateuch (*Leviathan* [London: Andrew Crooke, 1651]), although he did think that Moses wrote Deuteronomy 12–25. He is the first European to commit this view to writing; like Spinoza, he was not merely interested in a discussion of theology for its own sake, but for the sake of politics.

11. Not long after Spinoza, the French Catholic Hebrew scholar Richard Simon (1638–1712), in trying to refute the views of Spinoza, concluded that the Pentateuch contains numerous additions, inspired by the Holy Spirit but nevertheless post-Mosaic. Simon's writings caused considerable controversy and were suppressed. They did not gain a broader influence until they were popularized by the German biblical scholar Johann Semler (1725–91).

12. Astruc was not interested in post-Mosaic elements of Genesis, which occupied Spinoza and Ibn Ezra. Astruc wanted to understand how the information contained in Genesis could have come to Moses, who lived hundreds of years after the last recorded events in Genesis (and over two millennia after the events covered in Gen. 1–11, according to a literal reading of the genealogies in Genesis). Astruc was adamant that Moses did not receive this by divine revelation. He felt that Genesis is a simple record of events as one finds elsewhere in the Pentateuch or the Historical Books. Nothing there is said to be specially revealed to anyone, as opposed to the giving of the law or the inspiration of the prophets. For Astruc, Moses wrote as a simple historian who had in his possession these two memoirs (one using Elohim, and the other using Yahweh), which he edited into one document.

13. Another German Old Testament scholar, H. B. Witter (early 1700s), arrived at some similar conclusions several years before Astruc, but without gaining wide influence.

14. Wellhausen's magnum opus is *Prolegomena to the History of Ancient Israel* (New York: Meridian, 1957). The original English translation is *Prolegomena to the History of Israel*, trans. J. Sutherland Black and Allan Enzies (Edinburgh: Adam and Charles Black, 1885). The German original was published in 1882, though an earlier version came out in 1878.

15. Here Wellhausen followed the work of fellow German Old Testament scholar Karl Heinrich Graf (1815–69).

16. Wellhausen was influenced here by another fellow German, Wilhelm Vatke (1806–82), who adapted a Hegelian notion of history to biblical studies—movements breed countermovements that are eventually synthesized to a fresh third movement. Hegel's influence on Wellhausen was likely indirect at best. Others have seen in Wellhausen's arrangement of the sources an "evolutionary" development from simple to complex, which might suggest that Wellhausen was influenced directly by Darwin, but this does not seem to be the case.

17. Wellhausen's understanding of D was largely dependent on the work of W. M. L. de Wette (1780–1849), who argued that the "finding" of the "book of the law" under Josiah in 2 Kings 22:8 was political propaganda. De Wette argued that the book of Deuteronomy was actually written during this time to foster political and religious unity under Josiah's reign.

18. Wellhausen's anti-Semitism, prevalent in Germany at the time, is hardly veiled, and it is no surprise that one Jewish scholar referred to Wellhausen's brand of higher criticism as "higher anti-Semitism" (Solomon Schechter, "Higher Criticism—Higher Anti-Semitism," in *Seminary Addresses and other Papers* [Cincinnati: Ark Publishing, 1915], 36–37).

19. Although treating this issue fully would take us far afield, I should mention at least a common line of defense for Mosaic authorship: Jesus seems to attribute authorship of the Pentateuch to Moses (e.g., John 5:46–47). I do not think, however, that this presents a clear counterpoint, mainly because even the most ardent defenders of Mosaic authorship today acknowledge that some of the Pentateuch reflects updating, but taken at face value this is not a position that Jesus seems to leave room for. But more important, I do not think that Jesus's status as the incarnate Son of God requires that statements such as John 5:46–47 be understood as binding historical judgments of authorship. Rather, Jesus here reflects the tradition that he himself inherited as a first-century Jew and that his hearers assumed to be the case.

20. I wish to be clear that by citing Spinoza in this way, I am not giving blanket support to all of Spinoza's thought! Spinoza is simply an early example of a viewpoint about the Pentateuch that has stood the test of time, and whatever other issues there might be about his life and thought, they are irrelevant here.

21. Daniel E. Fleming, "History in Genesis," *Westminster Theological Journal* 65 (2003): 251.

22. Two important responders to the Documentary Hypothesis are Umberto Cassuto, *The Documentary Hypothesis and the Composition of the Pentateuch*, trans. I. Abrahams (Jerusalem: Magnes, 1983); and William Henry Green, *The Pentateuch Vindicated from the Aspersions of Bishop Colenso* (New York: John Wiley, 1863); Green, *The Higher Criticism of the Pentateuch* (1895; repr., New York: Charles Scribner's Sons, 1916).

23. Walter Brueggemann, *Theology of the Old Testament: Testimony, Dispute, Advocacy* (Minneapolis: Fortress, 1997), 74–75.

24. The Hebrew Bible is divided into three sections: Law (Pentateuch), Prophets (which includes many of the Historical Books), and Writings. The third section includes Psalms, Proverbs, Job, Song of Songs, Ruth, Lamentations, Ecclesiastes, Esther, Daniel, Ezra, Nehemiah, and Chronicles. Chronicles has a long history of being last among the writings, but some early traditions have it first among the Writings, before Psalms. At any rate, none of the Hebrew traditions have it among the Prophets (meaning right after 2 Kings).

25. The term "Septuagint" (Greek for "seventy") reflects the legend found in the *Letter of Aristeas* that the Hebrew Old Testament was translated into Greek in seventy-two days by seventy-two translators (six from each of the twelve tribes of Israel) in the third century BC. Its actual origin, like that of the Hebrew Bible, is far more complex.

26. "Forever" in the Old Testament does not mean "eternity" but rather an imprecise, long-enduring span of time.

27. Chronicles has its own unique theology that includes a diminishment of David's sins, an emphasis on the unity among the Israelites, an emphasis on the temple and Solomon's role in building it, and a theology of "immediate retribution" (not being held responsible for the sins of the ancestors but only for one's own). Most books of Old Testament introduction will address this. For a scholarly discussion, see Sara Japhet, *The Ideology of the Book of Chronicles and Its Place in Biblical Thought* (Frankfurt: Peter Lang, 1989).

28. In the Old Testament "messiah" does not carry the overtones it does in common Christian usage. It means "anointed one," and all kings in the Old Testament were anointed. Messianic hope refers to the expectation that God would one day put his appointed king back on the throne to lead Israel.

29. Chronicles seems to suggest that Adam is Israel's ancestor specifically. This is not unique to Chronicles, and we will look at this more in chap. 4 below.

30. The term "Deuteronomistic History" is academic shorthand for Joshua through 2 Kings because these books reflect the theology of Deuteronomy, such as the importance of a central place of worship (Deut. 12) and the consequences of worshiping foreign gods (Deut. 13), especially by imitating Canaanite practices of "altars . . . sacred stones . . . Asherah poles" (NIV: Deut. 7:5; 12:3; 16:21–22).

31. These statistics are compiled from the indexes in Barbara Aland et al., eds., *The Greek New Testament*, 4th rev. ed. (Stuttgart: Deutsche Bibelgesellschaft, 1993), 887–900.

Chapter 3: Stories of Origins from Israel's Neighbors

1. Technically speaking, *Enuma Elish* is not so much a "creation story" as it is a story of the ascendancy of Marduk, the patron god of Babylon at the time, with an account of cosmic origins supporting that main theme.

2. A summary can be found in Alexander Heidel, *The Babylonian Genesis: The Story of Creation*, 2nd ed. (Chicago: University of Chicago Press, 1963), 82–140, with diagram on 129; Bernard F. Batto, *Slaying the Dragon: Mythmaking in the Biblical Tradition* (Louisville: Westminster John Knox, 1992), 76–77.

3. Biblical scholars are generally in strong agreement that the conventional translation of Gen. 1:1 is wrong ("In the beginning God created the heavens and the earth" [NIV]). This implies "creation out of nothing" (ex nihilo; cf. 2 Macc. 7:28), which is what neither Genesis nor other ancient Near Eastern stories depict. Genesis begins with the assumption that the waters (the "deep") and the earth are already there. God separates the waters to make the sky and reveal the land, and then fills sky, earth, and sea with plant and animal life. For this reason, most scholars today translate verse 1 similar to what we see in the NRSV: "In the beginning when God created the heavens and the earth." This clause then introduces v. 2, which depicts the prior chaotic state. In other words, Gen. 1:1–2 together lay out the chaotic conditions: "In the beginning when God created the heavens and the earth, the earth was formless and void and darkness covered the face of the deep." God's first creative act is in verse 3 where he begins to order the chaos: "Then God said, 'Let there be light.'" Genesis 1 is not interested in the ultimate origins of the chaotic matter.

4. Although not as clear a parallel, in *Enuma Elish* this sequence concludes with the building of a temple. There is no temple in Gen. 1, but some suggest that the ordered cosmos is God's cosmic temple. For a recent, popular take on seeing the cosmos as God's temple, see John Walton, *The Lost World of Genesis One: Ancient Cosmology and the Origins Debate* (Downers Grove, IL: InterVarsity, 2009), 78–86. I look at this notion a bit further in chap. 4 below.

5. Incidentally, this is relevant to the issue of the relative dating of the biblical and Mesopotamian material. The polemical function of Gen. 1 requires that the Mesopotamian stories, whether written or oral, be older—otherwise there is nothing against which to polemicize.

6. I treat this general point at greater length in my *Inspiration and Incarnation: Evangelicals and the Problem of the Old Testament* (Grand Rapids: Baker Academic, 2005) and flesh this out a bit more in thesis 7 of the conclusion below. Also, my late colleague at Westminster Theological Seminary, J. Alan Groves, would muse on how

interesting it was that "God let his children tell his story." Thanks to my former student Dr. Brad Gregory for bringing to mind this reminiscence.

7. Although it is wholly absent in Babylonian stories, the Egyptian Memphite Theology (eighth-century text, second-millennium origin) has the god Ptah bringing the elements of the cosmos into being by his speech. As with other examples in this chapter, direct dependence of Israelite thought on Memphite Theology.

8. Translations of these stories are not hard to find. One convenient (and affordable) source is Bill T. Arnold and Bryan E. Beyer, eds., *Readings from the Ancient Near East* (Grand Rapids: Baker Academic, 2002). See also the one-volume edition (with a foreword by Daniel E. Fleming) of James B. Pritchard's classic anthology *Ancient Near Eastern Texts: An Anthology and Pictures* (Princeton: Princeton University Press, 2010).

9. Gen. 1:26 ("Let *us* make humankind in our image") reflects a notion of a divine council as found in other religious texts, but that council has no functional role whatsoever in ordering chaos. Gen. 1 diminishes ancient stories by presenting the divine council as anonymous bystanders. Two other options for understanding "sons of God," unlikely in the view of most scholars, are (1) the godly line of Seth (see Gen. 4:26) or (2) tyrannical rulers (since ancient kings were often accorded some divine status). A brief and helpful overview of the options may be found in John H. Walton, *Genesis*, The NIV Application Commentary (Grand Rapids: Zondervan, 2001), 291–95. Walton sees a clear connection between the "sons of God" taking human wives and Gilgamesh, who is portrayed as two-thirds divine and one-third human and who deflowered brides-to-be (the right of first night).

10. The following chart is slightly adapted from Daniel C. Harlow, "Creation according to Genesis: Literary Genre, Cultural Context, Theological Truth," *Christian Scholars Review* 37, no. 2 (2008): 163–98; and Harlow, "After Adam: Reading Genesis in an Age of Evolutionary Science," *Perspectives on Science and Christian Faith* 62, no. 3 (September 2010): 179–95.

11. Adapted from Harlow, "After Adam," 184. Harlow's chart is a slight adjustment of Batto's chart in *Slaying the Dragon*, 51–52. See also Batto's succinct retelling of *Atrahasis* on 27–33.

12. A handy place to begin is John H. Walton, "Genesis," in *Zondervan Illustrated Bible Backgrounds Commentary*, ed. John H. Walton, 5 vols. (Grand Rapids: Zondervan, 2009), 1:10–42. Walton's footnotes will guide readers to valuable sources of information.

13. This is a Sumerian myth. Alternatively, this myth may be referring more to an uncultivated land in need of fresh water rather than a garden paradise—although Gen. 2 also presents the original earthly state as uninhabitable land.

14. Nippur was an important city in Sumerian culture, from which numerous cosmogonies (texts of cosmic origins) were generated. Scholars distinguish this tradition from the Eridu tradition, which includes such texts as *Enki and Ninhursag*, *Enki and Ninmah*, and *Ewe and Wheat*, as mentioned here. The volumes by Clifford and Sparks in the bibliography provide more detail.

15. On this see Batto, *Slaying the Dragon*, 51–62.

16. See Walton, "Genesis," 28–29, and footnotes for details.

17. This is an Akkadian myth that shares similar themes with the second creation story: "Adapa" likely means "human," as does "Adam"; it is a story of primeval humans and the problem of divine knowledge; presence of a crafty being (a serpent and the god Ea); pride; missed opportunity for immortality; deception of humans; and eating of food as a metaphor for knowledge/immortality. See Kenton L. Sparks, *Ancient Texts*

for the Study of the Hebrew Bible: A Guide to the Background Literature (Peabody, MA: Hendrickson, 2005), 318.

18. A Sumerian myth. Although there is no conflict as in the biblical story, Dumuzi and Enkimdu are gods who represent shepherds and farmers trying to gain the favor of the goddess Inanna.

Chapter 4: Israel and Primordial Time

1. There is no positive, direct evidence for Israelite presence in Egypt or a massive departure of 600,000 men (see Exod. 12:37–38 and Num. 1:46). If one includes women and children, plus others (see Exod. 12:38), I estimate that number to be around 2,000,000. It stretches the imagination to think that a group that large, which then spent forty years wandering around the wilderness, would leave Egypt without a trace in either Egyptian literature or the archaeological record. However, there are indirect suggestions that some type of authentic historical memory is at work: the Joseph story represents well some aspects of Egyptian life; there was a clear Semitic (not identifiable as Israelite) presence in Egypt at a time roughly corresponding to the Joseph story, and Semitic slaves were used as labor on building projects in the Nile Delta (where the Israelites were enslaved according to Exodus); the names Moses, Aaron, Phinehas, and others are of Egyptian origin; the storehouses Pithom and Rameses (Exod. 1:11) are clearly historical, and their locations have likely been identified in the Nile Delta. The archaeological evidence for the conquest of Canaan is more problematic. The archaeological record presents a far more complex and lengthy picture than what we find in the book of Joshua. The best-known example is Jericho, which was destroyed by Joshua according to Josh. 6, but according to the archaeological record was clearly not occupied or destroyed anywhere near the time depicted in the book (thirteenth century BC). The same holds for Ai and Gibea. Two other cities, Hazor and Lachish, were destroyed according to the archaeological record, but about 100 years apart, not soon after each other, as we read in Josh. 10:31–32 and 11:13. It seems clear to most biblical archaeologists that "Israel" was not an outside population that imposed itself upon the Canaanite population but rather largely Canaanite in origin, perhaps influenced by a small group of outsiders. The Israelites shared with Canaanites such things as pottery style, alphabet, and worship (the Canaanite high god was called El, which is also used of Israel's God over 200 times in the Old Testament), thus further suggesting significant cultural identity between the two.

2. A lot has been written on this, some of which is listed in the bibliography. The books by Clifford, Batto, and Simkins are great resources. For other biblical passages not discussed here, see Job 9:8; 26:7–13; 38:1–11; Isa. 27:1. See also Ps. 65:6–7; Isa. 66:1–2; Jer. 27:5; Hab. 3:1–15.

3. I use "instantiation" to mean a concrete manifestation of something abstract or in this case beyond the boundaries of human history.

4. For these examples specifically, see John R. Levison, *Portraits of Adam in Early Judaism: From Sirach to 2 Baruch*, Journal for the Study of the Pseudepigrapha: Supplement Series 1 (Sheffield: Sheffield University Press, 1988), 44–45, 89–96.

5. All of these connections are discussed in more depth in Jon D. Levenson, *Creation and the Persistence of Evil: The Jewish Drama of Divine Omnipotence* (San Francisco: HarperSanFranciso, 1988), 53–127.

6. C. S. Lewis, "Myth Became Fact," in *God in the Dock: Essays on Theology and Ethics*, ed. Walter Hooper (Grand Rapids: Eerdmans, 1970), 63–67; Lewis,

Surprised by Joy: The Shape of My Early Life (New York and London: Harcourt Brace Jovanovich, 1955), 236.

Chapter 5: Paul's Adam and the Old Testament

1. An important treatment of this theme is James Barr, *The Garden of Eden and the Hope of Immortality* (Minneapolis: Fortress, 1992).

2. Israel's national history, beginning with Abraham, seems to be one extended drama of how Israel tries to fulfill the role that Adam was to have played in Genesis: obedient servant of God being prepared to take its place as God's chosen means to call the nations to God himself. This is introduced already in the promise to Abraham to be a blessing to the nations (Gen. 12:1–3). Israel, however, aborted its redemptive role, which was then fulfilled by Christ in his death and resurrection. For a detailed yet succinct explication of one approach to understanding this Adam theology, see N. T. Wright, "Adam, Israel and the Messiah," in *The Climax of the Covenant: Christ and the Law in Pauline Theology* (Minneapolis: Fortress, 1993), 18–40. Since the topic of this part of the book is bringing Paul and evolution into meaningful theological conversation, our focus will remain on how Paul saw Adam's disobedience as the cause of universal sin and death.

3. Adam may be alluded to in Ezek. 28:11–19, a lamentation over the king of Tyre. This king sought to deify himself (28:2), but his downfall is sure (vv. 9–10). Verse 13 says the king of Tyre was "in Eden, the garden of God"; "created" by God; and "blameless in your ways" (v. 15). Although there is no mention of Adam, Eden is named, which suggests that Ezekiel was familiar with a garden story, but more than that is hard to say. Isaiah 43:27 says that Israel's "first ancestor sinned," but this is surely not a reference to Adam. Abraham is referred to this way in 51:2–3, and some commentators suggest Jacob.

4. Another interesting explanation is to read *'adam* (in Hosea 6:7) as "ground" or "earth," or even "dirt." If this is the correct reading, we would have something like, "They treated my covenant like dirt"; yet this does not take into account the other geographic indicators of this passage. On this reading, see Douglas Stuart, *Hosea–Jonah*, Word Biblical Commentary 31 (Waco: Word, 1987), 98–99, 110–11.

5. John Calvin, *Commentaries on the Twelve Minor Prophets*, vol. 1, *Hosea* (Grand Rapids: Baker Academic, 1989), 235.

6. On the sinfulness of the nations, see, e.g., Ps. 53.

7. Notice that Wis. 10:4 attributes the ultimate cause of the flood to Cain, not Adam. The Mishnah (*'Abot* 5.2) attributes the ten-generation delay between Cain and the flood to God's patience.

8. Paul's use of this passage in Rom. 10:6–8—to speak of faith in Christ *and not the law*—is a wonderful example of his creative use of the Old Testament in general. We will look at five other examples more closely in chap. 6, below.

9. Some might object that Ps. 51:5 is fully in step with Paul's view of Adam as the cause of human sinfulness: "Indeed, I was born guilty [NIV: "sinful"], a sinner when my mother conceived me." This may appear convincing at first blush, but it does not support the argument, mainly because there is no indication of the main point of contention, that David's congenital condition is caused by Adam. David's point is not a brief allusion to a primordial cause for his behavior, but a graphic illustration of how utterly corrupt he is. His sin with Bathsheba, which included the murder of

her husband, Uriah, has exposed to David how deeply sinful he is. In other words, what he did is not just a momentary lapse in judgment (as modern American politicians are so prone to say) but an exposure of his own heart, and so he pleads with God to create in him a "clean heart" (v. 10). We should not minimize David's words, but neither should we extrapolate from them a "theology of original sin" in the Old Testament as a whole. Here David is speaking from the deep pain of the consequences of his choices and how he has sinned against God in the process. We will return briefly to this issue in chap. 7 below.

10. Movement toward spiritual perfection, or maturity, is in view, not a "moral" perfection, as the word "perfect" is often assumed to mean. Irenaeus puts it this way: "It certainly is in the power of a mother to give strong food to her infant, [but she does not do so], as the child is not yet able to receive more substantial nourishment; so also it was possible for God Himself to have made man perfect from the first, but man could not receive this [perfection], being as yet an infant"; *Against Heresies* 4.38.1; in *The Ante-Nicene Fathers: The Writings of the Fathers Down to A.D. 325*, ed. Alexander Roberts and James Donaldson (Buffalo: Christian Literature Publishing Co., 1885), 1:521. Theophilus argues in the same manner (e.g., *To Autolycus* 2.25–26). See the discussion in Peter C. Bouteneff, *Beginnings: Ancient Christian Readings of the Biblical Creation Narratives* (Grand Rapids: Baker Academic, 2008), 71, 79, and the summary on 87.

11. According to this reading, Adam and Eve were not born immortal, but immortality remained available to them through access to the tree of life as long as they obeyed the prohibition. As I mentioned in chap. 4, this may explain in part the logic of why Adam did not die "on the day" he ate of the fruit, as Gen. 2:17 promises. "Death" may simply refer to the introduction of mortality as the result of being barred from the tree of life. His actual and inevitable death only came much later, at 930 years of age (5:3).

Chapter 6: Paul as an Ancient Interpreter of the Old Testament

1. An influential and hefty treatment of this phenomenon is by Michael Fishbane, *Biblical Interpretation in Ancient Israel* (Oxford: Clarendon, 1985).

2. It is possible that Neh. 8:8 refers to the need to translate the Hebrew Torah into Aramaic so that the people could understand it, since by then Aramaic had become the dominant popular language of the Jews. Note the contrast with the incident in Isa. 36:11 that took place in 701 BC. Sennacherib's field commander threatens King Hezekiah's men with sure destruction. Hezekiah's men ask the commander not to speak in Hebrew because it will upset their people.

3. The standard English translation of these works is the massive two-volume edition, James H. Charlesworth, ed., *The Old Testament Pseudepigrapha* (Garden City, NY: Doubleday, 1983–85).

4. This translation is by D. J. Harrington in Charlesworth, *Old Testament Pseudepigrapha*, 2:321–22. See also the *Book of Biblical Antiquities* 13.8–9. Adam transgressed God's ways, and as a result *death* (not sin) was "ordained for the generations of men." Paradise (the garden) is lost to humans "because *they* have sinned against me."

5. The translation is by A. F. J. Kjiln and found in Charlesworth, *Old Testament Pseudepigrapha*, 2:640.

6. Throughout the thirteen letters traditionally ascribed to Paul (Romans–Philemon), the Old Testament is cited in seven of them for a total of 103 citations (Romans, 59x;

1 Corinthians, 17x; 2 Corinthians, 10x; Galatians, 10x; Ephesians, 5x; 1 Timothy, 1x; 2 Timothy, 1x). In the thirteen letters, the Old Testament books cited most frequently are Psalms (29x), Isaiah (27x), and Deuteronomy (18x). The other books are Genesis (11x), Exodus (7x), Leviticus (5x), Hosea (3x); 2 Samuel, 1 Kings, Job, Jeremiah, Ezekiel, and Habakkuk (2x each); Numbers, Proverbs, Joel, Zechariah, and Malachi (1x each). There is, however, a general scholarly consensus that Paul did not write all of the letters ascribed to him, namely, Ephesians, Colossians, 2 Thessalonians, 1 and 2 Timothy, and Titus. My examples below are taken from letters that are not disputed.

7. Grammatical irregularities led early interpreters to find some hidden meaning in this grammatical phenomenon. For example, if a singular form appeared when a plural was expected, it prompted some to conclude that the many were acting as one or were considered as one. A specific example from rabbinic literature (*Genesis Rabbah* 99.7) has to do with Gen. 49:6, which (in Hebrew) says that Levi and Simeon slew "a man." This verse refers to the incident in Gen. 34, where they slew "every male" (see 34:25) for raping their sister Dinah. This rabbinic text explains this theologically: in God's eyes, all the Shechemites were "as one." From the viewpoint of Hebrew grammar, this is hardly necessary. Singulars can act as collective nouns (as we will also see in our example below). These early interpreters knew that perfectly well, but the presence of the grammatical issue was considered a divine invitation to move deeper into the text, beneath the surface, and uncover more that the text has to offer.

8. The Hebrew is singular ("he"), which either refers to Babylon's king or, more likely, refers to the people collectively, as NRSV has it, and that is a common occurrence in biblical Hebrew. The point I am making here does not hang in the balance.

9. The "faith" Paul speaks of is a controversial topic. In Gal. 2:16, Paul uses the phrase "faith of Christ" (*pistis Christou*) to describe how one is justified before God. This phrase can either mean *our faith* in Christ (the traditional understanding) or *Christ's faithfulness* in willingly dying on the cross for our benefit. New Testament scholars are quite divided on which is the proper interpretation of *pistis Christou*. (The scholarly literature on this is enormous, but a relatively recent volume provides a good overview of the issues: Michael F. Bird and Preston M. Sprinkle, eds., *The Faith of Jesus Christ: Exegetical, Biblical and Theological Studies* [Carlisle, UK: Paternoster, 2009]). How Paul understands "faith" in 2:16 will influence how one understands "faith" in his citation of Hab. 2:4 in Gal. 3:11. When Paul cites, "the one who is righteous will live by faith," he may mean that the individual is made righteous by *his own faith in Christ* (as opposed to works). Conversely, Paul may be saying that *Christ is the faithful one* whose faithfulness and righteousness is defined by going to the cross. As I said, this is a controversial topic and taking a strong stand may not gain you many friends. Thankfully, for our purposes, settling the matter is not absolutely central (and it is entirely possible that both meanings are at work in Gal. 3:11). Either way, Paul is saying that the individual's faithfulness in keeping the law, the very point Habakkuk makes, has no place in the gospel—and Paul uses Hab. 2:4 to make that point!

10. For an example elsewhere in Romans, see Paul's litany of citations in Rom. 3:10–18. Paul groups together several passages, mainly from the Psalms, to support his contention that Jew and gentile are all alike under sin (see v. 9). Although this is a possible implication of these passages, in their original Old Testament context they do not appear to be making this point. Another celebrated example is Rom. 10:6–8, where Paul's use of Deut. 30:13–14 is clearly creative.

11. Actually, his citation includes Isa. 59:21 and possibly 27:9 (Jer. 31:33–34). But for us the heart of the matter concerns 59:20.

12. The Hebrew of this verse has the redeemer as coming *to* Zion (the preposition *lamed*). The Septuagint is similar in that it uses the preposition *heneken*, which means "for the sake of." Both agree that Zion, the people of God, is the destination and the object of salvation.

13. The translation is by D. J. Harrington in Charlesworth, *Old Testament Pseudepigrapha*, 2:317.

Chapter 7: Paul's Adam

1. But note that in Rom. 5:14, Paul refers to death as reigning from Adam to *Moses*. Since there is no question that Paul thought Moses to be a historical figure, naming them both suggests that Adam was a historical figure for Paul as well.

2. N. T. Wright, *The Letter to the Romans*, vol. 10 of *The New Interpreter's Bible* (Nashville: Abingdon, 2002), 523.

3. George L. Murphy, "Roads to Paradise and Perdition: Christ, Evolution, and Original Sin," *Perspectives on Science and Christian Faith* 58, no. 2 (June 2006): 109–18. Murphy's treatment of original sin is succinct and accessible, including valuable bibliographical references to important academic works on the subject.

4. On this point, see J. R. Daniel Kirk, *Unlocking Romans: Resurrection and the Justification of God* (Grand Rapids: Eerdmans, 2008).

5. An influential article in the early years of this debate, and still so, is Krister Stendahl, "The Apostle Paul and the Introspective Conscience of the West," *Harvard Theological Review* 56 (1963): 199–215; repr. in *Paul among Jews and Gentiles* (Philadelphia: Fortress, 1976), 78–96.

6. E. P. Sanders, *Paul and Palestinian Judaism: A Comparison of Patterns of Religion* (Minneapolis: Fortress, 1977).

7. Two important treatments to consider are James D. G. Dunn, *Jesus, Paul, and the Law: Studies in Mark and Galatians* (Louisville: Westminster John Knox, 1990); and N. T. Wright, *What St. Paul Really Said: Was Paul of Tarsus the Real Founder of Christianity?* (Grand Rapids: Eerdmans), 1997. An excellent online source for learning about the New Perspective on Paul is "The Paul Page" (www.thepaulpage .com). This site includes essays, book reviews, challenges to the New Perspective, bibliographies, and more.

8. Paul employs a similar rhetoric of reversal in Gal. 4:21–31, where the slave woman Hagar stands for Mount Sinai and the law, meaning "the present city of Jerusalem" (v. 25), and the free woman Sarah stands for "the Jerusalem that is above" (v. 26). Here too the law is the problem, not the solution.

9. Those interested in gathering a more detailed sense of the issues could begin by reading recent commentaries, which reflect a breadth of opinions on Rom. 5:12–21, such as those by Cranfield, Moo, Wright, Dunn, and Murray (see the bibliography). One perennial exegetical problem is v. 12, where Paul says something that seems to be out of accord with what we have seen in vv. 18–19. In the latter, Adam's trespass leads to death and condemnation for all, but in v. 12 we read that death and sin entered the world through one man, "so death spread to all *because all have sinned*" (emphasis added). The phrase "because all have sinned" is a bit striking: it suggests that human death is not Adam's doing but the result of individual responsibility.

One might have expected "because *Adam* sinned" in view of vv. 18–19. Augustine, working from the mistaken Latin translation at the time, read "because" as "in him" (*in quo*, v. 12), meaning "in Adam." Scholars across the ideological spectrum recognize, however, that the Latin is incorrect and the original Greek (*eph hō*, v. 12) means "because." Perhaps Paul is saying, "You need Christ because of what you have done [v. 12], and your connection to Adam means you cannot do anything about it [vv. 18–19]." That may be, but Paul does not forge that connection, and we are left to figure this out on our own.

Conclusion

1. Augustine, *The Literal Meaning of Genesis*, trans. J. H. Taylor, 2 vols. (New York: Paulist Press, 1982) 1:42–43.

2. The flood story in Gen. 6–9 is typically considered to be a composite of two Israelite versions, J and P (two of Wellhausen's four sources and still routinely recognized as such today). The scenario I am suggesting here pertains only to the J version. The P version was combined with J at some later point, perhaps when the first creation story (also P) was added, as I mention in the next paragraph.

3. Herman Bavinck, *Reformed Dogmatics*, vol. 1, *Prolegomena*, trans. J. Vriend (Grand Rapids: Baker Academic, 2003), 434–35, emphasis added. My own thoughts on this are expanded in "Preliminary Observations on an Incarnational Model of Scripture: Its Viability and Usefulness," *Calvin Theological Journal* 42, no. 2 (2007): 219–36. By citing Bavinck, I do not mean to suggest that he would apply this principle precisely as I do to this same issue.

4. This thesis lies behind my *Inspiration and Incarnation: Evangelicals and the Problem of the Old Testament* (Grand Rapids: Baker Academic, 2005), mentioned in the introduction.

Bibliography

The topics addressed in this book are wide-ranging, including not only evolution and faith but also much of modern biblical scholarship on Genesis and Paul. The bibliography below, therefore, includes the sources cited in the book (with the exception of works only alluded to), as well as numerous other books and articles that I find particularly helpful for readers interested in entering the discussion. Yet it is a brief and selective bibliography.

Anderson, Bernard W. *Chaos versus Creation*. Philadelphia: Fortress, 1984.
————, ed. *Creation in the Old Testament*. Issues in Religion and Theology 6. Philadelphia: Fortress, 1984.
Anderson, Gary A. "Biblical Origins of the Problem of the Fall." *Pro ecclesia* 10, no. 1 (2001): 17–30.
————. *The Genesis of Perfection: Adam and Eve in Jewish and Christian Imagination*. Louisville: Westminster John Knox, 2001.
Arnold, Bill T. *Genesis*. New Cambridge Bible Commentary. Cambridge: Cambridge University Press, 2010.
Arnold, Bill T., and Bryan E. Beyer, eds. *Readings from the Ancient Near East*. Grand Rapids: Baker Academic, 2002.
Augustine. *The Literal Meaning of Genesis*. Translated by J. H. Taylor. 2 vols. New York: Paulist Press, 1982.
Barr, James. *The Garden of Eden and the Hope of Immortality*. Minneapolis: Fortress, 1992.

Batto, Bernard F. *Slaying the Dragon: Mythmaking in the Biblical Tradition.* Louisville: Westminster John Knox, 1992.

Bavinck, Herman. *Reformed Dogmatics.* Vol. 1, *Prolegomena.* Translated by J. Vriend. Grand Rapids: Baker Academic, 2003.

Bouteneff, Peter C. *Beginnings: Ancient Christian Readings of the Biblical Creation Narratives.* Grand Rapids: Baker Academic, 2008.

Brown, William P. *The Seven Pillars of Creation: The Bible, Science, and the Ecology of Wonder.* Oxford: Oxford University Press, 2010.

Brueggemann, Walter. *Theology of the Old Testament: Testimony, Dispute, Advocacy.* Minneapolis: Fortress, 1997.

Calvin, John. *Commentaries on the Twelve Minor Prophets.* Vol. 1, *Hosea.* Grand Rapids: Baker Academic, 1989.

Carlson, Richard F., and Tremper Longman III. *Science, Creation and the Bible: Reconciling Rival Theories of Origins.* Downers Grove, IL: InterVarsity, 2010.

Cassuto, Umberto. *The Documentary Hypothesis and the Composition of the Pentateuch.* Translated by I. Abrahams. Jerusalem: Magnes, 1983.

Charlesworth, James H., ed. *The Old Testament Pseudepigrapha.* 2 vols. Garden City, NY: Doubleday, 1983–85.

Childs, Brevard S. *Myth and Reality in the Old Testament.* Studies in Biblical Theology 27. London: SCM, 1960.

Clifford, Richard J. *Creation Accounts in the Ancient Near East and in the Bible.* Catholic Biblical Quarterly Monograph Series 26. Washington, DC: Catholic Biblical Association of America, 1994.

Collins, Francis S. *The Language of God: A Scientist Presents Evidence for Belief.* New York: Free Press, 2006.

Coyne, Jerry. *Why Evolution Is True.* Toronto and New York: Viking, 2009.

Cranfield, C. E. B. *Romans.* International Critical Commentary. 2 vols. Edinburgh: T&T Clark, 1980–83.

Dunn, James D. G. *Jesus, Paul, and the Law: Studies in Mark and Galatians.* Louisville: Westminster John Knox, 1990.

———. *Romans.* Word Biblical Commentary. 2 vols. Dallas: Word, 1988.

Enns, Peter. *Inspiration and Incarnation: Evangelicals and the Problem of the Old Testament.* Grand Rapids: Baker Academic, 2005.

———. "Preliminary Observations on an Incarnational Model of Scripture: Its Viability and Usefulness." *Calvin Theological Journal* 42, no. 2 (2007): 219–36.

Falk, Darrel R. *Coming to Peace with Science: Bridging the Worlds between Faith and Biology.* Downers Grove, IL: InterVarsity Press, 2004.

Fishbane, Michael. *Biblical Interpretation in Ancient Israel.* Oxford: Clarendon, 1985.

Fleming, Daniel E. "History in Genesis." *Westminster Theological Journal* 65 (2003): 251–62.

Fretheim, Terence E. "Is Genesis 3 a Fall Story?" *Word & World* 14, no. 2 (1994): 144–53.

———. *The Pentateuch*. Nashville: Abingdon, 1996.

Giberson, Karl W., and Francis S. Collins. *The Language of Science and Faith: Straight Answers to Genuine Questions*. Downers Grove, IL: InterVarsity, 2011.

Glover, Gordon J. *Beyond the Firmament: Understanding Science and the Theology of Creation*. Chesapeake, VA: Watertree, 2007.

Green, William Henry. *The Higher Criticism of the Pentateuch*. 1895. Reprint, New York: Charles Scribner's Sons, 1916.

———. *The Pentateuch Vindicated from the Aspersions of Bishop Colenso*. New York: John Wiley, 1863.

Haarsma, Deborah B., and Loren D. Haarsma. *Origins: A Reformed Look at Creation, Design, and Evolution*. Grand Rapids: Faith Alive, 2007.

Harlow, Daniel C. "After Adam: Reading Genesis in an Age of Evolutionary Science." *Perspectives on Science and Christian Faith* 62, no. 3 (September 2010): 179–95.

———. "Creation according to Genesis: Literary Genre, Cultural Context, Theological Truth." *Christian Scholars Review* 37, no. 2 (2008): 163–98.

Harrell, Daniel M. *Nature's Witness: How Evolution Can Inspire Faith*. Nashville: Abingdon, 2008.

Heidel, Alexander. *The Babylonian Genesis: The Story of Creation*. 2nd ed. Chicago: University of Chicago Press, 1963.

Hess, Richard S., and David T. Tsumura, eds. *I Studied Inscriptions from before the Flood: Ancient Near Eastern, Literary, and Linguistic Approaches to Genesis 1–11*. Sources for Biblical Theology. Winona Lake, IN: Eisenbrauns, 1994.

Ibn Ezra, Abraham Ben Meir. *Ibn Ezra's Commentary on the Pentateuch*. Vol. 1, *Genesis (Bereshit)*. Translated by H. Norman Strickman and Arthur M. Silver. New York: Menorah, 1988.

Irenaeus. *Against Heresies*. In vol. 1 of *The Ante-Nicene Fathers: The Writings of the Fathers Down to A.D. 325*. Edited by Alexander Roberts and James Donaldson. Buffalo: Christian Literature Publishing Co., 1885.

Japhet, Sara. *The Ideology of the Book of Chronicles and Its Place in Biblical Thought*. Frankfurt: Peter Lang, 1989.

Jerome. "The Principal Works of Jerome." Translated by W. H. Fremantle. In *Nicene and Post-Nicene Fathers of the Church*. Vol. 6, *Letters and Select Works*. Series 2. Reprint, Edinburgh: T&T Clark, 1989.

Kirk, J. R. Daniel. *Unlocking Romans: Resurrection and the Justification of God*. Grand Rapids: Eerdmans, 2008.

Kugel, James L. *The Bible As It Was*. Cambridge, MA: Belknap, 1999.

———. *Traditions of the Bible*. Cambridge, MA: Harvard University Press, 1998.

Kugel, James L., and Rowan A. Greer. *Early Biblical Interpretation*. Philadelphia: Westminster, 1986.

Lamoureux, Denis O. *Evolutionary Creation: A Christian Approach to Evolution*. Eugene, OR: Wipf & Stock, 2008.

———. *I Love Jesus and I Accept Evolution*. Eugene, OR: Wipf & Stock, 2009.

Levenson, Jon D. *Creation and the Persistence of Evil: The Jewish Drama of Divine Omnipotence*. San Francisco: HarperSanFrancisco, 1988.

Levison, John R. *Portraits of Adam in Early Judaism: From Sirach to 2 Baruch*. Journal for the Study of the Pseudepigrapha: Supplement Series 1. Sheffield: Sheffield University Press, 1988.

Lewis, C. S. "Myth Became Fact." Pages 63–67 in *God in the Dock: Essays on Theology and Ethics*. Edited by Walter Hooper. Grand Rapids: Eerdmans, 1970.

———. *Surprised by Joy: The Shape of My Early Life*. New York and London: Harcourt Brace Jovanovich, 1955.

Longman, Tremper, III. *How to Read Genesis*. Downers Grove, IL: Inter-Varsity, 2005.

Middleton, J. Richard. *The Liberating Image: The Imago Dei in Genesis 1*. Grand Rapids: Brazos, 2005.

Moo, Douglas. *Romans*. Grand Rapids: Zondervan, 2000.

Murphy, George L. "Roads to Paradise and Perdition: Christ, Evolution, and Original Sin." *Perspectives on Science and Christian Faith* 58, no. 2 (June 2006): 109–18.

Murray, John. *The Epistle to the Romans*. Grand Rapids: Eerdmans, 1968.

Niditch, Susan. *Chaos to Cosmos: Studies in Biblical Patterns of Creation*. Chico, CA: Scholars Press, 1985.

Polkinghorne, John. *Quarks, Chaos and Christianity: Questions to Science and Religion*. Rev. ed. New York: Crossroad, 2005.

Polkinghorne, John, and Nicholas Beale. *Questions of Truth: Fifty-One Responses to Questions about God, Science, and Belief*. Louisville: Westminster John Knox, 2009.

Poole, Michael. *Questions of Faith: Exploring Science and Belief*. Peabody, MA: Hendrickson, 2007.

Pritchard, James B. *Ancient Near Eastern Texts: An Anthology and Pictures*. Princeton: Princeton University Press, 2010.

Rendsburg, Gary A. *The Redaction of Genesis*. Winona Lake, IN: Eisenbrauns, 1986.

Sanders, E. P. *Paul and Palestinian Judaism: A Comparison of Patterns of Religion*. Minneapolis: Fortress, 1977.

Schechter, Solomon. "Higher Criticism—Higher Anti-Semitism." Pages 35–39 in *Seminary Addresses and other Papers*. Cincinnati: Ark Publishing, 1915. http://www.bombaxo.com/blog/?p=1453.

Simkins, Ronald A. *Creator and Creation: Nature in the Worldview of Ancient Israel.* Peabody, MA: Hendrickson, 1994.

Smith, Mark S. *The Priestly Vision of Genesis 1.* Philadelphia: Fortress, 2009.

Sparks, Kenton L. *Ancient Texts for the Study of the Hebrew Bible: A Guide to the Background Literature.* Peabody, MA: Hendrickson, 2005.

————. *God's Word in Human Words: An Evangelical Appropriation of Critical Biblical Scholarship.* Grand Rapids: Baker Academic, 2008.

Spinoza, Benedict. *Theologico-Political Treatise.* Edited by Jonathan Israel. Translated by Michael Silverstone and Jonathan Israel. Cambridge Texts in the History of Philosophy. Cambridge: Cambridge University Press, 2007.

Stendahl, Krister. "The Apostle Paul and the Introspective Conscience of the West." *Harvard Theological Review* 56 (1963): 199–215. Reprint, pages 78–96 in *Paul among Jews and Gentiles.* Philadelphia: Fortress, 1976.

Stuart, Douglas. *Hosea–Jonah.* Word Biblical Commentary 31. Waco: Word, 1987.

Walton, John H. *Ancient Near Eastern Thought and the Old Testament: Introducing the Conceptual World of the Hebrew Bible.* Grand Rapids: Baker Academic, 2006.

————. "Genesis." In *Zondervan Illustrated Bible Backgrounds Commentary.* Edited by John H. Walton. 5 vols. Grand Rapids: Zondervan, 2009.

————. *The Lost World of Genesis One: Ancient Cosmology and the Origins Debate.* Downers Grove, IL: InterVarsity, 2009.

Wellhausen, Julius. *Prolegomena to the History of Ancient Israel.* New York: Meridian, 1957.

Westermann, Claus. *Creation.* Philadelphia: Fortress, 1974.

Wright, N. T. "Adam, Israel and the Messiah." Pages 18–40 in *The Climax of the Covenant: Christ and the Law in Pauline Theology.* Minneapolis: Fortress, 1993.

————. *The Letter to the Romans.* In vol. 10 of *The New Interpreter's Bible.* Nashville: Abingdon, 2002.

————. *What St. Paul Really Said: Was Paul of Tarsus the Real Founder of Christianity?* Grand Rapids: Eerdmans, 1997.

Young, Davis A., and Ralph F. Stearley. *The Bible, Rocks and Time: Geological Evidence for the Age of the Earth.* Downers Grove, IL: InterVarsity, 2008.

Subject Index

Scripture Index